Mirth, Madness, & St Magnus

and the eccentric Sheriff Thoms

Paul J. Sutherland

30/11/2013 .

Published by The Orcadian (Kirkwall Press)

Hell's Half Acre, Kirkwall, Orkney, KW15 1GJ

Tel: 01856 879000 Fax: 01856 879001

www.orcadian.co.uk

Book sales: www.orcadian.co.uk/shop/index.php

ISBN No: 978-1-902957-59-3

Printed in Orkney by The Orcadian, Hatston Print Centre,
Hell's Half Acre, Kirkwall, Orkney, Scotland, KW15 1GJ

Mirth, Madness, & St Magnus

and the eccentric Sheriff Thoms

Paul J. Sutherland

The Orcadian
2013

In memory
of my parents

MALCOLM SUTHERLAND
(1925 – 1988)

PAMELA V. SUTHERLAND
née FLETT
(1932 – 2006)

Contents

Introduction

Sheriff George Hunter Macthomas Thoms is one of the most significant figures in the last two centuries of Orkney's history. His intervention certainly changed the story of St Magnus Cathedral with dramatic effect.

As minister of the cathedral from 1990-2001, I would see the good Sheriff's name often, since it was enshrined in the glass of the great East rose window. Indeed, his name and his titles could hardly be avoided. But while I knew that his financial legacy had helped to save the cathedral from the potentially disastrous effects of a slow but steady deterioration in its fabric, I knew little about the character of the man himself.

"Weel, ye ken noo," as the Lord on His judgment throne is reputed to have told a baffled sinner who had pleaded in vain, 'Lord, Lord, I didna ken, I didna ken.' And I am right glad that I ken noo about this extraordinary sheriff, thanks to this magnificent book.

To say that Sheriff Thoms was a kenspeckle figure would be to understate his eccentricity. He could be vain, pompous, posturing and absurd, but he was also kind, compassionate, and far-seeing. A jocular self-described 'funny man' whose humour could sometimes get a bit much, he was also serious, scrupulous and clever. A bachelor sheriff with a flirting waistcoat and a laughing waistcoat, who played tricks on children, he was much respected for his legal skills. While his vanity and pretentiousness were risible, he was clearly a generous and expansive host who was much loved by his friends.

I will say no more, because there is so much more in the book. Mirth, Madness and St Magnus is a terrific read. I expected to be informed by this book, and I was; but I was also moved, enthralled and entertained by it. Some parts are laugh-aloud funny.

George Thoms was certainly unconventional, and sometimes a bit weird, but was he off his head? This question lies at the heart of the narrative, thanks to a court case that gripped and entertained Scotland. The sheriff's will, which granted £60,000 - a figure which would nowadays exceed £6 million - to the Provost and Magistrates of Kirkwall for the restoration of St Magnus Cathedral, was contested by some of Thoms' relatives.

Paul Sutherland is not just a fine prose stylist; as a lawyer himself, he leads the reader deftly through a legal quagmire. The top lawyers involved seemed as keen to burnish their public reputations as wits and savants as anything else, but the stakes were very high.

While we know that the case will end in a victory for Kirkwall and its great cathedral, the tale of how it got there is riveting.

Read this fine book, be informed by it, enjoy it, and laugh with it. But at the same time be grateful for the saving and development of this precious jewel in Orkney's crown, and for the cussed, absurd and generous sheriff who helped to make it possible.

Ron Ferguson

Acknowledgements

Many people have helped me in the eleven or so years since I first set out to tell the story of Sheriff Thoms. First of all, I would like to thank the former Chief Librarian of Orkney Library, Bobby Leslie and his staff, who provided me with the photocopy of the 340-page court transcript that was my first and most detailed source; former Orkney Archivist, Alison Fraser, and Shetland Archivist, Brian Smith, and their respective assistants; and the staff of Shetland Library. The other main libraries and archives I consulted were the North Highland Archive in Wick, the National Archives of Scotland, the National Library of Scotland, Edinburgh Central Library, and Dundee Central Library.

Among the other institutions and private individuals I contacted with specific queries or who helped me track down sources or potential illustrations are: The Advocates Library; the Society of Writers to H. M. Signet; the Royal College of Surgeons, Edinburgh; the Royal College of Physicians, Edinburgh; Grand Lodge of Scotland; the Royal Company of Archers; the Northern Lighthouse Board; the Royal Dornoch Golf Club; the University of Dundee; Coggeshall Museum; the National Portrait Gallery; the Scottish National Portrait Gallery; the Mitchell Library; the late Lord Clyde; Lord Craigmyle; Stephen Dean, Gordon J. S. Lindhorst; Norman Macdonald; Robert Bell; David Partner; John Stevens; the late Douglas Barker; the late Jack Donaldson; Duncan Mackenzie, Procurator Fiscal Depute, Lerwick; Barry Reid, former Sheriff Clerk Depute, Lerwick; Janet McEwan, Sheriff Clerk Depute, Wick; Anne Moore, Sheriff Clerk Depute, Kirkwall; Bryce Wilson; A. W. Wright; J. F. Bowman; P. Benyon; Harry Gray; David Sutherland; the Wick Society; David Greenhalgh; Anne Sinclair of the George Waterston Memorial Centre, Fair Isle; Tom Muir of Orkney Museum; David Mackie of Orkney Library Photographic Archive; Ian Tait and Jenny Murray of Shetland Museum; Martin Findlay; and the respective curators of St Giles and St Magnus Cathedrals.

I am grateful to the Trustees of the Estate of the late Stanley Cursiter and Orkney Islands Council for permission to reproduce the watercolours of the Cathedral restoration; to the Faculty of Advocates for the portrait of the Lord Justice-Clerk; to Sheriff Principal Sir Stephen Young, Bart., for the cartoon and painting in Kirkwall Sheriff Court; to Sheriff Colin Scott Mackenzie for the cartoon of the Trondra lasses; to Shetland Museum and Ian Tait for the portrait of Thoms as Magnus Troil; and to the Orkney Museum and David Mackie for the portrait of Thoms as Vice-Admiral.

I would like to express my special thanks to Andrew MacThomas of Finegand and Brian Turnbull, great-great-nephews of Sheriff Thoms, for their helpful comments and information, photographs of their ancestors, and generally for the tolerance they have shown towards a stranger exploring their family history.

The first draft of the book was read and commented upon by Dr R. P. Fereday, William P. L. Thomson, Brian Smith, Dr Mort Diament, R. R. Shaw, Agnes Wilson and Andrew MacThomas. Remaining errors are of course my own.

Finally I would like to thank James Miller and Drew Kennedy of *The Orcadian* for transforming my typescript into the handsome volume you hold in your hands.

P. J. S.

Lerwick,
25th October 2013.

I

An eccentric benefactor

Few are given a memorial as grand as that of Sheriff Thoms. While other people honoured in Kirkwall's St Magnus Cathedral may have a discreet plaque or the occasional ornate tombstone, Thoms has the great East Window, the most magnificent in the building. Rising almost to the full height of the eastern gable, the thirteenth-century window, with its tall paired lights and central rose above, has been filled with twentieth-century stained-glass depictions of the Crucifixion and the Ascension.[1] Along the bottom runs an inscription. It reads: 'To the Glory of God and in Memory of George Hunter Macthomas Thoms, Sheriff and Vice-Admiral of Orkney and Zetland, and Sheriff of Caithness, Orkney and Zetland, 1870 – 99.' What Sheriff Thoms did to be

The great East Window, dedicated to the memory of Sheriff Thoms. (Picture: Martin Findlay)

so honoured was to leave most of his estate to the Provost and Magistrates of Kirkwall for the purpose of restoring the cathedral. It was no small sum, either. The estimated value following his death in 1903 was around fifty to sixty thousand pounds, equivalent to anything between six and twelve million today.[2] The design of the East Window glass and the wording of the dedication were, in fact, specific conditions of the bequest.[3] Yet before the restoration could commence, or Thoms' name achieve its glazed and leaded immortality, an attempt was made to overturn his will on the grounds of an insanity that was alleged to have encompassed everything from believing himself a Highland

1

Chief to imposing fines on his cat. A sensational court case ensued, in which the life of the late Sheriff was exposed to judicial and public scrutiny. It was a life of some peculiarity, to say the very least.

Sheriff Thoms' background was not an unusual one for a man of his position and time. George Hunter Thoms (the Macthomas, as we shall see, came later) was born at Dundee on 3rd June, 1831, into a well-established mercantile family.[4] He was the elder son of Patrick Hunter Thoms (1796 – 1882), a merchant who was to be Provost of Dundee from 1847 to 1853 and, by purchase, proprietor of an estate in Forfarshire. Although only some five hundred acres, that property gave Thoms senior the status of a laird and the ability to style himself 'of Aberlemno'. His main interests, however, remained commercial and in Dundee, where he lived at The Crescent, a large house on the western outskirts overlooking the Tay.[5]

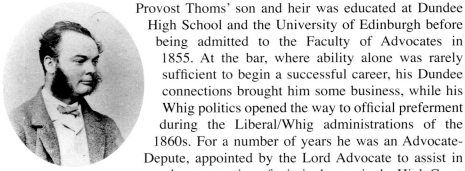

Thoms about the time he became Sheriff. A young Kirkwall lady remarked: 'I could call him nothing but a beau.' (Orkney Library Photographic Archive).

Provost Thoms' son and heir was educated at Dundee High School and the University of Edinburgh before being admitted to the Faculty of Advocates in 1855. At the bar, where ability alone was rarely sufficient to begin a successful career, his Dundee connections brought him some business, while his Whig politics opened the way to official preferment during the Liberal/Whig administrations of the 1860s. For a number of years he was an Advocate-Depute, appointed by the Lord Advocate to assist in the prosecution of criminal cases in the High Court of Justiciary, and in that capacity prosecuted on the first High Court circuit to take place in his home town. Then, in August 1870, he was appointed Sheriff of Caithness, Orkney and Zetland.[6]

The office Thoms held was that of what is now called Sheriff Principal. Although that term was also used informally in his day, his official title was simply Sheriff of the county.[7] As such, in the three counties that comprised his sheriffdom he had a wide range of judicial and administrative functions. His jurisdiction in civil and criminal matters was extensive, and included not just the proceedings of the Ordinary Court but also the Sheriff's Small Debt Court, which sat periodically on circuit as well as in the main court towns.[8] As local representative of the Crown he was charged with maintaining the Queen's peace, and thus had a supervisory role in the investigation and prevention of crime. In a somewhat anomalous situation, he had the power of appointment and direction of the Procurators Fiscal who prosecuted in his court, although they were answerable to the Lord Advocate in the discharge of their duties. Amongst many other functions, the Sheriff was also returning officer for parliamentary elections.

Most of the Sheriff's duties however could be, and usually were, delegated to the Sheriffs-substitute. These were the judges resident in each of the County towns of Wick, Kirkwall and Lerwick, and were, to confuse matters further, normally just called 'Sheriff' as well.[9] They heard the bulk of cases at first instance, while the Sheriff Principal heard appeals from his substitutes' judgements in civil matters. This did not preclude the Principal from hearing cases at the initial stages as well. In fact, he was statutorily obliged to hold a certain number of such courts in his sheriffdom each year. The reason for this obligation was that the post of Sheriff of a county was not a full-time one. Such Sheriffs remained advocates at the bar in Edinburgh and were entitled to practise as such, provided they did not engage in any cases from their own sheriffdom. In Orkney and Shetland the requirement was to hold four courts each year, but as these could be held on consecutive days, and whether or not there was any business to transact, they were often a mere formality. [10]

Whether they were formalities or not, Thoms entered into his shrieval duties with enthusiasm. His sheriffdom, it was said, was this lifelong bachelor's chief interest in life.[11] Not confining himself strictly to his official tasks, he showed an active concern for the well-being of the three counties under his charge. On his trips north, which were mainly in the summer months, he also found time to mix business with the pleasures of the County society in which he moved: shooting, riding, golfing, sailing;[12] and displaying all the while a marked eccentricity.

Thoms became a familiar and distinctive figure on his travels, both in dress and manner. Like many another Victorian gentleman, he remained pretty faithful to the fashions of his young adulthood. In his case that meant more than a touch of the mid-century 'swell': long side-whiskers of the type known as 'weepers', low turn-down collar, narrow bow tie and a waistcoat which was often fastened only by the lower buttons as if, in the words of one acid commentator on such matters, 'the swelling soul in the wearer's bosom had burst all the rest.'[13] Usually clad in tweeds, he often wore 'a special hat which did service for a great many years,'[14] knickerbockers and, completing the *ensemble*, a pair of Fair Isle hose 'rather highly coloured for the average man.'[15] The inhabitants of Avoch in the Black Isle, where Thoms was a regular visitor at the Manse, called him 'the little Irishman'.[16] Further north, having accompanied Thoms up from Granton on the paddle steamer *St. Magnus* for his first sittings in Kirkwall, the Orkney Sheriff-substitute James Robertson thought his new superior 'a nice jolly fellow'.[17] Rather less impressed was a young Kirkwall lady who was formally introduced to the new Sheriff at a ball and received a dance from him.

She recalled being amused at his 'inordinate conceit and vanity', adding that she could call him 'nothing but a beau.'[18] Friend and foe alike spoke of the conceit he had for himself: 'his besetting sin.'[19] Some of his brother advocates remarked upon it, too.[20]

Thoms in his long-coveted role, and uniform, as Vice-Admiral of Orkney and Shetland. 'A damn fine Admiral you are,' said a genuine tar, 'when you don't know port from starboard.'

One way in which this characteristic manifested itself was in his attempts to magnify the status of his position. The post of Sheriff of Orkney and Zetland carried with it the office of Vice-Admiral. Although this was a judicial office, dealing with matters such as wreck and salvage, whose separate jurisdiction had been merged with that of Sheriff, Thoms not only had his entitlement to the post confirmed by the Admiralty (eventually - it took him eleven years), but went so far as to procure an appropriate uniform.[21] One colleague suspected he had designed it himself.[22] In fact, it appears to have been the regulation full-dress uniform of the 1880s, with its gilt buttons in two rows of ten, epaulettes, lace, sword and all.[23] Thus attired, the Vice-Admiral can be seen yet in a carefully composed photograph, his stance more suited to the quarter deck than the bench, left hand on hip, right hand on telescope, his eyes scanning an imaginary horizon, and his charts spread out before him.

But the uniform was not just for the photographer's studio. It did sometimes see the sea. As a Sheriff of maritime counties, Thoms was one of the Commissioners of Northern Lighthouses, and thus joined his colleagues on their yearly tours of inspection round the Scottish coasts and islands on the Lighthouse Board vessels *Pharos* and *Pole Star*. Hay Shennan, for a number of years Thoms' substitute in Shetland, recalled how his be-uniformed superior knocked on a colleague's cabin door at 7 am, offering what he called 'the elixir of life': a cocktail of champagne and the laxative Gregory's Mixture.[24] Thoms it seems had a very Victorian obsession with 'keeping the works going',[25] particularly when at sea, and pressed his Gregory upon fellow passengers with proselytising zeal.[26]

The uniform may also have been in evidence on 23rd June, 1886, when Vice-Admiral Thoms headed the party of VIPs on board the ss *Earl of Zetland* as she became the first vessel to berth at Lerwick's newly-constructed Victoria Pier. It was a day for uniforms, for earlier he had also required to don his masonic

OPENING OF VICTORIA PIER

The opening of Lerwick Harbour Works. ss Earl of Zetland with Vice-Admiral Thoms on board becomes the first vessel to berth at the new Victoria Pier on June 23, 1886. (Shetland Museum and Archives)

regalia. As Provincial Grand Master of Caithness, Orkney and Zetland, he had laid the foundation stones of the Grand Hotel and Lerwick Poorhouse (a strange pair of buildings, it was wryly noted at the time, to begin together).[27] Indeed, there was a flurry of public building activity in the Northern Isles in the late nineteenth century, and Thoms was rarely far from the centre of it. When new county buildings, comprising court houses and prisons, were erected in Kirkwall and Lerwick, Thoms presided with due ceremony at their opening. Then when those two burghs also built new town halls, he donated a stained glass window to each.[28]

The foundation stone of Kirkwall Town Hall was laid, along with that of the Masonic Hall, by the Earl of Mar and Kellie, Grand Master Mason of Scotland, on 20th August, 1884. On the same day, Thoms was installed as Provincial Grand Master. At the ensuing banquet Lord Mar proposed a toast to Thoms, and the Sheriff replied in characteristic vein. He stated that:

> . . . the last time he had made a speech in this hall, it was upon a very interesting topic – viz:- Darning. (Loud Laughter) There was nothing more important than darning. – (renewed laughter) – as it was closely related to wet feet and cold in the head. (Laughter.)

5

Thoms did indeed darn his own Fair Isle socks,[29] but there were some other practices he wished to advocate too:

> He now embraced in the class of good deeds which he had commended in the cause of that civilisation which had so much struck Lord Mar, dancing, kissing, and calisthenics. (Loud Laughter). He could appeal to those gentlemen who knew something of the ladies whether these things had not been the cause of that civilisation which had so much astonished Lord Mar, - (Laughter) – and which showed that the mischief done by Mother Eve in the Garden of Eden had been redeemed by the young ladies on these model islands. (Laughter, and applause).

Later, in proposing another toast, Thoms remarked that he had:

> ... got himself examined by the doctor and was told that he had nine cracks in his heart. (Loud Laughter.) He told the doctor that just corresponded with the number of his rejections. (Loud Laughter.)[30]

On one of these foundation-laying occasions, however, Thoms was a notable absentee. When HRH Prince Alfred, Duke of Edinburgh and second son of Queen Victoria, came to Lerwick in January, 1882, to inspect the Royal Naval Reserve, of which he was then commander, the opportunity was taken to have him lay the foundation stone of the Town Hall. Thoms did not attend. He explained privately afterwards that it would have been awkward, as he held a higher naval rank than the Prince.[31] Given that the Duke of Edinburgh was not only a Prince of the Blood but had been serving in the navy since the age of fourteen, there would have been more than one reason for a civilian Vice-Admiral such as Thoms to feel a little awkward, but, in truth, his explanation must have been tongue-in-cheek. His appointment as Vice-Admiral had not yet been confirmed, nor had he been going to attend even before it was known that Prince Alfred would be there. Despite his absence on the day, he still contrived to have his apologies intimated before the loyal toast and his thoughts on the occasion and his offer of a stained-glass window read out later to the Prince and assembled guests.[32]

No, Thoms was not easily abashed. Finding himself in Kirkwall when the Channel Fleet paid one of its visits there, he donned his uniform, mustered a crew of the smartest boatmen he could find and, standing proudly at the helm of his 'barge', headed out to pay his respects to the Admiral in command. Unfortunately, Vice-Admiral Thoms, having stuck close to his desk and never gone to sea, did not know that he was supposed to come alongside to starboard. As he clambered aboard at the flagship's port side, a crewman put him right:

> A damn fine Admiral you are, coming on board so, when you don't know port from starboard.

The officers who overheard were hard pressed to contain their amusement.[33]

Thoms' taste for self-aggrandisement did not escape more gentle ridicule, either. When he presented the Lerwick County Buildings with a set of Union Flags, one large and one small, to be flown whenever he or the Lord Lieutenant were in the county, another advocate penned some appropriate lines:

A New 'Northern Streamer'

Oh! the Union Jack is a rare old flag,
And it waves o'er many a sea;
Brave lives have been given to guard the rag
From danger and insult free;
It recks not the thrust of the foeman's spear,
It laughs at the rushing bombs,
But now it's to rise to a higher sphere,
It's to float over ADMIRAL TH-MS.

For TH-MS is a high and a mighty swell
In the regions of Ultima Thule,
He's nearly as big as 'The Duke hersel','
If you reckon his dignities duly;
The Mariner bold and the Udaller old,
The people on shore and on board-ship,
The Old Man of Hoy and the youngest small boy,
They all must give way to his Lordship.

'Tis right, when a Sheriff so grand and so proud
Goes down in his velvet and splendour,
That his presence august should be known to the crowd
And be hailed by each Minna and Brenda.
So he carries two flags to the North Countree,
And he says in presenting each pennant,
'The big one, you see, is to float over Me,
And the small o'er the Lord Lieutenant.'

There are times, perchance, when the flags may fly
Though neither great man may be there,
When a Prince of the blood may be born or die,
Or the great house of TH-MS have an heir.
But never, except for some mighty event,
Shall the big Union Jack be unfurled,
Which flutters in gladness at TH-MS' descent
On the Ultima Thulian world![34]

There was plenty of bunting fluttering in Lerwick on 20th August, 1880. That was the day of the newly-formed Lerwick Boating Club's first regatta, and Thoms was at the centre of the action. A women's pulling race had been advertised, and three girls from Trondra who wanted to compete in it had rowed to Scalloway and had their boat taken by cart over the hills to Lerwick, only to discover on arrival that they were the only entry and there would be no race. Fortunately, help was at hand. It was decided that they should race against two sailors from HM Cutter *Eagle,* which was lying at anchor in the harbour, and 'the worthy Sheriff of the County' volunteered to steer. In no time Thoms and his crew had shown the navy clear blue water, and when they crossed the finishing line still well ahead it was to ringing cheers from a throng of small boats.[35] The incident afforded such amusement to Thoms and others that one of his friends had a sketch of it drawn by, it was said, *Punch* cartoonist Linley Sambourne, and sent it to him as a Christmas card.[36] It also became something of a standing joke at regatta time. As late as 1888 it was reported that the Trondra lasses had withdrawn from a rowing race when they learned the Sheriff and Vice-Admiral was unavailable to be their coxswain.[37] Two weeks later the local press published a letter from Thoms, explaining that his absence was due to the last-minute change of the date of the regatta and urging the regatta committee to adhere to the date they fix 'so as to prevent disappointment both to myself and my Trondra crew.'[38] His 'crew', it seems, could be rather fickle. In 1883, Thoms

'Ye Trondra Lasses, their Victorie', with Vice-Admiral Thoms in his element at the helm. Sketch bequeathed by Thoms to be hung in the Sheriff's chambers at Lerwick, where it still remains. (courtesy of Sheriff Colin Scott Mackenzie).

had told the regatta prize-giving, to loud laughter, that he was in very bad spirits because the Trondra girls would have nothing more to do with him. He had tried every means in his power to bring back their affections, he said, and had even gone to the island and distributed sweeties among them, but all to no purpose. They seemed to have taken a deep-seated objection to him, and that objection was, he believed, that they thought he was too heavy in the stern.[39]

But there was more to Thoms' extra-official involvement in the affairs of his Sheriffdom than self-indulgent frivolity. His intervention in the Lerwick harbour works was a most practical one. Although he did lay the foundation stone with masonic honours on yet another day of civic bunting and frolic, he had earlier volunteered to guarantee personally any shortfall of the ten thousand pounds required to get the project under way.[40]

Shetland knitters, too, had cause to thank him, and not just for buying loud socks. To bring Shetland knitwear before a wider public he secured a stall at the Edinburgh International Exhibition of 1886. He then asked Mrs Muir, of the Lerwick hosiery firm Schoor, Currie & Co,[41] to take charge of it for him, as he was impressed with that firm's policy of paying their knitters in cash for their work instead of the old practice of truck or paying in goods. The stall was manned by six girls, three from Fair Isle and three from elsewhere in Shetland. Thoms paid all expenses, arranged accommodation, and handed over all profits to the knitters. Each month, six new girls took over, and they and Mrs Muir would be invited to tea at Thoms' house at Charlotte Square, where ladies would provide music and entertain them, and the host would be 'full of fun and humour' himself. He was most particular that the girls saw as much of the city as possible, and gave each of them five shillings pocket money for that purpose.[42] Several of the girls liked Edinburgh enough to stay on and find work after their tour of duty at the exhibition was over.[43]

Between May and October, 1886, some two-and-three-quarter million visitors poured through the exhibition site in the West Meadows,[44] and the Shetland and Fair Isle Knitters' stall was one of the star attractions. It was certainly of striking appearance, framed as it was by the four enormous whale jawbones that still stand at 'Jawbone Walk' today, having been, at Thoms' suggestion, donated to Edinburgh after the exhibition.[45] These bones were draped with lace curtains and herring nets of different hues, with the flags of Great Britain, Denmark and Norway at the corners and the arms of the Burgh of Lerwick on the front. Underneath hung various items of Shetland knitwear, while the girls sat below as if working at their own crofthouse hearths, a 'kishie' or straw basket of peats by their side.[46] The Shetland writer Jessie M. E. Saxby suggested they wear 'the old national peasant dress': dark blue skirts, jackets of brighter blue or pink figured calico confined at the waist and throat by dark blue ribbon, scarlet kerchiefs, and 'rivlins' or shoes of untanned hide,[47] a suggestion which, curiously enough, caused the girls of Mrs Saxby's home island of Unst to refuse to attend.[48] As the girls sat carding, spinning and knitting, they were asked numerous questions, all of which they answered with:

> . . . modesty and intelligence, to which the pretty Shetland accent adds unconscious piquancy.[49]

There was the odd bit of banter with expatriate Shetlanders, too.[50]

A good deal of the attention the stall received was a result of the adventure, that February, of the Shetland woman Betty Mouat, on whose behalf Thoms had also busied himself.[51] Travelling to Lerwick on the smack *Columbine* to sell her shawls,

The Zetland & Fair Isle Knitters' Stand at the Edinburgh International Exhibition of 1886. Financed and organised by Sheriff Thoms with meticulous attention to detail, it was a huge success, even being visited by Queen Victoria. The knitters sit beneath an arch made by whales' jawbones which now stands at Jawbone Walk, Edinburgh. (Shetland Museum and Archives).

she had found herself adrift alone when the two crewmen, having taken to the ship's boat in a vain attempt to save their drowning captain, had been unable to get back on board. The wind had suddenly filled the smack's sails, carrying the helpless passenger off out of reach and sight to her presumed death in a stormy North Sea. When word reached Britain nine days later that the vessel had, in fact, drifted ashore on the Norwegian coast with Betty half-starved but safe, the news caused a national sensation. Arriving in Edinburgh on her way home, she was immediately visited by Sheriff Thoms, who put her under the care of his own doctor and reported to her landlord on her well-being. He also bought one of her shawls, which was probably the one later displayed in a glass case on the Shetland stand.[52]

Thoms showed the shawl to Prince Albert Victor, elder son of the Prince and Princess of Wales, on the day he opened the exhibition,[53] and no doubt it was also viewed by his parents and sisters when they visited in October,[54] and by Queen

Victoria herself in August. On each occasion, Thoms was there in his Vice-Admiral's uniform to present appropriate items of knitwear to the royal ladies. Presenting the Queen with an Unst shawl, he made a short speech thanking Her Majesty for her kind patronage, outlining the history and importance of the Shetland knitting industry, and adding:

> The antiquated system of barter in disposing of their knitting still remains, and it is to introduce the knitters to better commercial ideas and relations that they have been brought south in monthly relays of six to this Exhibition. They go home with all their earnings, and what with these, the Parcel Post, and new commercial connections formed here, we may hope for a brighter hope for their industry.

The Queen returned the following day and purchased several more shawls.[55]

Thoms' 'unwearied energy and interest'[56] had paid dividends. The stall proved such a success – it won a gold medal, too - that Mrs Muir herself decided to organise one at the Glasgow Exhibition two years later. Thoms volunteered to pay the ground-space dues of £8. After that, the knitters were able to have a stall at each subsequent Scottish exhibition, where they continued to win prizes and royal patronage. Although he no longer made a financial contribution, Thoms continued to show a friendly interest.[57]

Mrs Muir found Thoms very kind and a thorough gentleman, but a sharp businessman, most particular in every little matter. This attention to small details, coupled with a pointed mode of expressing himself in writing or speech, was apparent in everything he did. His promotion of an Orcadian craft industry provides an example.

At the end of March, 1890, the Orkney-chair maker, D. M. Kirkness, received a letter:

Dear Sir,

> You supplied me with a straw chair in the end of November. I wish you to get made and send me another of smaller size as I propose to send both to the Exhibition to open here in beginning of May to see if it can do good to the Industry. The Local Industries of Scotland are to have a stall. As there is no time to be lost as it will require to be painted and varnished here to avoid scratches in transit, you will send it to the address of Messrs Sheppard, Painters, George Street, to whom I have given instructions as to colour &c. You will of course send the account to me.

Yours obedly.,

Geo. H. M. Thoms.

Kirkness did as he was told – almost:

13 Charlotte Square,

Edinr., 17 April, 1890

Dear Sir,

I had your Mem of 15th. as to your sending a straw backed chair <u>with drawer</u> <u>under</u> <u>seat</u>. I never ordered such and it will be returned to you if possible by tomorrow's steamer. A drawer under the seat gives it altogether the appearance of a night stool and makes it inappropriate as a drawing-room chair. Your photograph by which I ordered the chair shews no such drawer. You will never get customers at the Exhibition for your nightstool. I wished to advertise this as an Orkney native industry and if you can send me (to the care of Sheppard & Son, Painters, George Street) a chair of the smallest size according to the photograph <u>without</u> a <u>drawer</u> <u>underneath</u> immediately it may be in time for the Exhibition still.

Yours obedly.,

Geo. H. M. Thoms.

The effort was worth it. In June came another letter:

Dear Sir,

I have been today at the Exhibition and congratulate you at making a hit with the Orkney Chairs. 'Liberty' the great art furniture man, Regent Street, London, has taken them up and you must make hay (in this case chairs) while the sun shines – that is while the London season lasts. If you cannot get workers enough in Orkney you will get plenty in Zetland. And as this is a rare piece of good fortune I told Miss Glendinning who is in charge of the stall and is in communication with you, that rather than let this Golden opportunity pass if you could not undertake the orders she was to apply at the next stall – the Zetland and Fair Isle workers, and she would get the address of a Zetlander who could supply the chairs you could not undertake. Why not take all the orders and then run up to Lerwick by steamer and arrange for assistance yourself? I am to be in Lerwick – address County Buildings – on 21st. and could see you on 23rd. and assist you.

Yours obedly.

Geo. H. M. Thoms

I was right in telling you to make the chairs <u>open below the seat.</u>

To Thoms' annoyance, Kirkness did not seize the opportunity to the extent he urged. Even so, Kirkness enjoyed a full order book for his chairs from then on, a fact he attributed largely to Thoms' help. To show his appreciation, in 1896 he sent the Sheriff an Orkney chair he had made from oak taken from the cathedral. Thoms was delighted at the gesture but insisted on sending a cheque for £1: 10/- in recompense. In the light of the comments on his chair designs, one of the last contacts Kirkness had with Thoms was somewhat ironic: he had to mend the Sheriff's commode.[58]

Whenever he arrived in Kirkwall, Thoms would take an early opportunity to either call upon the Provost or send for him to discuss developments in the burgh and matters he had read about in the local press since his last visit. He was willing to give generously to worthy causes – the library, the hospital, the school, for example - and equally ready to refuse.[59] He was also free with advice, on one occasion even urging the County Council to send someone to a forthcoming Board of Trade conference on light railways which he thought would be of use in Orkney.[60] And all along he showed a marked interest in St Magnus Cathedral.[61]

One day in the 1870s or early eighties, policeman Isaac Costie was walking along the street in Kirkwall when he suddenly found himself buttonholed by Thoms and asked if he was aware of damage being done to the cathedral. When he said he was not, he was told 'that shows you have not been attending to your duty', and was peremptorily marched up to the front door of the building to be shown a small chip which had been knocked off one of the pillars. He was then given a lecture on the importance of the building and how it was not to be allowed to be destroyed by 'boys or other malicious persons.' Thoms then spoke to Costie's superior, Superintendent Grant, with the result that the boys of the town were banned from playing in the cathedral's doorways, and thenceforth the Kirkwall police had specific instructions to keep an eye on the building.[62]

Neither did Thoms miss an opportunity to remind the magistrates of their duties towards the cathedral. When a young man from Aberdeen had the ill luck to be carving his name on the tower parapet with a mallet and chisel just as Sheriff-substitute Armour came up to admire the view, and thus found himself before Sheriff Thoms on a charge of malicious mischief, Bailie Nicol Spence was one of the witnesses. After Spence had given evidence, Thoms invited him onto the bench for the remainder of the proceedings. Although the defence pointed out that the tower's stonework was already well-covered with initials and names, including that of Prince Alfred (apparently painted a yard and a half long), Thoms was unimpressed. He found the accused guilty and imposed a fine of one pound or a month's imprisonment.[63] Afterwards, he explained to Bailie Spence that he wished to give a lesson to the magistrates as to how they should deal with offences towards the building. He pointed out the dangers of allowing visitors unaccompanied to the tower, urged the town council to take some steps to put the cathedral in better repair, and stated that he would be willing to give some financial assistance to enable them to do so.[64]

This was not the only time he vainly attempted to get the Town Council to galvanise itself into action. To the Town Clerk, William Cowper, he suggested that if they drew up a scheme of restoration and advertised for subscriptions all over the world 'wherever there is an Orcadian', they would soon raise enough money. He himself would not be the last or least to give his subscription. Cowper thought it would never work.[65] Thoms had made a similarly unsuccessful effort publicly some years earlier, in 1886 at the opening of Kirkwall Town Hall, urging his listeners with words which would prove punningly prophetic: 'wherever there is a will, there is a way.'[66] More directly prophetic, however, was what he said on a social visit to Kirkwall doctor James S. S. Logie. When Logie said that he hoped some day some rich Orcadian would restore the cathedral, Thoms gave an emphatic reply: 'The day will come, and the man will come.' After Thoms had left, Dr Logie turned to his wife and said, 'I am sure it is in his 'noddle' to do it himself.'[67]

In the south, too, Thoms took an interest in the wider community. He was involved at both ends of the educational spectrum, as not only a Life Governor of University College, Dundee, and a member of the committee responsible for erecting new buildings for Edinburgh University, but also a director of the United Industrial School of Edinburgh, an institution which, he believed, had:

> . . . successfully solved the problem of educating Protestant and Roman Catholic children together in secular knowledge and separately in religious knowledge.[68]

For the Juridical Society of Edinburgh he delivered extra-mural lectures for two sessions on the topic 'The Law of Scotland as a System of Equity', and he was the learned author of a *Treatise on Judicial Factors, Curators Bonis, and Managers of Burghs,* which ran to a second edition,[69] and some articles on the office of Procurator Fiscal. These articles he planned to expand into a book, and he also gathered materials for a history of the Admirals of Scotland and a collection of old documents relating to Orkney.[70] He was a Member of the Royal Scottish Geographical Society, a Fellow of both the Society of Antiquaries of Scotland and the Royal Society of Edinburgh, and a member of the Royal Company of Archers (the Queen's Bodyguard for Scotland), as well as chairman of the Metropolitan Cemetery Company and a director of the Edinburgh Sanitary Protection Association (an organisation to promote better sewers).[71] However:

> In no public work of this kind has he ever taken a keener interest or

brought about results more satisfactory to himself, or of more lasting benefit to the public, than in the restoration of St Giles's cathedral, Edinburgh, where he worshipped.[72]

Although his father had been a Free Kirk elder,[73] Thoms formed a high-profile attachment to this most 'establishment' of Established churches, an attachment celebrated in three further humorous poems by a legal colleague.[74] As 'an enthusiastic brother of those masons who built it',[75] he was one of the instigators of its restoration and became vice-chairman of the committee of subscribers. The appointment of the publisher and ex-Lord Provost Dr William Chambers of Glenormiston as chairman was Thoms' suggestion. Later, when money ran short, Chambers financed the remainder of the restoration out of his own pocket and thus, in Thoms' view:

> . . . raised an imperishable monument to himself, while doing a patriotic service to his country.[76]

A kenspeckle and convivial figure in Edinburgh society, Thoms was a regular dinner and dance guest.[77] One evening in February, 1878, for instance, he was to be found gracing the St Andrew's Boat Club Fancy Dress Ball in the guise of Magnus Troil of Burgh Westra, Great Foud of Zetland, a character from Scott's *The Pirate* holding a similar office to his own.[78] Thoms himself kept a hospitable table and a well-stocked cellar. His prestigious New Town address of 13 Charlotte Square, where he had moved from Great King Street in 1885, had a large back drawing room which doubled as a ballroom. The floors were covered with long mats which could be rolled back easily to facilitate dancing, and on the wall above the entrance was painted the third line of the 100th Psalm: 'Him serve with mirth.'[79]

That Thoms liked to enjoy himself, there is no doubt. His wealth and position in life – and his bachelorhood - enabled him to indulge his fancies pretty freely. The duties of a Sheriff then were not particularly taxing. The salary he received for discharging them, combined with any earnings he may have had from the Bar[80] and, after his father's death, the Aberlemno and Dundee properties, supported him in a manner to which anyone would happily become accustomed. It was a fairly sunny existence while it lasted, but when Thoms was around sixty the shadows began to fall. The next dozen or so years would see a slow but inexorable decline into painful and debilitating illness, a decline halted only by death.

With hindsight, the deterioration in his health could be said to have begun in the spring of 1891 with a severe attack of gout. He had suffered from that disease for years, but this time the attack came in combination with influenza and double pneumonia, laying him up for twelve weeks. Although he made light of it – apologising to the London Caithness Association for his absence from their first annual dinner on the grounds that he was confined to Blanket Bay with two anchors down[81] - he had, in fact, been lucky to pull through. It was thought, too, that he had suffered a slight shock or stroke which left him paralysed down one side for several days and affected his speech. Although he seemed to recover, from that point on his mobility, speech and general health grew gradually worse. His speech was greatly affected by a recurring abscess in his upper jaw. This flared up in 1893 and again in 1895, on each occasion being operated on to remove decayed bone. In the autumn of the former year, he had also taken suddenly ill when in Caithness. He suffered a seizure while dressing for dinner at Stemster, and his Edinburgh doctor had to engage an attendant to go north to look after him for a few weeks and bring him home. After that he always needed the services of a manservant to help him around and otherwise attend to him. He developed a foul discharge from his nose and mouth, his speech became indistinct as if his tongue were too big, and in around 1898 running sores broke out all over his body and his head.[82]

For at least the last six or seven years of his life it was obvious to everyone that Thoms was physically a broken man. His habitually cheery look had gone. At home he sat often with his head sunk upon his breast, a cap on his head, his cold hands in gloves or a muff, and a plaid about his legs. His sores had to be cleaned and dressed twice a day, and he continually used a handkerchief to wipe the discharge from his nose and mouth. Any room he used had to be kept well-ventilated to disperse the smell of his sores, and scented ribbon was burned for the same purpose.[83]

Yet he would not give in to what assailed him. Showing an indomitable will to live[84] and refusing to admit he was ill, he even resented being asked how he was. 'Perfectly well. Perfectly well. All except my legs,' remained his standard reply almost to the end,[85] usually followed by some quip about his going to get himself a new pair,[86] for illness, while subduing it, never quite killed off his humour.[87] He remained Sheriff until 1899, and until the previous summer travelled north to carry out his duties as before, although sometimes only able to hold courts in his lodgings.[88] In these later years he spent longer in the north, basing himself at Kirkwall for several weeks each summer.[89] On his last visit, in 1898, he was there for three months, but that was as far as he got.[90] His attempt to reach Shetland was frustrated by the weather when the steamer was forced to turn back, and he did not try again.[91] When out and about in his Sheriffdom he came to rely on two sticks for support.[92] Later, he was led along by his manservant taking both hands and walking backwards before him.[93] In the end he used a bath chair. He was more or less carried to and from it, and he required similar assistance to get on and off the bench.[94] Back in Edinburgh, he liked to go out for a drive in a cab almost every day.[95] When, in 1898, the horse bolted down Liberton Brae and the cab overturned, Thoms was carried out unconscious. Despite suffering minor head injuries and being badly shaken, he insisted on going out again the next day.[96] He went on holiday, too, to Moffat in 1900 for example, and to Gullane in 1901.[97] In the latter place he was seen being wheeled around in his bath chair, a veil over his face to keep the flies from the pus.[98]

In the spring following his retiral Thoms removed from Charlotte Square to a new suburban villa at 26 Cluny Drive. There his health continued its slow deterioration. In neither 1902 nor 1903 was the weather good enough for him to go away, and in the autumn of the latter year his final decline began. Confined to bed under the full-time care of a nurse, he slipped gradually into a semi-comatose state and became unable to retain nourishment. Then on a Sunday evening, 25th October, 1903, at about ten o'clock, Thoms' suffering was finally over.[99]

His nephew Alfred's was just beginning.

A late portrait of Sheriff Thoms in uncharacteristically plain clothes.

17

II

A disappointed nephew

If Kirkwall was the winner in Thoms' last will, his nephew Alfred was the loser, for it was he who had stood to inherit what was left, instead, to restore St Magnus Cathedral. What came between him and his expectations may well have been a game left knee.

Alfred Thoms, nephew of the Sheriff, and prime mover in the attempt to overturn his will.

Alfred Patrick Thoms was the elder son of Thoms' only brother. Born in 1871, he grew up in Dundee, where his Uncle George was a frequent visitor to the family home during his childhood.[2] Surviving estimates of Thoms' fondness for his relations vary. One person said the only relative she ever heard him speak of with any tender emotion was his late mother, but that is probably putting it too strongly, since he showed a good deal of kindness and generosity to his nephew.[3] He wrote Alfred when the latter began his arts course at St Andrews in 1889, saying, amongst other things, that he hoped he was taking up golf, and letting him know that he had written Old Tom Morris, the celebrated Open Champion and St Andrews club-maker, to open an account for him. Later, he asked what Alfred intended to do as a career. On learning of his nephew's wish to become a Writer to the Signet, Thoms offered to pay his fees for the WS Society, then around £500.[4] After consulting his father Alfred declined the offer on the grounds that it was far too large a sum to accept. Having graduated MA in 1892, Alfred went to Geneva and took another degree there. On his return, he apprenticed himself to a Writer to the Signet in Dundee for three years. All the while he had maintained a regular correspondence with his uncle. When he came to Edinburgh to attend the law classes in the autumn of 1896, he began to visit him frequently as well.

It was at this stage that the subject of Thoms' will first came up. In the autumn or early winter of 1897, Alfred was visiting his uncle at Charlotte Square when the latter told him he was to be his principal beneficiary, and would get Aberlemno and The Crescent as well as the Charlotte Square house and some of his moveable property (ie, property other than land or buildings). He said he did not want Alfred to sell the house but to live in it, as he had taken a great deal of trouble with it and there was no better house anywhere. Alfred assured his uncle he would, thanked him for what he proposed to do, and said:

> I hope your health may be restored, and that it may be long before the succession opens.[5]

There was only one formal condition to the bequest, namely that Alfred assume the name 'Macthomas'. This was because Thoms believed himself to be Chief of the Clan Macthomas of Glenshee, or as he liked to refer to himself 'Ye MacComish', and had already assumed the additional name himself. Of this belief, Alfred said his uncle:

> . . . invented it himself, and by dint of repeating it very often he came to believe it....He attached very great importance to his position as the imaginary head of this clan, and took an immense pride in it.[6]

He even designed a clan tartan.[7]

Another way in which the clan chief's pride manifested itself was in book form. In 1887, a Blairgowrie schoolmaster named William McCombie Smith had published a book entitled *Memoir of the Family of McCombie, a branch of Clan McIntosh*. Shortly afterwards Thoms contacted the author, stating he had read his work with great interest and that it was a tradition in his family that they were descended from McComie Mor of Glenshee. He provided Smith with his family tree. Although Smith tried to find evidence of Thoms' descent from the Glenshee clan, he did not manage to find anything more concrete than tradition. He obviously thought it sufficient, for in 1888 he acceded to Thoms' suggestion that he produce a new edition to include the story of Thoms' family. This duly appeared in 1890, not only financed by Thoms but also, it seems, partly written by him.[8] The new edition was entitled *Memoir of the Families of McCombie and Thoms, originally McIntosh and McThomas* and contained chapters on Thoms and his father.[9] If they were indeed written by Thoms himself, he evidently did not believe that self praise was no recommendation. He presented Alfred with a copy of the new edition, inscribed 'To my dear nephew Alfred, from his affectionate uncle, Geo. H. M. Thoms, Ye MacComish.' Other copies were given to his servants, whom he urged to read it, to friends,[10] and to the Shetland Literary and Scientific Society.[11] According to a story that went the rounds in Kirkwall at the time, he even sent a copy to Queen Victoria.[12]

A particular bugbear of the fastidious clan chief was the spelling of the clan name. Thoms was adamant that the 't' in Macthomas had to be lower case. He emphasised the point strongly to Alfred, wrote a nasty letter to the wife of an old friend who had got it wrong,[13] and generally flew into a rage whenever it was misspelt. Strangely enough, Smith's book spells it with a capital throughout.

According to Alfred's account, he agreed to take the name 'Macthomas', with a small 't', when the condition was first mentioned to him by his uncle in 1897. Then, towards the end of February the following year, Thoms noticed that he had not taken it yet, and challenged him about it. Alfred explained that he had promised to take the name upon his surviving his uncle and the succession opening. At this, Thoms burst out with great emotion, 'You may die before me, and then you will never keep your promise.' He became so worked up that he was trembling all over. He demanded that Alfred take the name immediately. The latter, having urged his uncle to calm himself as such emotion was not good for him, said he would think the matter over and come back to speak to him about it again in a few days. On his return, he claimed, things went even worse. He told his uncle that he thought if he changed his name then people might think that he was toadying to him for the sake of improving his prospects. This lit Thoms' short fuse. 'It will cost you a mint of money if you don't take the name,' he cried, turning purple in the face and foaming at the mouth. Alfred was afraid the succession would open there and then. He begged his Uncle George to calm himself, said he would write him with his decision, and then took his leave. The letter he sent was to the effect that he was unwilling to take the name under threat of disinheritance. This seemed to mollify Thoms. He apologised to Alfred, saying he would never think of threatening him as he was 'his own laddie', and he thought all the better of him for not kowtowing to him. He said he would still like it very much, though, if he took the name, and it would be much more convenient for him to do so then than later. After discussing the question with Thoms' solicitor, Alfred agreed to do so.[14]

For a while Alfred's relations with his uncle were good. There was one unexplained outburst at the end of 1899 when, according to Alfred, Thoms suddenly demanded, 'Do you wish to kill me?', but that was apparently an isolated incident. Then came Alfred's knee problems.

Alfred had what he called 'a serious accident' to his left knee in December, 1897, through doing gymnastics. He did not take his doctor's advice to lay up, but by May, 1900, the knee had got so bad that he had to give up work and go away. He consulted the London specialist, William Watson Cheyne, a Shetlander more famous as a pioneer of antiseptic surgery, and was told that if he did not keep off town pavement he would become permanently lame. So he took himself off to Ilfracombe, Brighton, Bournemouth and other resorts for the next two and a half years until his knee had recovered. He did not return to Edinburgh till the autumn of 1902.

It was this absence which seems to have poisoned Thoms' relations with him. The uncle came to regard the nephew as an idle fellow, who was sitting back on his oars waiting for his inheritance and was not going to practise his profession.

When Alfred returned to Edinburgh he felt there was a distinct change in his uncle's demeanour towards him. He did not say much, but looked at him in the coldest way. Relations were not helped when Thoms urged Alfred in vain to set up his plate in Dundee.[15] Alfred had passed the necessary exams and had been admitted as a Writer to the Signet in July, 1903, but although he made enquiries in Dundee that September, he did not find partnership terms that he considered acceptable. By the time of Thoms' death he was working as head clerk in an Edinburgh law office to gain practical experience. He only commenced practice on his own account some seven months after his uncle's death.

Despite the apparent coolness between uncle and nephew, during Thoms' final illness Alfred visited regularly. When on one visit he sympathised with his uncle for having a bad throat, Thoms just managed a hoarsely spluttered reply: 'My throat is perfectly right.' On Saturday, 24th October, Alfred offered to read him the 23rd Psalm, but he shook his head. The following afternoon he visited again. He told his Uncle George how very sorry he was to see him so ill and thanked him for all his past kindnesses to him. At this, Thoms tried very hard to speak but could only manage fragments of words. From these, Alfred formed the opinion that he wanted to change his will. It seems Alfred may have had some inkling that he had been passed over. Perhaps, though, that was all his uncle was trying to tell him.

Whatever the case, Alfred was a bit slow in realising the possible urgency of the situation. Only at half past nine that evening did it occur to him that maybe he should do something. What he did was call on a Mr Babington, one of the partners of Thoms' solicitors, Messrs Melville and Lindesay, in Wemyss Place. Babington suggested Alfred speak to his partner, Mr Wood, who acted personally for Thoms. This required a cab, because Wood lived at Buckingham Terrace out the Queensferry Road. On arriving at Wood's, Alfred asked the cab driver to wait, and went in to see the solicitor. Wood thought it best to speak to Thoms' doctor before taking any action. This was Doctor Affleck, who lived in Heriot Row, just beyond where Alfred had started from. So back they and the cab went. Satisfied by what the doctor told him, Wood then needed an independent witness. He decided to take one of his staff who lived in Royal Circus. Not only was that in precisely the opposite direction to Thoms' house, but the witness could not at first be found. Eventually he was. Then he and Wood, plus an anxious Alfred, a fortunate cabbie and a less fortunate horse all headed out to Cluny Drive.

There is something reminiscent of Conan Doyle in all these scurryings across a darkened city in a four-wheeler, though of course Alfred Thoms was not armed with Dr Watson's service revolver. He was in fact carrying something much more useful in the circumstances: the form of docquet of notarial execution required when a testator is physically unable to sign his name. He had cut it specially from one of his legal reference books.

But it was all too late. When they arrived at Cluny Drive it was eleven o'clock and Thoms was already laid out under a sheet. Worse still, Alfred found his uncle's manservant, Adam Melrose, in what he described as 'a state of horrible elation', and was, he claimed, ushered by him into the drawing room to be told, 'Your uncle has left me thousands.'

What he had left, and to whom, was specified in a will dated 16th March, 1903. Though this was Thoms' last will, it was certainly not his first, or even his second. It was, in fact, something like his eighty-fifth testamentary writing, including codicils.[16] His previous will was dated 21st March, 1893, and in it he left the residue of his estate (ie, what remained after satisfying specific legacies, executry expenses, etc) to his nephew Alfred on condition that he use and constantly retain the name 'Macthomas'. If he refused to comply with that condition, the residue was to go to Alfred's brother Henry, or Harry, subject to the same condition. The 1893 will also contained the following unusual provision:

> I wish to be buried from St Giles' cathedral in the Metropolitan Cemetery, Morningside, in a wicker or other slight coffin, so as to have a chance to be in early at the general scramble at the resurrection.

During the next ten years Thoms made twenty-three codicils altering or adding to this will. One of them contained the direction that his body be cremated and the *residuum* put in a jar in the Ladies' Vestry at St Giles, a retiring room added to St Giles at Thoms' expense and which had his coat of arms carved into the fabric. He told T. W. Ranken, the Orkney Sheriff Clerk, of this direction one night at Kirkwall as they walked across the Ayre together on their way to dine at Grainbank. Why, asked Ranken, did he want his ashes to be put there? Because, Thoms replied, he wanted to see what the ladies did.[17]

In the end he left slightly more conventional instructions. He was cremated in Glasgow and his ashes buried in Morningside Cemetery, the service being performed by the minister of St Giles and the funeral undertaken by a joiner from Torphichen Street.[18]

The 1903 will was five closely-written pages long and, apart from the residuary provision which gave most of his fortune to Kirkwall, contained a fair number of specific and pecuniary bequests. These

TO THE GLORY OF GOD
AND
IN HONOUR OF S. MARGARET
1891

Thoms' coat of arms in the Ladies' Vestry or Retiring Room of St Giles cathedral, Edinburgh. Constructed at Thoms' expense, it is now the souvenir shop.

ranged from leaving St Giles' Kirk Session five thousand pounds for the musical service in the cathedral and a further sixteen hundred pounds for two assistants to supply the daily service, to bequeathing his ex-Lighthouse Board door knocker to the Society of Antiquaries of Scotland. Some friends got pictures or books, his sister Grace got the mourning ring he had purchased on the death of their 'dear sister Eliza', and he requested his Trustee to arrange for two of his pictures to be hung in Lerwick Sheriff Court, one being of himself in fancy dress as Magnus Troil from Scott's *The Pirate*, the other the sketch of 'The Trondra Lasses: their Victorie.' He left a thousand pounds to the widow of an old school friend, Mrs Mary Irvine, whom failing, to her daughter Emily who had acted as his amanuensis. Five hundred pounds went to his cousin, Mrs Ella Smith, and a hundred each to three godchildren,

Thoms as Magnus Troil from Walter Scott's *The Pirate*. Bequeathed to be hung in Lerwick Sheriff Court it was instead thrown into a lumber room. It has only recently been restored and put on display. (Shetland Museum and Archives).

one of whom was also to have the premiums paid on her endowment policy. There was also a bequest of a hundred pounds to William McCombie Duguid, his fifth cousin, representing in the female line the McCombie branch of the Clan Macthomas, fifty pounds to the clan historian William McCombie Smith, and five pounds to the Orkney and Zetland Association of which he had been president for many years.

His valet Adam Melrose's 'horridly elated' anticipation was justified. He and his wife, and the survivor of them, received a liferent tenancy of the Cluny Drive property, rent-free, refurbished as necessary, with the use of all usual household plenishings and an annuity of £100 per annum. He was also left Thoms' fur cloak and the other items of his wardrobe.

Alfred and his brother were not exactly 'cut off with a shilling' either, though it must have seemed like it, particularly to the former. He received the liferent of Aberlemno, worth about £170 a year, while his brother got the more lucrative liferent of The Crescent, earning him just under five hundred pounds a year. They also received quite a number of family heirlooms and other items, albeit accompanied by the testator's rather biting humour. They were left his curling stones, for example, 'to make men of them', Alfred was the recipient of two screens of flowers hand-painted by Thoms' mother, and Harry received 'the copper gong which has been my companion through my years of ill health.' Alfred was also left the grants of arms of Thoms and his father, the latest (1903) edition of a standard work on Scottish heraldry, and yet another copy of William McCombie Smith's book so he would understand their significance. Finally, in a quite deliciously mischievous touch, Alfred was to receive an address that had been presented to Thoms on his retiral by the Sheriff-substitute, Honorary Sheriffs-substitute, Members of the Bar and officials of the Sheriff Court of Orkney. The address was contained in a casket made of old oak from St Magnus Cathedral.

Alfred obviously did not appreciate these provisions, and decided to challenge the will. First, however, he attempted a compromise. If the Provost and Magistrates of Kirkwall were not to oppose his action, he informed them through his solicitors, he would be willing to pay them a sum of money, to be negotiated, which they could spend at their discretion on erecting the memorial window and carrying out other works on the cathedral. The proposal was rejected.[19]

Proceedings were raised in the Court of Session in April, 1904. The pursuers (those raising the action) were Alfred, Harry and their three sisters. The defenders (those sued) were William A. Wood CA, the trustee and executor appointed under the 1903 will, and incidentally the brother of Thoms' solicitor John Philp Wood WS, together with all the beneficiaries under the will other than the pursuers. The action was for reduction of the will, to have it declared null and void. The action also sought to reduce a number of the codicils made by Thoms since 1893 so that, with a few minor changes, the 1893 will, alone, would be left standing and effective, leaving Alfred as the main beneficiary.

The grounds of reduction were twofold: first, that on the dates of making the codicils and the will, Thoms was not of sound disposing mind, so they could not be regarded as his deeds; and, second, that these deeds were impetrated from Thoms by his manservant Melrose by fraud and circumvention when Thoms was weak and facile in mind and easily imposed upon.[20] The latter ground came as something of a surprise to Melrose, since Alfred had not only frequently expressed gratitude to him for his care of his uncle, but had assured him that he had nothing to fear from the action as it would only affect Kirkwall.[21]

The alleged facts the pursuers sought to rely on to establish these grounds can be grouped under a number of heads. First, they relied upon Thoms' noted and long-standing eccentricity. They then went further and said that he had come to suffer from insane delusions. These included the belief that he was chief of the Macthomases. Another was that he was financially poor. They also argued that St Magnus Cathedral was in a good state of repair and that no-one in possession of his sanity would leave such a large sum for its restoration. Underlying all

25

of this was his ill health which, the pursuers claimed, had so weakened his reason as to make him incapable of understanding the effect of his purported testamentary writings and lay him open to the malign influence of Melrose the valet.

The written pleadings and other preliminary stages having been concluded, the case came before the Lord Justice-Clerk, Sir John H. A. Macdonald, and a civil jury of twelve men[22] on Saturday, 4th February, 1905. It would last five days. Counsel for the parties included some eminent figures. Leading for the pursuers was Frank Towers Cooper KC (1863 – 1915), an Englishman whose father edited *The Scotsman*. He was assisted by William Hunter, afterwards a Lord of Session, and William W. R. Garson. A contemporary profile describes Cooper as 'an excellent advocate – alert, resourceful and persistent', with a peculiarly lucrative practice acting for the class of clients who:

> . . . provide luncheon for their counsel, their agents, their skilled witnesses, and themselves. They are chiefly bodies corporate; on behalf of the unincorporated individual who leaves you to forage for your own refreshments Mr Cooper 'attends' comparatively seldom.[23]

How well Alfred victualled him is not recorded. Cooper had originally been only junior counsel in the case, supporting Lord Advocate Charles Scott Dickson KC, MP, and soon-to-be Solicitor-General E. T. Salvesen KC, but these two had ceased to act by the time the case came to trial.[24]

For the first defender (William A. Wood, Thoms' Trustee) appeared Thomas Shaw KC, MP, James Avon Clyde KC and John G. Jameson. Shaw (1850 – 1937), the son of a Dunfermline baker, was a high-flier in both the law and politics. On the radical wing of the Liberal party, he had been MP for the Hawick burghs since 1892 and Solicitor-General for Scotland in Lord Rosebery's administration. After ten years in opposition, he would soon be Lord Advocate when the Liberals regained power at the end of 1905, before going to the House of Lords as a Lord of Appeal in 1909.[25] A gifted orator with a literary bent, Shaw excelled in jury trials.[26]

Clyde, no less effective on questions of fact before a jury, but reputedly Shaw's superior in purely legal matters, also combined law and politics, albeit with less emphasis on the latter and that on the Unionist side. A few months after the Thoms case, he became Solicitor-General in the dying days of the Balfour government, although he was not yet an MP, and in 1916 was appointed Lord Advocate in Lloyd George's coalition. He would end his legal career as Lord President of the Court of Session and Lord Justice-General from 1920 to 1935.[27]

The Provost and Magistrates of Kirkwall were the only beneficiaries actively to defend the action, and were represented by Alexander L. McClure, Advocate.

As the principal beneficiaries, they agreed to indemnify Thoms' trustee for the expenses of defending the will. The trustee would be responsible for most of that defence, but the Provost and Magistrates would deal with the reasonableness of the bequest. To that end, McClure led the evidence of two architects and cited a considerable number of witnesses, mainly from Orkney, who had to travel down to Edinburgh without in the end being called. Otherwise, his was mainly a watching brief.[28]

Before examining the evidence that was led, it is worthwhile pausing for a moment to consider just what an odd case this was. Here was the second most senior judge in Scotland presiding over a hearing to determine the sanity of a man who had been a judicial colleague. Seven members of the Faculty of Advocates were gathered before an eighth to argue the mental capacity of one of their brethren. Four of the seven were or would later be Sheriffs themselves, with Cooper and McClure's appointments as such having been announced that very week.[29] The closer one looks, the more incestuous the whole business appears. Jameson, junior counsel for the trustee, was the son of Thoms' old friend Lord Ardwall, who would be one of the trustee's witnesses. Cooper had lived two doors from Thoms in Charlotte Square.[30] Above

Sir John H. A. Macdonald, Lord Justice-Clerk. An old colleague of Sheriff Thoms, he presided in his will case with the appropriate mix of firmness and dry wit. For the occasion he would have worn the more workaday short wig, and civil robes faced in crimson with crimson or scarlet crosses. (portrait by George Fiddes Watt, 1911, reproduced courtesy of the Faculty of Advocates).

all, the Lord Justice-Clerk had been a Sheriff at the same time as Thoms,[31] a brother-in-arms in the Royal Company of Archers, and a convivial companion on the *Pharos* and elsewhere, offers of laxative concoctions notwithstanding.[32] Indeed, in his charge to the jury, he said they had all known Thoms and that no-one who had known him could doubt that he had been eccentric. Then, having reviewed the stories of his old colleague's eccentricity that had been brought out in evidence, he threw in a couple of his own for good measure.[33]

The pursuers' case began on the Saturday morning with an opening speech by Hunter, explaining the nature of the case and what the pursuers would be seeking to prove, after which their first witness took the stand. He was the Rev.

John Mackenzie Gibson, aged 69, formerly minister of the Parish of Avoch in Ross-shire, and an intimate friend of Thoms for some forty-seven years. He was therefore an ideal first witness. He could speak to the whole period under consideration and thus give the jury an outline of the ground to be gone over repeatedly later. Further, as a minister he was likely to be trusted implicitly, especially as he had no obvious axe to grind in the matter. With him began four days of evidence. With him, too, began the humour, not always intentional, that was to be a marked feature of the case. It came not just from witnesses and counsel, but often from the presiding judge as well. An early example was when Cooper, for the pursuers, asked the reverend gentleman about Thoms' taste in purgatives:

(Q.) Was he addicted to taking Gregory's mixture? (A.) – He was.

The Lord Justice-Clerk. – That was not a sign of insanity when I was a boy. (Laughter.) Witness – He called it 'the element of happiness'. (Renewed Laughter.)[34]

After Mackenzie Gibson, twenty other witnesses took the stand for the pursuers, with the evidence of a further three being taken on commission as they were either unfit to attend or abroad. Most of them described the eccentricities of the late Sheriff in considerable detail, and these eccentricities were many and various. His sartorial individuality, for example, did not stop at his socks. He had a number of waistcoats made with elasticated sides to wear when dining. At least one such he dubbed his 'Laughing Waistcoat', and had those words or 'Laughing Vest' embroidered in gold upon its red material.[35] He also had a 'Flirtation Waistcoat', but as to what its special features may have been the evidence is mercifully silent.[36] Once, when dining at Musselburgh after a round on the links, he insisted on throwing back his golfing jacket to show all the ladies of the party his laughing waistcoat, and tried to get them to abandon stays and take to gussets instead.[37] This, it should be remembered, was at a time when the gentleman's shirt was still regarded as an item of underwear, and therefore not for exposure to the tender gaze of ladies except at the stiffly-starched collar, cuffs and front. Nor do contemporary manuals of etiquette recommend the relative merits of whalebone or elasticated corsetry as a suitable conversational topic in mixed company.

Even Thoms' other waistcoats were not entirely normal. On their front, from his watch chain, he hung a silver broken heart; to mend the cracks in his own heart or in those of any jilted ladies he encountered he was said to carry gutta-percha; and, when attending weddings, his waistcoat pockets were filled with camphor in order, he said, to 'keep away matrimonial infection.'[38] Perhaps the most unusual thing he carried around with him, though, was a schoolmaster's tawse.

The tawse or strap was always, it seems, at hand to be produced whenever he encountered any small boys. A Kirkwall witness, whose evidence was not in the end used in court, the widow of Police Superintendent Grant, recalled a typical incident. Thoms had been on a regular tour of inspection of

A schoolteacher's tawse or strap of the kind carried by Sheriff Thoms to tease any children he encountered. Presumably his was fairly small, as he carried it in his pocket with his gloves and handkerchief.

the police station, which then stood at the foot of Wellington Street. Mrs Grant was coming down the stairs followed by the Sheriff, with her husband bringing up the rear, when a little boy who was in the habit of begging for bread from her came in at the outer door and asked her for a 'piece'. On seeing this, Thoms began to fumble in the tail pocket of his coat and, whipping out a tawse of yellow leather, waved it in the air with the words 'Look at that, my little boy!' As Mrs Grant put it, the boy 'gave one yell and went out through the door flying'.[39]

On another occasion, when Thoms was visiting the historian and Episcopal rector at Kirkwall, the Rev. J. B. Craven, he inadvertently pulled out the tawse with his handkerchief and gloves, only to put it away again without comment. With their common antiquarian and masonic interests, one might have expected Craven and Thoms to be friends, but in fact their relations were purely formal. When Kirkwall Town Council's lawyers interviewed Craven as a potential witness, he gave his views quite succinctly:

> I always thought the Sheriff was queer but I could not say he was off his head.[40]

He was not cited to give evidence.

Of those who did, many mentioned the tawse. Indeed, from the evidence led at the jury trial, and the precognitions or statements of those who did not give evidence, it is doubtful whether any child Thoms encountered escaped without at least seeing the implement and being teased with it. Although he also used it to give 'palmies', these it seems were playful rather than painful. Neither were children the only recipients: he once gave his Kirkwall landlady the strap for not waiting up to let him in.[41] Usually when the tawse was produced it was closely followed by sweets. With typical thoroughness Thoms had a batch of sweets prepared by Fergusons, the Edinburgh Rock manufacturers, before setting off for his sheriffdom. These would be made up in small packets for distributing to children. On the lighthouse cruises, Thoms would ascertain, as the ship approached a lighthouse, how many keepers' children were there, and take the appropriate number of boxes ashore with him, the sweets in one pocket, the tawse in the other. Then, after he had made a pretence of strapping the boys, the sweets would be distributed.[42] Sometimes he would make a child hold out its hand for a 'cut' from the tawse, only for him to put sweets there instead.[43] At the end of the cruise, Thoms would divide the remaining sweets among the crew for their own children.[44]

Through twenty-first century eyes it is a little difficult to view Thoms' behaviour towards children in the innocent spirit in which it was almost certainly intended. The spectacle of a middle-aged to elderly bachelor roaming the country whipping small boys and giving sweets to little girls is the sort of thing liable to bring a modern child-care professional out in a cold sweat. Moreover, his behaviour at a Kirkwall children's party seems, when set down in print, at best macabre and at worst positively sadistic:

> [H]e threatened to take out some of the children's tongues. He had a penknife in his hand and put the children in an abject state of terror. He told them he had some sheep's tongues in the lobby which he was to put in instead.

The witness's explanation somehow offers little reassurance:

> This was purely done as a joke and he was never done joking where children were concerned and teasing and frightening them.[45]

And yet this witness was the mother of one of the children present, saw nothing wrong in his behaviour, and went on to testify to his fondness for children.[46] Her daughter, too, recalled how he took a delight in children and in joking and teasing with them.[47]

Neither were children just convenient butts for his humour. He does seem to have taken a genuine interest in them, impressing observers with his memory for all the lightkeepers' families,[48] always enquiring after the children of his friends and colleagues – Sheriff Shennan's son, for example, was 'my young friend Ronald'[49] – and following their later careers not only with interest but often practical assistance, too. Amidst the teasing, he was not above making a fool of himself as well. In the summer of 1881, at a picnic at Sundibanks in Shetland, he went to assist some youngsters who were tossing each other in a blanket. After helping to toss a couple of them, the Sheriff and Vice-Admiral gamely took his turn in being thrown Sancho Panza-style into the air.[50]

There is ample evidence from adults that the children liked Thoms. More significantly, there is also evidence to that effect from people who had encountered him when they were children. Nonetheless, not all children can have appreciated his rather heavy-handed humour. Mrs Grant's children usually tried to get out of the way when the Sheriff arrived, though that may have been partly down to their picking up on their parents' anxiety at his imminent inspection. When the sweets came out, their mother said, they were 'usually about hands'.[51] The Edinburgh Rock evidently did not sweeten the attitude of his young cousin Helen Fleming, however:

> . . . he was given to making jokes and was so pleased with them that he continually repeated them....he did not change unless it were to become more monotonous.[52]

Nor, apparently, did he make a hit with the young James Cullen Grierson, son of Shetland landowner A. J. Grierson of Quendale and later a solicitor in Lerwick. His precognition is one of the most disparaging of the late Sheriff:

> Even as a boy...I remember him as the laughing stock of the community, he used to always call at my father's house and was an object of great amusement to myself and my sisters, he would probably bring along a halfpenny worth of sweets for each of the girls which he would present to them with the manner of making them a handsome present, he always talked of the number of times he had been in love, and how his heart was all cracked and mended up with Gutta-percha.

> The whole talk was not that of a man of robust mind, but rather of one so eccentric and odd as to be verging on insanity. We always treated him as a buffoon and fool.

He then went on to tell the story of the blanket-tossing incident, adding 'I merely quote this as showing the respect which his Lordship inspired.'[53] The last time Grierson saw Thoms was in the summer of 1897. The Sheriff called upon Grierson's mother to express his condolences on the death of her husband. According to her son, Thoms did not seem quite sure why he had come. He never stuck to any topic for long, but soon drifted off disjointedly into the old talk of the number of times he had been in love and the cracks in his heart. He also presented Grierson's sisters with two little packages of Edinburgh Rock, although they were grown up by then, and he apologised for the smallness of the present but said he was not so well off as he used to be. Grierson thought that as well as being physically enfeebled Thoms was mentally weak, too.[54]

Although Grierson modified the remarkably sour tone of his precognition when giving evidence in court, it is quite clear that it reflected his opinions.[55] He did acknowledge the kindness Thoms had shown him as a young man and later, but his account of Thoms' last visit shows little sympathy. The pathos of an ill old man clinging to the habits and conceits of better days, as if in so doing he could convince himself and those around him that neither he nor they had changed, seems largely to have passed Grierson by. His attitude remained disparaging.

There may be several reasons for this. In adulthood, he had, unlike Thoms, put away childish things. He may have done so even before he first met Thoms;

children can be very contemptuous of what they perceive as childishness. Moreover, and unusually for a member of the landed classes, he was a leading Rechabite and keen proselytiser for the Temperance cause.[56] He is unlikely, therefore, to have approved of Thoms' brand of high living. But the main reason for his poor opinion of Thoms is quite clear. Grierson was a solicitor, had practised in Thoms' court since 1886, and did not recall the experience with affection.

III

Thoms as Sheriff

The manner in which Thoms discharged his judicial duties was not dwelt upon in the will case to any great extent, with just two witnesses, Grierson and a Thurso solicitor, David Keith Murray, discussing it in detail. There was not much need for it to be concentrated upon. Thoms had retired almost four years before he signed his will and there were plenty of examples from his private life to prove his underlying eccentricity. Yet the topic remains an important one, and not just because it was plainly what Shaw was referring to in his memoirs when he wrote that some of the most peculiar things Thoms did were not brought out in evidence.[2] The office Thoms held was one of considerable responsibility and power, upon the exercise of which hung the courses of lives and livelihoods. Moreover, he held his office at a time of political and social change and of popular agitation for such change, especially in the matter of crofters' grievances. Sheriffs were required not only to determine cases brought to alleviate such grievances, but also to deal with those whose agitation for change had put themselves on the wrong side of the law. This could bring the conduct of a Sheriff under close public scrutiny.

The prime example of this was Thoms' friend and colleague William Ivory, Sheriff of Inverness.[3] In the winter of 1881/2 the crofters of the Braes in Skye, inspired by the success that open defiance had brought their Irish counterparts,[4] began to withhold their rents, and when a Sheriff Officer attempted to serve summonses of removal, he was assaulted by a crowd and the notices burnt. To arrest those responsible, Ivory brought in over fifty Glasgow policemen and went with them on their early-morning mission. Although they apprehended their quarry, the Sheriff and his posse were surrounded, assaulted and stoned by a large crowd of crofters and their womenfolk, and it was only after a number of baton charges that they were able to reach safety. With this skirmish, 'the Battle of the Braes', began the crofting agitation that soon spread throughout the Highlands and Western Isles and continued until the passing of the Crofters Holdings (Scotland) Act 1886 and beyond. The appointment of a Royal Commission under Lord Napier and Ettrick in 1883 encouraged crofters to organise themselves and express their grievances fully, even in the non-Highland counties of Caithness, Orkney and Shetland, and when crofting tenants were given the vote in time for the 1885 General Election, the whole controversy was kept simmering away nicely.

Back in Skye, Sheriff Ivory saw unrest spread from the Braes to Glendale and elsewhere. More policemen were assaulted, more Sheriff Officers deforced in the execution of their duty, and soon whole districts became 'no-go areas' for the forces of law and order. Eventually, Ivory succeeded in having military assistance brought in, but it was at a cost to his own reputation.[5] Although some recognised the unenviable position he was in and supported him accordingly,[6] his critics were much more vociferous. Ivory

William Ivory, Sheriff of Inverness, whose obstinate and high-handed behaviour during the crofters' agitation aroused much criticism.

was, it seems, a little man with rather a large sense of his own importance, and his high-handed and unbending attitude added to his problems. Criticism of his suitability for office extended right up to Cabinet level, while Donald Cameron of Lochiel, Highland landowner, Conservative MP and member of the Napier Commission, wrote to A. J. Balfour, when the latter was Scottish Secretary, complaining of Ivory's 'obstinacy and conceit', 'want of tact and judgement' and of 'being in point of fact almost off his head.'[7] Some contemporary criticisms of Sheriff Thoms were remarkably similar.

We have seen that Thoms possessed a number of quite pronounced personal characteristics. Apart from his general eccentricity, he had a finical attention to detail combined with a sharp mode of expression and a no-less-pointed sense of humour; he was exceptionally vain, with an almost limitless capacity to draw attention to himself, however ridiculous he might appear in the process; and he had a tendency to irascibility, possibly accentuated by his gout and other ailments. Whilst one or two of these traits, in small doses, might be tolerable in a judge, or even an advantage, it does not take much imagination to see how the wrong combination could provoke public criticism and a strained relationship with colleagues, superiors and subordinates.

Thoms' organisational abilities and drive did produce some benefits. In the year following his appointment, for example, he drew up a curriculum of study for apprentice law agents.[8] He required to do this because, at the time, none of the lawyers in his Sheriffdom had organised themselves into the local faculties that ordinarily would have regulated such training.[9] Eventually, Thoms managed to persuade the solicitors in both Caithness and Orkney to form faculties, and then spent a fair amount of money helping to finance their law libraries,[10] though his offers to do the same in Shetland seem to have fallen on stony ground.[11] One of Thoms' ideas that did prove a universal success, however, was his arranging monthly tabulated returns from each of the chief constables and procurators fiscal in order to keep himself informed of the number and nature of crimes in his sheriffdom. It was copied by his successor, who continued the practice when promoted elsewhere.[12]

Although such administrative efficiency did not attract public attention, other aspects of Thoms' sheriffship certainly did, particularly in cases with a political or crofting aspect. In August, 1883, for example he made an intervention in the struggle between Lieutenant-General F. W. Traill-Burroughs and his Rousay crofters which, although relatively minor, is revealing of his attitude to such matters. In the heated situation that followed some of Burroughs' tenants giving evidence to the Napier Commission, and thus promptly earning eviction, the laird received a juvenilely-written letter containing a threat to his life and bearing a Rousay postmark. Burroughs made a great deal of it and so, obligingly, did Thoms. About to head to Shetland on the fishery cruiser HMS *Firm*, Thoms had the vessel diverted to Rousay instead and, while the Procurator Fiscal, John Macrae, Superintendent Grant and the Fiscal's clerk went off to the Sourin school to investigate the matter, the Sheriff, along with Sheriff-substitute Mellis and some of the ship's officers, paid a social call on the laird. This led to another less-threatening anonymous correspondent branding the Sheriff and his party 'all toadies'.[13]

The gunboat HMS *Firm* on which Thoms made his intervention in the dispute between General Burroughs and the Rousay crofters. (Shetland Museum and Archives).

Another protracted and bitter dispute between crofters and their landlord occurred at Cunningsburgh in Shetland in the early 1890s. Bruce of Sumburgh had, some years previously, fenced off part of the common grazings for his own exclusive use, but the fence had been allowed to fall into disrepair. Thus the crofters' sheep were gaining access to and feeding off the landlord's pasture. Bruce's shepherd began to impound the sheep and levy fines for their return, as he was entitled by statute to do. The crofters, however, attempted to get the sheep back by force, intercepting the shepherd whenever he and his men tried to drive the sheep to the pounds.[14] In a heated series of confrontations, the shepherd was accused of assault, had a court order, lawburrows, taken out against him to secure his future good conduct, and then was accused of breaching the order.[15] Subsequently, a number of Cunningsburgh crofters also found themselves on the wrong side of the law, being prosecuted for breach of the peace. Their case was heard by Thoms on his annual visit to Shetland, and when he handed down sentences of imprisonment, he was roundly condemned for it in the local press.[16]

That was criticism for Thoms' sentencing at the end of a trial. A few years earlier we find press criticism for something he did before a trial had even started. The depredations that steam trawlers from the south inflicted upon local fisheries were an issue generating almost as much heat as the crofting question. When, in March, 1885, some of these trawlers attempted to land their catch at Wick, they were attacked by local fishermen. Although the alleged rioters were imprisoned on remand, they found they had a friend in high places when their bail bond was signed by the Provost of Wick, William Rae. Thoms thought little of the burgh's chief magistrate mixing himself up in the matter and took the most public opportunity imaginable to say so. The trial was about to start, and Thoms was already on the bench. Every available seat in court was packed with spectators, including the jury box as there was no jury in this case. It was there that Rae was heading when Thoms suddenly addressed him – 'screaming at the top of his voice' according to the provost:

> I cannot extend to you, Provost Rae, the usual courtesy of asking you to take a seat on the bench, on account of having signed the bail bond for these men.

Rae said he didn't quite understand his Lordship, so Thoms repeated himself. Rae asked him what authority he had for objecting to that. When Thoms dismissed him with a wave of the hand and the words 'No answer, please', the Provost said he would answer him elsewhere; and he did. He wrote demanding an apology from Thoms, and then had the whole of the ensuing ill-tempered correspondence printed in his own newspaper, the Liberal *Northern Ensign*, from which it was copied in other sympathetic journals. If Rae's intentions in signing the bail bond had been to gain political capital, he extracted every last farthing's worth from the sequel.[17]

Of all the late Victorian cases in Thoms' sheriffdom, however, the most controversial must be that of the Rev. Matthew Armour. Free Church minister in Sanday and a champion of the crofters there, he was charged with a breach of the peace at a Conservative election meeting during the General Election of 1885. The alleged conduct complained of was to attempt to address the meeting instead of confining himself to asking questions, and to refuse to obey the chairman. Although the precise nature of Armour's behaviour was disputed, there was no doubt that the meeting broke up in disorder. Outside, the disorder grew violent, when some of the young Sanday men harassed the Tory candidate and his friends as they attempted to make their way back to their lodgings through the dark November evening, jostling them, pelting them with clods of earth, knocking off their hats and attempting to trip them up with sticks. That the Conservative candidate was the Honourable Cospatrick Thomas Dundas, whose brother, the Earl of Zetland, was landlord to many of the Sanday crofters, only added to the fun. The beleaguered Conservatives gained the comparative safety of the inn at Castlehill, but even there some window glass was put in before the mob dispersed.

Rev. Matthew Armour, the Free Kirk minister whose imprisonment for disrupting a Conservative election meeting in Sanday may have been at Thoms' instigation.

Although Armour had no involvement in this rioting, the fact that it occurred plainly influenced the decision to prosecute him and to sentence him to four days' imprisonment without the option of a fine. In the event, he was only in prison for a matter of hours, being released pending an appeal which was ultimately successful. Nevertheless, that he was prosecuted at all provoked a torrent of condemnation, both locally and nationally, from press and from pulpit and from the High Court bench.[18]

Thoms did not preside at the trial. That dubious honour went to his Kirkwall substitute, John Campbell Mellis. Mellis, therefore, bore the brunt of the criticism, and it is Mellis whose name is remembered in connection with the case. Yet how much his conduct owed to his superior's direction or influence needs to be considered. Thoms was not a man to leave those below him – whom he always referred to as *his* Substitute, *his* Fiscal and *his* Clerk[19] - in any doubt as to what he thought they should be doing and how. The example Shaw gave, in his anecdotage, to illustrate his remark that some of the most peculiar things Thoms did were not brought out in evidence was that, instead of waiting for his substitutes' judgements to be appealed against, Thoms sometimes just scored them out, sheet after sheet, and put in judgements of his own.[20] Further, he had a direct involvement in the earlier stages of the Armour case as well as in other cases relating to public disorder during the same election.

The Sanday events were not, in fact, the only riot to occur in Orkney during the electoral campaigning of 1885. Kirkwall saw a similar outbreak of disorder. Whereas the county constituency saw a straight fight between Liberal and Conservative, the Burgh of Kirkwall (which then returned a member to Westminster along with the other Northern Burghs of Wick, Dingwall, Dornoch, Tain and Cromarty) had a contest between two Liberals, the sitting member

John Pender and the radical J. McDonald Cameron. Trouble started after Pender addressed a meeting in the Temperance Hall on the evening of 25th November, 1885, the night after the Sanday disturbances. On leaving the hall, Pender and his supporters found themselves having to run the gauntlet of a mob of opposition supporters who had put out the gas lamps between Mill Street and the Castle Hotel to aid their nefarious purposes. These were much the same as those of the Sanday youths, with a particular emphasis on pelting their opponents with bags of flour. After Pender reached the safety of his hotel, whitened but unharmed, a large crowd of supporters of both sides surged and eddied across Castle Street, carrying in its midst the struggling figure of a lone policeman who had seized hold of one of the troublemakers and was stoutly refusing to let him go till he found out his name, despite having his helmet smashed from his head by a stick, his belt cut from his waist and his legs kicked black and blue, all amid shouts of 'Smash the b-----!' and 'Throw him into the Peerie Sea!'[21]

Thoms, in his sheriffdom because of the election, investigated the matter personally, committed seven men and youths for trial, and then presided at the trial himself.[22] This was still perfectly proper procedure in the nineteenth century. At the trial he sat with both Mellis and the Sheriff-substitute of Shetland, David J. Mackenzie.[23] He was evidently determined to show just what a serious matter this was, and also to demonstrate to his substitutes how such offences should be dealt with. The reason such public demonstration of the matter's seriousness was considered necessary can be gathered from remarks made by the solicitor for some of the Sanday rioters, Andrew Thomson, who said that what had occurred in Sanday had occurred at political meetings in Orkney since time immemorial and had not thitherto been interfered with by the authorities. The agent for the Kirkwall accused, J.A.S. Brown of Stromness, said that mobbing and rioting had not been added to the calendar of crime in Orkney and Shetland, that this was an election squabble and there had been some rough horseplay, but he thought there should be a little licence given on such an occasion. Thoms disagreed, and proceeded to set out the line the authorities were now going to take. It was an uncompromising one:

> The prosecution had been a sad revelation to him, because he was naturally proud of that county, and so were Orcadians generally, as being a law-abiding county, where law was respected and the intelligence of its inhabitants was such that they boasted of its few policemen, and could, even in their present elections, show no illiterate voters compared with the 2,000 in Ross-shire. But not even in Ross-shire was there mobbing and rioting to disgrace the people. For Orkney that unenviable distinction had been reserved. There could be no doubt of that disgrace. The evidence in the case showed that there was organised obstruction of the law, and invasion of the public peace by assault on a magistrate, on a candidate for

the people's suffrages, on the police force, and private citizens, as well as malicious mischief by extinguishing the gas lamps with the undoubted object of preventing identification, and thus escaping detection . . . In a free country like this, where open discussion was permitted by the press, and at meetings which any one could convene, the law very properly forbade all such violence, in the interests of the rioters themselves as well as the law-abiding citizens. He was sorry for the respectable position of all those whom he found guilty of all the charges libelled; and he regretted more that some of the guilty were of immature years . . . No one could be in such a mob and plead that he did nothing. There was too much inertness on the part of the bystanders, and the failure to render assistance to the police was simply disgraceful. Orcadians must now understand that if they were present in such a mob they must actively take the side of law and order or take the consequences. A lawless spirit was abroad, and the cowards who would not assist in resisting it were participators in it.

Six of the accused were convicted and sentenced to periods of imprisonment of between seven and ten days, to the shocked silence of the public benches and widespread anger outside. Although representations on the severity of the sentences were made to the Home Secretary, he declined to intervene.[24]

Having cleaned up the lawless streets of Kirkwall and made them a safe place once more for respectable politicians to walk, Sheriff Thoms intended to go to Sanday to do the same. An outbreak of stack-burning in Caithness caused a change of plan. While Thoms crossed the Pentland Firth to deal with the incendiarism, he sent Mellis and Procurator Fiscal Macrae to Sanday to investigate the disturbances there. This they spent two days doing, after which Mellis instructed Macrae to raise summary complaints of mobbing and rioting against those who had harassed the Tories outside the meeting, and of breach of the peace against Armour. The charge against Armour included the allegation that he had brandished a stick or other weapon at the platform party, but when no satisfactory evidence of that came out at the trial Mellis instructed the Fiscal to delete those words from the libel. Although this removed the most serious element of the charge, Mellis still proceeded to convict and imprison, albeit after an adjournment and 'very serious and anxious consideration' as to what the appropriate sentence might be.[25] There seems to have been a determination to make an example of Armour, come what may. Whether that was down to Thoms or to Mellis alone it may never be possible to say with certainty. Armour's supporters, though, had no doubt. His friend, colleague and biographer, the Rev. Alexander Goodfellow, wrote of Mellis that he was 'supposed to be but a mere tool in the hands of another.'[26] There can be little question which 'other' he had in mind.

When Thoms became publicly involved in the aftermath of the Armour trial there were no signs of his being abashed at its outcome. Although the Sanday minister had been cleared and the authorities responsible for his prosecution and conviction condemned at all hands, some of Armour's friends showed no inclination to let the matter drop. The Rev. John Jamieson, Free Church minister of Firth, in particular, relentlessly pursued the question of how much the prosecution had cost the public purse. When the Commissioners of Supply refused to tell him, he sought the assistance of the Sheriff Principal. This is the reply he got:

> The Sheriff of the County has to acknowledge receipt of the letter from the Reverend John Jamieson, Free Church Minister, Firth, Finstown, Orkney, as to business of the Commissioners of Supply of the County of Orkney. The Sheriff, while declining to correspond on this subject with his reverence, begs to express the hope that he may be able to assist his reverence, however humbly, by correspondence or otherwise, in the discharge of those overwhelmingly important duties as to the spread of the Redeemer's kingdom within the Sheriff's jurisdiction, which demand the whole of his reverence's time, attention, and energies.[27]

Perhaps in his younger days Thoms had had his fill of being preached at by Free Kirk ministers.[28] In any event, if this letter was intended to annoy Jamieson it succeeded only too well. 'His reverence' complained to the Home Secretary and Thoms was required to apologise.[29]

Whilst Thoms had the necessary resilience, not to say bloody-mindedness, to deal with such public criticism, Mellis was not so fortunate. His personal background, too, made him particularly vulnerable in this case. Although all three principal actors in the Armour prosecution, Thoms, Mellis and Macrae, had come of Free Church families but had gone over to the Established or Episcopal Churches in adulthood, Mellis moreover was the son and brother of Free Kirk ministers and had trained for the ministry himself before turning to law.[30] According to Goodfellow, Mellis was 'naturally…full of kindness and had no vindictive spirit';[31] but he was in poor health, and his resulting absences caused a backlog of work which, it was said, began to prey on his mind. How much the Armour case and its aftermath did so, too, we can only speculate. In the autumn of 1887, answering a friend's enquiry for his health, Mellis replied, 'I am in the Valley of the Shadow of Death.' When, a few weeks later, he moved from the shadow to the substance, it was by his own hand.[32]

It would be easy to characterise Thoms' behaviour in all these cases as arising from reactionary political bias. It would be easy but unfair, for there is, in fact, a more obvious common thread which runs through these incidents as well as some others where Thoms' conduct provoked public criticism, but where there was no political aspect. The common feature is a jealous protectiveness of the rule of law and due process, combined with an abhorrence of disorder. Anything Thoms perceived as a threat to the administration of justice or the Queen's peace was liable to provoke a reaction, not to say over-reaction. Examples can be given from each part of his Sheriffdom. In Lerwick, his imposition of a fine of ten pounds or two months' imprisonment on each of two men who had obstructed and assaulted a Customs officer in the execution of his duty caused much unfavourable comment in the town.[33] In Kirkwall, a bankrupt who had not made a full disclosure of his assets, some of which subsequently disappeared in mysterious circumstances, was sentenced to sixty days' hard labour, earning Thoms the condemnation of a leading article in *The Orcadian*.[34] Finally, in Wick, he insisted that a bankrupt who had sold a cow from his sequestrated estate be prosecuted for theft. Although the accused was acquitted, this incident was recalled by the Thurso lawyer David Keith Murray when giving evidence of Thoms' alleged weakness of mind.[35]

Conversely, where those in conflict with their supposed betters resorted to legal process, Thoms treated them fairly and impartially. In another Cunningsburgh sheep-poinding case in 1892, crofters who had sued the impounder of their sheep successfully recovered part of the money that had been demanded for the return of their animals. In his judgement Thoms wrote:

> The Sheriff in the interest of the public peace has to commend the pursuers' conduct in paying the defender's demands under protest, and afterwards seeking the Court's aid to fix the sum really due. This contrasts favourably with the conduct of others who, instead of letting matters be thus settled, have kept the district for two years in a state of lawless agitation. The Sheriff hopes that all parties will avoid causes of bitterness in the future but if any irritation does unfortunately occur, the parties must not take the law into their own hands, now that the more excellent plan of an appeal to the law has been shown to be practicable.[36]

Sound advice, but just how practicable it appeared to a crofter on the breadline is open to question.[37]

Off the bench, Thoms' attitudes were fairly progressive for his time, albeit within the limits of Victorian economic liberalism. As might be expected in a man of his commercial background, he believed in the virtue of trade as a means of spreading prosperity. In a speech he made after laying the foundation stone of Lerwick Harbour works, he eschewed his usual jokiness to give a detailed analysis of the benefits similar developments had wrought elsewhere and which Shetland might now expect.[38] If this was advocating the 'trickle-down' effect of capitalism, he sought a more direct flow of economic benefits when he championed the right of the Shetland knitters to be paid in cash, making himself in the process an unlikely ally of the Radical MP Charles Bradlaugh. When the anti-truck legislation was amended in 1887 to outlaw the payment of knitters by barter, Bradlaugh wrote a letter to *The Times* in which he referred with approval to Thoms' 'persistent agitation' over nearly twenty years for a change in the law,[39] and he again paid tribute to his efforts in a speech at Edinburgh the following year.[40] In education, too, Thoms was reformist. In 1871, he represented Kirkwall at a meeting of the Convention of Royal Burghs at which the Scottish Education Bill then being steered through Parliament by Lord Advocate Young was discussed. This was the measure that would introduce free and compulsory elementary schooling throughout Scotland. When discussion of the Bill threatened to become lost in a flutter of petty objections, Thoms made a successful plea for the Convention to approve the Bill in general principle first, as he was afraid that:

> . . . now, when the prospect of a good educational measure was within the grasp of the people, it would [be] frittered away in details.[41]

Thoms was quite prepared to show some understanding to those at the bottom end of the social scale, at least when they played by the rules and did not challenge the system. His sentencing in general criminal matters does not seem over-severe, and at times he was quite lenient. A Lerwick drunk, for example, who staggered home to the wrong house – his old one – was let off with a warning despite having had an unpleasant fracas with the new householder during which he kicked a hole in the door.[42] In Kirkwall, in 1885, we find him hearing the case of a woman who had assaulted her sister-in-law in a small shop in the Long Close.[43] Although she pled guilty, her solicitor led evidence in mitigation from two neighbours to the effect that she was 'a quiet industrious woman' who had suffered 'persistent persecution' from her sister-in-law for years. When Thoms came to pass sentence he said that the accused's conduct really deserved all praise, and should she be reviled again as she had been – for an assault, he said, could be committed with the tongue as well as with the hands – she should take action against her assailant. He then told her to go home with her friends.[44]

As one would by now expect, Thoms' general conduct on the bench had its idiosyncrasies. An entertainingly scabrous account, to which we shall return, is found in the precognition of Alexander Sutherland SSC, who had practised law in Wick and, subsequently, Lerwick. According to Sutherland:

> The advent of his arrival [*sic*] was invariably the signal for a full turn out of the public to see the 'fun', and they were seldom disappointed. He played to the gallery in the Court, and was greatly pleased at any cheap popularity . . . There was nothing too silly for him.[45]

He certainly made jokes on the bench, but one of the Kirkwall Bar officers was of the opinion that his jokes were usually to the point of the case. The example he gave seems rather more point than joke. When a Burray youth, who was sued for maintenance of an illegitimate child, admitted paternity but said he could not afford to pay anything, he was told that he should have counted the cost before he commenced operations.[46] Similarly, a colleague of the assaulted Lerwick Customs Officer, who had stood by and done nothing while the assault took place, was informed to laughter from the public benches that his presence had been 'purely ornamental'.[47] When Andrew Thomson, the agent for the Kirkwall bankrupt, elicited from a Crown witness that he did not know who had removed the items that had disappeared, Thoms interjected: 'Oh, they may have been removed by an angel.' *The Orcadian's* leader described this remark as having been made with the Sheriff's 'usual good taste'.[48]

The solicitors who appeared before him were often on the receiving end of Thoms' sharp tongue. Another Kirkwall Bar officer said the Sheriff would take the rise out of an agent if he could.[49] That suggests a degree of subtlety which was not always present. Sutherland again:

> I have seen many scenes while Sheriff Thoms was on the Bench, quite unbecoming the Bench. He always fell foul of the Agents, and used ungentlemanly language towards them . . . He could not do the right. He always fought the case for one side or the other. He has fought my case frequently, and if I attempted to say a word, he then turned and fought against me.[50]

A Lerwick solicitor making submissions to the bench found one of his points met with a cry of 'Fudge!'[51] W. P. Drever, defending the cathedral name-chiseller, mentioned the mallet. 'You should try it on your head,' said the Sheriff.[52] Then, in the Kirkwall bankruptcy case already mentioned, Andrew Thomson, who was obviously having a day in court he would rather have forgotten, uttered the cross-examiner's nightmare: the question that enables an opposing witness to blurt out some essential piece of evidence which the other side has tried but failed to elicit from him:

> The Sheriff – (addressing Mr Thomson) – It was not proved that those articles were in the possession of the bankrupt, and now you have done it yourself. (Laughter.)[53]

Something of the flavour of a criminal case before Thoms can be obtained from a report of a Lerwick summary prosecution for theft in 1889. The accused, a cartwright called Alexander Macdonald, had taken two pairs of boots home from Messrs Goodlad & Coutts to try on. He neither returned them nor paid for them. When defence agent Alexander Bain was cross-examining Coutts,

Sheriff Thoms interrupted him to say, 'You don't understand your case.' That is not the sort of remark a solicitor would ordinarily expect to have thrown at him from the bench. Bain's response:

> You are not entitled to tell me that I do not understand my case, with all due deference to your Lordship.

hastily qualifies indignation with conventional insincerity. At the close of the evidence, the Procurator Fiscal addressed the Sheriff for a conviction for theft, or alternatively fraud. Bain then made his submissions for the defence. He argued that no charge of theft or fraud had been proved, his client had got the boots in the ordinary course of business and he promised he would pay. At this, the Sheriff remarked that he might be willing to pay for the boots now that he was in the dock. While Thoms and Bain proceeded to argue, the prisoner leaned forward and tabled a guinea. Thoms said he thought the case was like that of a man who gets a pound to change and must either return twenty shillings or be guilty of theft or breach of trust. Bain said he did not think there was similarity between the cases at all. The Sheriff then asked Bain if he thought that a man who borrowed money to repay it on a certain day and failed to do so, or give any account, was not guilty of breach of trust or embezzlement. Bain did not think so.

> The Sheriff – Fortunately the judges in this Court have a higher sense of morality than that held by you.

Bain was still addressing the bench when Thoms said he was not going to hold the case proven, but he hoped it would be a lesson to the community. There had been a great deal of excuse used, but the goods were got on the second of February and here they were only paid for on the twenty-first of August. However, the prisoner would let this be a warning to him.[54]

The Procurator Fiscal in Lerwick, J. Kirkland Galloway, recalled that Thoms did some 'most outrageous things' on the bench. On one occasion Galloway had successfully applied to the Sheriff-substitute for a warrant to sell a boat. The other side appealed to Thoms. When the appeal called before him, he asked Galloway what he had to say. Galloway said it was not his appeal (it being usual for the appellant's solicitor to speak first and argue why the appeal should be successful). Thoms insisted, saying that if Galloway did not speak he would find against him. This he duly did, only to send for Galloway afterwards and ask him to enrol the case again. When Galloway refused, Thoms had it enrolled himself and found in Galloway's favour. On another occasion, Galloway thought Thoms had even torn out some interlocutors (court orders) he had already granted.[55]

Grierson spoke of a similarly cavalier attitude to normal procedure. Like Sutherland, he found Thoms not always willing to let agents conduct cases themselves. In one case:

> The moment I got up to examine my first witness, he told me to sit down, and examined him himself, he did the same with all the witnesses, would not indeed allow me to open my mouth, abused me when I did so, and then he gave Decree in favour of the Pursuer, which was natural, seeing he had conducted his case himself.[56]

James Cullen Grierson, Lerwick solicitor and critic of Sheriff Thoms. A photograph from an admiring profile in a Temperance Journal. (Shetland Museum and Archives).

Grierson's first case before Thoms was evidently the Customs Officer case already referred to. He acted for a third accused who was acquitted. This outcome, according to the solicitor who had stood up and argued for it, was 'not justice' because the facts in all three cases were the same. He thought Thoms was just doing him a good turn as he was a young struggling practitioner. If so, it was not appreciated. The same year, Thoms found in favour of one of Grierson's clients in a civil case. This, too, the solicitor considered an unwelcome success. The case was appealed to the Court of Session, who found in favour of the appellant without even hearing counsel. Of Thoms as Sheriff, Grierson concluded:

> I must say my whole recollection of him in the court was of a man of utterly unbalanced mind, and a most offensive judge to appear before.[57]

Alexander Sutherland's views were even more trenchant:

> . . . a case was considered as good as lost when one had Sheriff Thoms' decision in one's favour . . . I always regarded Sheriff Thoms as an unjust judge. Whether this was through want of principle or want of brains it is somewhat difficult to say, but I am inclined to the view that his mental capacity was weak. It was proverbial that he would decide in favour of the litigant he was best acquainted with. The public took this view and jeered at the idea of Sheriff Thoms administering justice. He was insufferably vain, and, in my opinion, a born cad. His eccentricities and aberrations were glaring, and I never regarded him as quite *compos mentis*. I always thought there was a screw loose, in short, a fool.[58]

Sutherland gave as an example the case of a young man near Thurso who had struck another on the head with a spade to the danger of his life. Thoms insisted on trying the case in Thurso, although the Sheriff Court was usually held in Wick. Sutherland, for the accused, argued this was an excess of jurisdiction and cited authorities to that effect. Thoms disregarded them and proceeded with the trial. Although Sutherland advised his client not to plead, the Sheriff forged ahead anyway, abusing Sutherland 'like a pickpocket' when he refused to take any part in the proceedings, examining all the witnesses himself and then convicting the accused. Then, after addressing the accused as if he had committed an offence deserving of the gallows, he fined him ten shillings. According to Sutherland, the small fine was to discourage any appeal. On another occasion, when an action for delivery of certain documents came before him at Wick, Thoms did not take the expected step of allowing a certain time for written defences to be lodged. Instead, he insisted that the defences be stated orally there and then. According to Sutherland, a scene then occurred lasting several hours, in the course of which the Sheriff-substitute, Harper, was called on to the bench, only to threaten to leave again unless Thoms withdrew a remark he had made. The case was subsequently appealed to the Second Division of the Court of Session. There, on hearing that it was an appeal from the Sheriff of Caithness, Lord Young enquired 'Is he still at large?' The appeal was granted without the appellant's counsel being required to speak.[59]

Lord Young had several swipes at Thoms from the bench of the Second Division despite, or perhaps because of, having been the Lord Advocate who recommended his appointment as Sheriff. Alexander Sutherland had an appeal there relating to an accident in a quarry. Young remarked that the Sheriff had fallen into the quarry himself.[60] In another successful Caithness appeal, Young said Thoms had knocked the process (the written pleadings, etc) all out of shape.[61] Even when he upheld Thoms' judgement he found fault with him.[62] Most remarkable of all, however, was Young's comment in another successful Caithness appeal of 1890 that Thoms' conduct of the case might be a good ground for petitioning the Secretary of State for his removal.[63]

A number of different factors may have contributed to Thoms' conduct on the bench. The onset of illness should not be discounted, though at the time of the incidents complained of, it is unlikely to have had a major influence. More to the point was the Sheriff's susceptibility to boredom. Arriving on the bench in Kirkwall one day, he said that there must be a cat there for it seemed to have run away with the pens, and there had been mice, too, and they had had nothing to eat but his blotting paper. He continued in this vein until he noticed that W. R. Mackintosh of *The Orcadian* was taking it all down. He immediately told him to stop as what he was saying was not meant to be reported in the newspapers. He said that the proceedings in a law court were as dull as ditchwater, and that they required a little humour to brighten them up. But if his little speeches were to be reported they would cease.[64]

More significant a factor in his behaviour on the bench than illness or boredom (although probably linked to the latter) was an almost pathological hatred of delay. 'Delay is dangerous' was a favourite cry,[65] and he missed no opportunity to administer a metaphorical dose of Gregory to the proceedings. At Kirkwall, one day in August, 1887, he sounded off on the topic through most of his time on the bench. It was a positive disgrace to the Court, he said, to have cases lying on hand so long as some of those which came before him that day. When John Macrae, appearing on behalf of W. P. Drever, Solicitor, who was unable to attend through illness, asked for

W.R. Mackintosh, editor of 'The Orcadian' newspaper, who also doubled up as the official court shorthand writer.

a continuation of the case on that account, the Sheriff said it was scandalous to have cases continued in that way. That the solicitor for one of the parties was laid aside through illness was no excuse. Some other agent could have taken the case. Having had his rant, though, he granted the continuation.[66] In a Shetland case appealed to him from the Sheriff-substitute three years later, he used the note to his interlocutor (ie, his judgement) to rap a few knuckles:

> The Sheriff's remonstrances as to the delays in this summary case have as yet been without effect. He hopes that this case will not be another Zetland scandal like the celebrated Abernethy cessio [a bankruptcy case which had dragged on for seven years[67]]. The defender's procedure since 20th June 1890 is not to the credit of the bar. On 10th October 1890, the Sheriff-substitute should not have thrown the reins away after the legislature had vested him with the power of saving another three weeks which have been lost.

Thoms objected to the Sheriff-substitute allowing time for the defender to make written answers to the pursuer's amendments of the pleadings, when both parties were in court and it could, he insisted, have been done there and then.[68]

Nineteenth-century Sheriffs had a power – in fact a duty – to excise from the parties' written pleadings any matter that they considered to be irrelevant or unnecessary. This was to be done at the procedural stage known as 'closing the record', when the parties' solicitors had finished adjusting their written pleadings and the next stage of procedure required to be determined. It could be done, indeed was designed to be done, even where neither side had any objection to any part of the other's pleadings. However, the author of one of the standard text books on Sheriff Court procedure said that this power was seldom resorted to and ought only to be used with the greatest caution. 'There is no duty more delicate for a judge,' the text book went on, 'than that of dictating to a party how he is to frame his pleading, or of restricting him as to what he may set forth.'[69] The learned author had obviously never seen Thoms in action, for delicacy was not Thoms' strong suit, and he used the statutory power zealously.[70] This is what was probably going on in July, 1890, when *The Shetland Times* reported that in Thoms' court the previous Wednesday the forenoon had been devoted to adjusting the record in two actions. When parties' agents resisted having the Sheriff take his blue pencil to their pleadings, any victory Thoms achieved for time-saving was bound to be pyrrhic. Perhaps he was trying something similar the day that Provost Nicol Spence heard him tell two solicitors appearing before him at Kirkwall:

> In this case there is a straight road and a circuitous road. The straight road is cheap and inexpensive, the latter tedious and expensive. You both want to take the circuitous road, but I will not allow you.[71]

It could be said with some justification that Thoms was ahead of his time, for Sheriffs today are encouraged to take a pro-active role in bringing the cases before them swiftly and effectively to an issue. At its best, his attitude showed an admirable concern for the litigant over the lawyer by cutting through the unnecessary and the time-consuming. But sometimes he went too far. In an appeal from a decision of the Caithness Sheriff-substitute, Thoms thought Sheriff Harper had allowed irrelevant matters to remain in the pleadings, and chose a dramatic way to show it. Producing a knife on the bench, he cut several pages out of the transcript of evidence before stitching what remained back together with needle and thread.[72]

What angered Thoms, above all, were cases where he thought delays and complications were being manufactured by the parties' lawyers in order to benefit themselves instead of their clients. This he thought particularly prevalent in Caithness. In a note to one of his interlocutors he opined:

> Procrastination is in Wick the soul of business.[73]

When D. K. Murray, appearing in a Wick intestate succession case, said there had been nothing to stop the deceased employing a solicitor to make his will, Thoms replied:

> That is true, but you may be sure that this crofter who saved £500 never employed a lawyer in his life.[74]

Thoms spoke bitterly to his Caithness friends about some of the Wick solicitors and their delays and sharp practices,[75] and, according to the Procurator Fiscal at Wick, while he took 'a most kindly interest' in the members of the Bar, to any of them he thought grasping or selfish he showed no mercy.[76] In particular, he condemned as a public scandal the conduct of litigation by trustees in Caithness sequestrations.[77] Presumably he thought the solicitors were dragging out the cases in the knowledge that their fees would be a privileged debt on the bankrupt estate.

One solicitor who incurred his wrath over the conduct of a sequestration was either Alexander Sutherland or his brother Symon,[78] a circumstance which Sutherland neglected to mention in his otherwise voluminous precognition. It may well explain why Thoms' nephews and nieces did not call him as a witness; that, and his obvious relish for overstatement. On his death in 1930, Sutherland was described as an 'original personality' with his white hair and silver-mounted cane, his large fund of reminiscences and his 'superb' telling of droll stories. There was no comment on their accuracy.[79] No other witness spoke of Thoms favouring his friends or called him a cad, nor for that matter did Sutherland himself back up his sweeping condemnation with any specific example of bias. Thoms himself, in one of his humorous speeches, declared:

> I have impressed it on people against whom I have decided that I was really their friend, and that the man who gets my decision is really my foe. (Laughter).[80]

Many a true word, for Thoms was just the man to ride roughshod over the feelings of friends and acquaintances in stubborn pursuit of what he thought was right.

And he sometimes was right, too. Sutherland's objection to Thoms hearing a case at Thurso, for example, and his subsequent refusal to take any part in the proceedings, were both equally unwarranted. Sutherland seems to have been unaware that the relevant legislation gave Thoms the power to hold courts in such places as he saw fit, or indeed that the Caithness court had sat at Thurso in the past.[81] Nor was Galloway right to refuse to speak first in an appeal. Thoms was merely following a common time-saving practice of the Court of Session in not asking an appellant's counsel to speak if, from an initial reading of the papers, the appeal seemed to be well-founded: precisely what had happened in the appeals mentioned by Sutherland and Grierson. But there was more to the behaviour of Sutherland and Galloway in these two cases than merely disagreeing with the Sheriff: in refusing to proceed they had openly defied him. This suggests not just a lack of respect on their part but a loss of authority on the part of the Sheriff, and these are two things which tend, when unchecked, to feed off each other. Thoms' manner on the bench probably fed both.

IV

The Sheriff v. the Lawyers

There can be little doubt that to appear as a solicitor before Sheriff Thoms was not always an easy experience. Stimulating might be a euphemistic way to describe it: always having to be on one's toes for the unexpected; the chance of a spot of public humiliation lurking around every corner. One of the Sheriff's least attractive judicial traits was to declare that a solicitor's arguments had made matters worse for his client instead of better.[2] It is no wonder that his relations with some of the local lawyers were fraught. Yet, whatever he might have said on the bench, Thoms usually left it there. Encountering Provost Rae the day after their courtroom clash, Thoms was taken aback to find himself 'cut'. He complained to the Wick Fiscal that this was needless, but 'seemed to be a peculiarity of the people here.'[3] For a similar cause he found himself in a potentially more serious stand-off with Sheriff Harper, the Caithness Sheriff-substitute. Ebenezer Erskine Harper – as his name might suggest, a man with a Secession Church background[4] - had taken offence at remarks made by Thoms in a note to one of his interlocutors. According to Alexander Sutherland, Thoms was in the habit of 'grossly insulting' his substitutes in this way. The next time Thoms called at Harper's residence, he found himself denied admittance. A correspondence ensued which Harper showed to Sutherland. The latter gave no details, but it is not hard to imagine the tone, if not the content.[5]

In Shetland, too, Thoms found public exception being taken to his remarks. According to Grierson, Thoms had a particular dislike of Lerwick solicitor J. B. Anderson. In an Inland Revenue prosecution around 1887, he 'nagged away' at Anderson all day before eventually calling him a 'pettifogger'. At that, apparently, Anderson and all the other agents present got up and left.[6] It is perhaps just as well that Thoms was not on the bench for the first Shetland prosecutions under the Truck Amendment Act, for Anderson, representing an accused hosiery merchant, asserted that if the Act was enforced it would be 'ruinous for the islands'.[7] Thoms' reaction on reading the Shetland papers that week may have been interesting.

Thoms was rather fond of giving the lawyers lessons. He may not have produced the tawse in court, but he certainly acted like a schoolmaster at times. 'You are both bad boys;' he told the Lerwick solicitors Galloway and John Small when they appeared before him one day in 1891:

> you were trying to cheat the Government with an unstamped document, and now you are trying to cheat each other. (Laughter.)[8]

But he was a teacher who lost the respect of some of his pupils, and discipline with it. His habit of publicly humiliating the duller and more recalcitrant ones cannot have helped. Nor can his disconcerting swings from jokey familiarity to pompous remonstrance.

It was in Caithness that matters reached their most serious, with the Caithness Faculty convening a meeting to discuss the role of the Sheriff Principal. The meeting took place in Wick on 16th July, 1888. In the chair was David Cormack, Clerk to the Pulteneytown Commissioners,[9] and also present were D.W. Georgeson and three Sutherlands: Alexander, whom we have already met; Hector, Town Clerk of Wick; and G. M. Sutherland, FSA(Scot.), subsequently Provost of the same burgh. Alexander and Hector were first cousins twice over, their parents being brothers married to sisters.[10] All those present it seems were Liberals – though not all on the same side of the recent Gladstonian / Unionist divide – and the third of the Sutherlands, in particular, had acted for many crofters in their grievances. He was the only lawyer there aged over forty. Georgeson, the youngest at no more than 23, had only commenced practice in Wick the year before.[11] The meeting was reported in detail in the press, with frequent applause throughout suggesting the attendance of the public, unless these five lawyers were particularly prone to mutual congratulation.

What triggered this meeting is not clear, but the recent vacancy in the Wick fiscalship was probably one factor. Wick Town Council had written Thoms asking that the new Procurator Fiscal be excluded from private practice and be one of the local Bar. A statement from the local Bar was adduced in support. In his reply, Thoms said that G. M. Sutherland had told him that the members of the Bar who were in favour of this course were concerned with their own interests rather than the principle of the matter. This resulted in a furious denial from Sutherland and the whole correspondence turning up in the columns of the *John O' Groat Journal*. In the midst of it all,

Ebenezer Erskine Harper, the Wick Sheriff-substitute who was not amused by Sheriff Thoms.

Sheriff Harper said he agreed that the Procurator Fiscal should not engage in private practice.[12]

It would be interesting to know if Harper offered encouragement to the Faculty

in its subsequent actions. Certainly, its meeting was fulsome in its praise of Sheriffs-substitute, whilst finding never a kind word for their superiors. Neither Thoms nor Harper nor any other Sheriff was mentioned by name. The main motion before the meeting was that the Faculty petition Parliament to abolish the office of Sheriff Principal[13] in respect that the Sheriff Principals' appellate jurisdiction over the decisions of the Sheriffs-substitute:

> (who are in many cases abler men than the Sheriff Principals) does not command nor deserve the confidence of the people of Scotland; that the salaries paid to the Sheriff Principals is [sic] a waste of public money, which could be utilized in providing a cheap appeal to a judge or judges of the Court of Session, who command and deserve the confidence of the public; and that the administrative duties of the Sheriff Principals would be better performed by the Sheriffs-substitute.

In proposing the motion, Hector Sutherland said that the office of Sheriff Principal was doomed; the question was only how soon that doom should take effect.

G. M. Sutherland, as well as saying that there was no need to go into the history of the office of Sheriff, and then proceeding to do so, came out with a statement which surely deserves a prize for disingenuousness. He held that:

> the question could be discussed independent of personal considerations.

There was little chance of that, given that these lawyers all practised exclusively or mainly in Caithness, that there was only one Sheriff Principal for that county, and that the office had been occupied by the same man for the last almost eighteen years. It could be nothing other than personal criticism of Thoms when Sutherland went on to say that the appeal from Substitute to Principal was very often an appeal:

> from a superior man to an inferior man, and very often from an experienced to an inexperienced lawyer.

He had not read of a like system anywhere in Europe:

> It would be very strange if a county judge in Ireland or England had to submit his decision to some briefless barrister on the floor of Westminster Hall.

The others made similar points. There was general praise for the skill, experience and acumen of the Sheriffs-substitute and condemnation of the lack of these qualities in the Principals. The anomaly of an appeal from one advocate to another was highlighted, and the practice of conducting appeals by sending the papers by post to the Principal without parties' agents necessarily having an opportunity to address him was criticised. Alexander Sutherland, in particular, showed that his gift for overstatement was not confined to his precognition sixteen years later. The criticisms that had been made were, he thought:

the present position of all the solicitors in Scotland.

The office of Sheriff Principal was:

the biggest sinecure of the present age . . . The principal Sheriffs were paid very handsome salaries for disposing of some three or four appeals in the course of a year, and having holiday trips to their respective counties. The office was useless, unnecessary and expensive, and the means of prolonging litigation.

After passing the principal motion unanimously, the meeting resolved to remit to a committee of three of their number the task of preparing a petition to Parliament and having it presented by James Caldwell, Liberal Unionist MP for the St Rollox Division of Glasgow and a solicitor himself,[14] along with a draft Bill to carry out their resolution. In the meantime, copies of all the resolutions passed at the meeting were to be forwarded to the Chancellor of the Exchequer, the Secretary for Scotland, the judges of the Court of Session, the Scottish MPs and the legal societies in Scotland.[15]

What these recipients made of the Caithness Faculty's campaign was not reported in the Caithness press, though some other reactions to it were. One such was a relentlessly sarcastic piece in the *Aberdeen Evening Express*. Wick, it said, was a place which did not have 'fail' in its vocabulary, and therefore:

it must be obvious to every one possessed of common-sense in any degree that Wick is competent to manage, not only its own affairs, but those of the whole kingdom of Scotland.

After outlining what the Faculty had said, the *Express* continued:

coming from Wick this ought to settle the question at once.[16]

Both that newspaper and 'A Caithness Procurator' (i.e. solicitor) writing to the *Scottish Leader* and *The Scotsman* speculated that there must be personal reasons behind the Faculty's actions. The anonymous Caithness lawyer also pointed out that there were sixteen practising solicitors in Caithness, of whom twelve were members of the Faculty, and only five attended the meeting. One of those absent was the Dean. Until the meeting, the writer claimed never to have heard a word against the double sheriffship, and he considered the large number of appeals brought to the Principal as being the best argument in its favour.[17]

There was also support for Thoms, of a sort, at a meeting of Wick Town Council on 26th July, when Councillor W. Brims gave notice of a motion to confer the Freedom of the Burgh on the Sheriff. Although the motion was not to be heard until a subsequent meeting, Brims proceeded to read an effusively-worded speech giving the reasons he thought Thoms deserved the honour. Both the Provost and another councillor objected to his doing so, but Brims doggedly carried on through several interruptions all the way to the optimistic conclusion that:

> he fully expected that the motion when it came up would receive the unanimous support of the Council.

In fact, his little speech merely provoked his opponents to propose several other names they thought more worthy of the honour, including Brims himself.[18] His motion was withdrawn.[19]

When Thoms returned to this volatile atmosphere of division and resentment a few months later, it was not long before an explosion occurred. The spark was provided by the case of Farquharson v. Cormack, which erupted into the 'scene lasting several hours' mentioned by Alexander Sutherland after Thoms had refused time for written defences. The court had appointed a Judicial Factor to preserve the assets of a bankrupt pending the appointment of the permanent Trustee in Sequestration to administer the estate. When the Trustee tried to take up his duties, however, the Judicial Factor refused to hand over the books and papers until his expenses had been paid. The Trustee sued for them. It was a fairly straightforward situation; or so at least thought Thoms, when the action called before him at Wick Sheriff Court on 19th November, 1888. He was therefore astonished when D. W. Georgeson appeared on behalf of the Judicial Factor and stated that his client was defending the action. When Thoms demanded that Georgeson state his defence there and then, Georgeson refused, and the arguments began. Sheriff Harper, the Sheriff-substitute, was with Thoms on the bench for at least part of the time, the spectators included several solicitors, and Georgeson was not alone, either. The action had not only been raised against the Judicial Factor, but also against Georgeson personally as the Judicial Factor's law agent, and he had therefore felt it necessary to engage Alexander Sutherland to represent his own interests. Thus, it came to pass that the court heard Georgeson arguing the case on behalf of the Judicial Factor, and then Sutherland making similar arguments on behalf of Georgeson.

Had some malevolent sprite wished to conjure up a scenario guaranteed to set Thoms and the Caithness lawyers at each others' throats, it could scarcely have done better. He had neither forgotten nor forgiven the remark of a Caithness solicitor about an earlier sequestration that 'lawyers must live'. Now in this case, while creditors awaited payment, all the Sheriff could see from his elevated position on the bench was the meagre fund from which the money was to come being frittered away in what he regarded as self-serving and time-wasting argument. A selection of the Sheriff's remarks shows the temper of the proceedings:

As a practising solicitor you ought to know the law.

You are all so slow here.

You seem to read nothing.

The threat of an appeal is too old-fashioned to influence a judge.

You all think that it is necessary to put your answers in writing, in order that you may have fees.

I regret that the law is not sufficient to protect clients from their agents.

Whether or not this last remark hit the nail on the head, it certainly caught Georgeson on the raw. He demanded to know whether Thoms was referring to him. Somewhat begrudgingly, and possibly after the intervention of Sheriff Harper, Thoms stated that he was not. Yet he still tried to have the last word. In the note to his interlocutor he wrote:

> The amount of delay through litigation, and the expenses thereby incurred, falling on the creditors in bankruptcies in Caithness, have lately become a public scandal. The Sheriff has attempted, by the dispatch with which the present proceedings have been conducted, and the economy thereby secured, to show all concerned that the Court are determined to attempt to remedy the evils mentioned. The dispatch did not interfere with the able debate with which the procurators for the defenders ultimately favoured the Sheriff. That should convince the procurators generally that procrastination does not aid them in attention to the true interests of their clients.[20]

Thoms' refusal to allow time for written defences had been quite wrong as well as counter-productive (the involvement of the appeal court settled the latter point as effectively as the former), but it was his manner and his remarks which really seemed to get under the skin of the solicitors. His repeated use of the term 'public scandal' particularly offended them. At a subsequent meeting of the Caithness Faculty they again raised the question of the 'double sheriffship', but this time there was not even a pretence of discussing the question separately from personalities. Once more David Cormack, D. W. Georgeson and the three Sutherlands were there, but this time the Dean of the Faculty, J. M. Nimmo, was in the chair. That is to say, he was in the chair until he realised what the others were going to discuss. 'I will not wait for that', he declared, just as Hector Sutherland was reaching full flow. 'You are not in order in interrupting me,' snapped Sutherland, before moving that Cormack take the chair. Nimmo then left the meeting, though the diplomatic effect of so doing was somewhat undermined by his stating that anything Thoms did was 'his misfortune, not his fault'.

In their leisure hours, Alexander Sutherland, Hector Sutherland and D. W.

Wick Old Players Cricket Club, 1890. Among those who sought Thoms' dismissal, Alexander Sutherland stands third from the left; D. W. Georgeson is two further places to the right in the broad-striped blazer; Hector Sutherland is the right-hand umpire; and Symon Sutherland is seated far right. (Wick Society).

Georgeson liked to turn out for the Wick Old Players Cricket Club,[21] but at the Faculty meeting they let rip with bouncers of a verbal kind. In fairness, they had faced some hostile bowling from the bench, too. Said Alexander Sutherland:

> . . . knowing the great privilege which he enjoys as a judge, how frightened we are, and how bullied we can be, he takes advantage of it. When in the course of our remarks before him, he interrupts us; and, if in his opinion, we have any little fault, in a petition, or other paper, he must point it out. He tells us we cannot make a record; that we cannot frame a paper; and that he cannot put new heads upon us. I would not care to exchange my head with Sheriff Thoms'. (Mr Georgeson – Of course, none of us would like to do that! – Laughter.)

Sutherland wondered where Sheriff Thoms had obtained his legal practice to come there and correct them. In Sutherland's six years spent in attendance at Parliament House he had not even heard Thoms make a motion in court:

> The only practice, and the only opportunity of his obtaining it arose from the reverses that his judgements received in the Court of Session. (Laughter.)

This time the meeting resolved to petition the Lord Advocate to bring in a Bill to abolish the office of Sheriff Principal,[22] after they had first compiled a dossier on the cases appealed from Thoms to the Court of Session. They were also to send copies of the report of their meeting to all Court of Session judges, Scottish Members of Parliament, Sheriff Principals and Sheriffs-substitute.[23]

Circulating the report may have prompted James Caldwell MP to ask the Lord Advocate in the House of Commons about Thoms taking a knife to the transcript of evidence,[24] but does not appear to have had much other effect. Elsewhere, the five Caithness lawyers were roundly condemned. A correspondent writing to the *Northern Chronicle* pointed out that they comprised less than a third of Caithness solicitors, added that anyone reading the report would be:

> disgusted at the language used towards a superior and at the bumptiousness of the speakers generally,

and asserted that in his campaign against legal procrastination, the Sheriff had the sympathy of the general population.[25]

While there was nonetheless a measure of support for the abolition of the office of Sheriff Principal,[26] both it and its incumbent in the Northern Counties survived the campaign. Indeed, far from being 'doomed', the office survives to this day, albeit much reformed. By contrast, the five solicitors who had launched the campaign against it suffered mixed fortunes. It seems there were too many lawyers for the amount of available business in Caithness at the time, which may explain an eagerness for making the most of any work that came along. Although D. W. Georgeson and Hector Sutherland continued to flourish, Alexander Sutherland moved away, first to Edinburgh and then to Lerwick, before returning to Wick in 1913.[27] As for David Cormack and G. M. Sutherland, their subsequent histories show that Thoms, for all his lack of tact, may have had a point, for in the early 1890s both men were sequestrated and both were also subsequently prosecuted for embezzlement. Cormack's crime, though committed in 1885, did not come to light until after Thoms' retirement. At the High Court in Aberdeen in June, 1900, he was convicted and sentenced to six months' imprisonment for helping himself to a thousand pounds intended for a public trust.[28] The allegations against G. M. Sutherland, on the other hand, surfaced when Thoms was still Sheriff, but all charges were dropped. The Sheriff's stubborn insistence that the case should have proceeded led to almost farcical results.

A sceptic might suppose at this point that there was a personal grudge behind Thoms wanting Sutherland prosecuted. Perhaps there was an element of that. However, even upon the most charitable interpretation, Sutherland's financial affairs were chaotic. He seems to have been less than careful in keeping his clients' funds separate from his own. Some serious allegations were made against him, and these properly justified a criminal investigation.

The main allegations were of embezzlement from a School Board of which

Sutherland was clerk. These were serious enough charges to merit prosecution on indictment at the instance of the Lord Advocate. The complexities of what had been going on with the Board's finances were such, however, that a detailed report from an accountant was deemed necessary to enable the prosecution to go ahead. This required to be paid for by the Board. The Board refused, and the Lord Advocate therefore decided to drop proceedings. There was probably more than economy behind the Board's reluctance. A certain amount of closing of ranks was going on, for, at the same time, one of Sutherland's disgruntled clients claimed to have been pressurised by a number of people, including two church ministers, to drop his complaint of embezzlement against the lawyer.[29] Thoms was not amused at the Lord Advocate's decision, but thought some of the lesser allegations merited summary prosecution without the necessity of an accountant's report. He accordingly instructed the Procurator

Fiscal at Thurso, James Brims, to raise a summary complaint. Thus, as Thoms saw it, Sutherland had been given the chance to clear his name. No doubt the accused appreciated the kindness. The Lord Advocate evidently did not, as he instructed Brims to abandon those proceedings, too. When Brims appeared in court before Thoms to seek to desert the charges, Thoms granted the motion out of deference to the Lord Advocate's wishes, but added a condition. This was that the various papers and records relied upon by the prosecution should remain in the custody of the Sheriff Clerk rather than be returned to their owners. Presumably Thoms wanted to safeguard the evidence in case proceedings were ever revived.

James Brims the Thurso Procurator Fiscal whom Thoms threatened to imprison.

There matters might have rested, had the Lord Advocate not requested sight of these papers and got Brims to uplift them from the Sheriff Clerk and send them south. When he returned them to Brims it was with an instruction to forward them to their original owners. Although Brims pointed out that the order of the Sheriff precluded that, the Lord Advocate insisted. Brims therefore felt he had no choice but to comply. It was at this point that Thoms probably should have let the matter drop. However, Brims was clearly in breach of the terms upon which he had uplifted the documents. Thoms therefore took out an order against him called a Caption, which authorised Brims' immediate imprisonment until the documents were returned. The Fiscal, not surprisingly, sought review of the Caption in the Outer House of the Court of Session and took out an interim interdict against the Sheriff and Sheriff Clerk to stop it being enforced meantime. The court found in favour of Brims. Thoms accepted the court's decision without appealing to the Inner House.[30]

From what we have seen of Thoms' heavy-handed dealings with his professional brethren, one might think it unlikely that any lawyer or court official anywhere would have had a good word to say about him. In fact, several were willing to praise him, and not just in Kirkwall where their home town was going to be sixty thousand pounds to the good. Those being complimentary included lawyers in private practice, Sheriff Clerks, Procurators Fiscal (where not threatened with imprisonment) and a Sheriff-substitute.

It cannot have been easy to have been one of Thoms' officials. Yet to balance the unseemly clash with Sheriff Harper in Caithness, we have the testimony of Sheriff Shennan in Shetland. In his view:

> Sheriff Thoms certainly was not without marked eccentricities, but underneath there was a strong vein of sound common-sense, and he gave me much sane advice.[31]

An example he gives relates to his duties as returning officer. Thoms thought it expensive and unnecessary that the Sheriff-substitute, as deputy returning officer, accompany the Shetland ballot boxes on the steamer to Kirkwall for the count. Instead, he ordered him to send them by registered post, an arrangement which worked quite satisfactorily.[32]

The views of Thoms' other substitutes are not known. Several, including Harper, were dead by the time of the will case. His last Substitute in Kirkwall, John R. Cosens, was himself the subject of courtroom tributes there a mere two months after he had led those to his old Principal with the words:

> Sheriff Thoms may have had his little idiosyncrasies – which one of us has not? – but no-one who knew our late Sheriff well will disagree with me when I say we have lost a kindly, hospitable and generous friend.[33]

As for Mellis, it would be harsh to hold Thoms responsible for his death. Neither should the suicide of Kirkwall Sheriff Clerk John A. Bruce in May, 1883, be seen as more than melancholy coincidence. He, it seems, had worries outside his official duties.[34] But what we can say is that Thoms was probably not the type of man that the depressed or vulnerable would feel able to approach for understanding or sympathy. Mellis, beset with worry over the backlog of cases mounting because of his ill health, may have baulked at unburdening his problems with someone who only weeks before had decried the poor progress of cases in his court and refused to accept illness as an excuse for delay.[35]

Galloway, the Lerwick Procurator Fiscal, despite his criticisms of Thoms' conduct on the bench, had been on terms of intimacy with him socially and considered him a sound businessman and a good commercial-law man.[36] Two other Lerwick solicitors, while describing the Sheriff's peculiarities and how his ill health slowed his mental powers on his last two visits north, were generally positive in their comments. John S. Tulloch spoke of Thoms' methodical way of doing business and the commonsense he displayed on the bench.[37] John Small echoed these sentiments, saying he had always found Thoms' judgements sound. He also spoke of the good advice that he used to dispense to agents, such as more than once telling them to render their accounts quickly while their clients could still remember the value of the work they had done for them.[38] Some solicitors evidently thought well enough of Thoms and, though not blind to his idiosyncrasies, could put up with them without adopting the attitudes of Alexander Sutherland and J. C. Grierson. It was probably Sutherland and some of his Wick colleagues from whom the Wick Fiscal Robert S. W. Leith was seeking to distance himself when he said:

> the Sheriff's decisions always gave reasonable satisfaction to the best of the Agents.[39]

For all that, it cannot be denied that the charges that Grierson and Sutherland levelled at Thoms had a sizeable core of truth. It is equally clear, however, that they were exaggerated. The idea, for example, that Thoms' decisions were invariably wrong and reversed on appeal is incorrect. Nor was Alexander Sutherland right to say of Thoms that:

> Totally ignoring the law, he made up his mind to reverse every decision of his Substitute. My view is that he did so out of sheer cursedness and vanity.[40]

Looking through the cases that merited mention in the local press (which in those days meant most of them) over several years, and in all three courts, shows a fairly normal mixture of successful, unsuccessful and mixed-success appeals from Substitute to Principal. In 1892 we even find Alexander Sutherland successfully persuading Thoms to refuse an appeal and uphold the judgement of his Substitute.[41] Although Grierson and D. K. Murray said that the Shetland and Caithness lawyers began to boycott Thoms, taking their appeals direct to Edinburgh instead, right up to the end Thoms still had cases to hear and appeals to deal with. Quite probably the lawyers avoided him when they had a case that they thought he would decide against them, but appealed to him when they thought they would win.

The comments of Lord Young should also be treated with caution. A brilliant advocate, Young's judicial career never reached the heights his talent perhaps deserved. Incisive, but caustic with it, his sarcasm was directed at counsel, witness and judicial colleague alike. Shaw said of him:

> His defect was his smile, which expressed a relish for the discomfiture of others. His smile followed his own sallies. Both cut deep.[42]

In falling foul of Young, Thoms was far from unique.

The example of Lord Young also serves to highlight that those most critical of Thoms were in some ways rather like him. While the solicitors who clashed with Thoms shared something of his peppery stubbornness, their criticisms of his judicial behaviour were remarkably similar to those often made about Young. Although Thoms was explosive where Young was cutting, both men were quick to form a view on the cases before them and then often lacked the necessary patience to allow counsel or agents to argue their points properly. Young was also inclined, like Thoms, to take over the questioning of witnesses himself. After one such lengthy intervention an exasperated advocate asked, 'Who's your next witness, my Lord?'[43] Ironically, considering the praise they received from the Caithness lawyers for righting Thoms' wrongs, Lord Young and his colleagues on the Second Division bench were themselves to provoke unprecedented public criticism from the legal profession.[44]

Lord Young. When hearing an appeal from Sheriff Thoms he asked, 'Is he still at large?'

A critical but balanced view of Thoms was provided by Duncan J. Robertson, Solicitor in Kirkwall and son of Sheriff James Robertson:

> I had no great opinion of Sheriff Thoms as a lawyer but as a man learned in the law that he made a good judge where common sense was required and he never allowed his assumed eccentricities to interfere with the essentials of his work. He was an obstinate and determined man.[45]

J. B. Anderson of Lerwick was surprisingly restrained, given the 'pettifogger' incident. In fact, he did not mention it at all. He said merely that he looked on Thoms as a man of some ability, but a little peculiar and very vain, before adding:

> He was a difficult man to get on with except by showing him considerable deference and he showed this very often while on the bench.[46]

Thoms certainly liked deference, and those who showed him it were likely to be treated with respect in return. A less deferential attitude to the Sheriff, though, was liable to meet with a less considerate response. It is perhaps significant that the people he got on best with – outside his immediate circle of intimate friends and family – were often those who would not then have been regarded as his equals; those, in fact, who knew their place and kept to it. The bar officers and policemen, the lighthousemen and seamen, the women and children, all generally got on well with him. The Lerwick Superintendent of Police even named his son after him.[47]

With fellow lawyers, though, there was a tension. They were his social equals and, so some of them thought, his professional superiors, in ability if not position. This no doubt gave rise to that peculiar form of inverted condescension that members of a learned profession reserve for those of their number who have been promoted above them. Thoms, for his part, was touchy and pretentious, but that hardly made him unique in the legal profession or elsewhere. It did, though, have a bearing on his perception of similar characteristics in others. While a touchy person tends to be so conscious of his own feelings as to be oblivious to those of others, a pretentious person can often seize on the pretensions of others while remaining blind to his own. Thus Thoms, in 'taking the rise out of' agents, was not just making sport of their pride, but storing up a good deal more resentment than he realised. Some of the results have already been described.

Yet most of the lawyers who appeared before Thoms managed to remain on good enough terms with him, whatever they thought of the experience. Those who did not may have allowed their own pride to take priority over the interests of their clients, and those interests are seldom served by antagonising a Sheriff, however unavoidable it may be. Of the three local bars in Thoms' sheriffdom, it seems his relations were best with that of Kirkwall. Perhaps the lawyers there were willing to show him more deference – at least to his face. At any rate, he thought highly enough of them to make them responsible for ensuring the proper implementation of his cathedral bequest.

Perhaps, if Thoms' relations with the Kirkwall lawyers had broken down as they did in Caithness, he would have felt less inclined to benefit the town in his will; perhaps not. At any rate, Wick received nothing from him. Lerwick, on the other hand, received two pictures of her late Sheriff, but the bequest was only partly implemented. When the portrait of Thoms as the character from *The Pirate* was sent to Lerwick Sheriff Court, its fate came to be discussed by Zetland County Council, the body responsible for the building. The council did not appear very grateful for Thoms' munificence. In fact 'derision' is the word Alexander Sutherland used to describe their attitude. Some twenty years earlier a leading article in *The Shetland Times* praising Thoms for his generous support of public causes in the county had looked forward to the day the portrait would be displayed, but these sentiments had evidently been forgotten.[48] One councillor argued that the bequest to hang the portrait in the hall of Lerwick Sheriff Court could not be implemented because the court had no hall. The meeting agreed, and the picture, instead of being hung, was unceremoniously consigned to a lumber room with a load of old rubbish. The argument against hanging it, which seems a little legalistic, not to say 'pettifogging', was advanced by Councillor J. B. Anderson. Revenge, as the saying goes, is the dish that people of taste prefer to eat cold.[49]

There was no such satisfaction for J. C. Grierson and D. K. Murray when they gave evidence in the will case. Murray, the Thurso solicitor, spoke of the Caithness Faculty meeting, and also of a case he had before Thoms in 1896 where he thought the Sheriff's mental powers so weakened that he was unable to grasp even the self-evidently simple point that a greater period of years encompassed a lesser period. In the space of a few questions of cross-examination, Thomas Shaw KC succeeded in demonstrating to the jury that it was Murray not Thoms who had singularly failed to grasp the point. Having made one Caithness solicitor look as though he did not know what he was talking about, Shaw then proceeded to discredit his colleagues:

> Is it the fact that the condemnation of the Sheriff arose largely from men in your profession who had made very large charges which the Sheriff was condemning, and gentlemen who also were subsequently sequestrated and some found guilty of embezzlement?[50]

Grierson's evidence met with similar treatment, and not just at the hands of opposing counsel, for the Lord Justice-Clerk seized on his account of the Customs case. In his charge to the jury he called it:

> . . . a still smaller affair altogether, but rather a funny one, because it was to bring out that there was something wrong with Mr. Thoms, because Mr. Thoms did not convict the gentleman's own client, but thought the case in regard to him was not proven. I think it extremely likely that the gentleman himself, knowing perfectly well that his client was guilty from the information he had, was very much surprised at his getting off.[51]

V

Thoms at home

Thoms' domestic eccentricities received much more attention in the will case than his judicial ones. These were the eccentricities that caught the attention of press and public, too, and proved a rich source of amusement as they saw just what had gone on behind the august facade of 13 Charlotte Square.

Hay Shennan recalled later that the Sheriff had organised his household with 'military precision.'[1] Like a ship of the line would surely have been a more appropriate analogy for a Vice-Admiral's establishment. Indeed, when Captain Obadiah Sutherland, master successively of the Northern Isles steamers *Queen*, *St. Nicholas* and *St. Clair*, called on Thoms at Charlotte Square to discuss lighthouse business, he found himself received in a small

13 Charlotte Square, Edinburgh, the prestigious residence of Sheriff Thoms from 1885 to 1900. On an inside wall was painted the text: 'Him serve with mirth.'

room fitted up as a ship's state-cabin.[2] To keep everything shipshape and Bristol fashion, Thoms drew up a set of rules rather in the form of an Act of Parliament. These he had printed and displayed in the hall, as much for the amusement of his friends as the regulation of his servants. The Lord Justice-Clerk remembered them and how, amongst other things, they listed the duties of each of the servants. Those of the housekeeper ended with the provision:

> The housekeeper will lock all doors punctually at ten o' clock, except when Mr. Thoms is out.[3]

Breach of the rules was punishable by a fine, which was marked up on a slate and entered in a fines' book, although it seems payment of the fines was not always exacted. The usual fine was a penny, but lateness in the morning was punished at the rate of a penny for every five minutes. True to his judicial oath, Thoms administered justice without fear or favour, affection or ill-will, fining his servants, his friends (both when they were guests in his house and when he was a guest in theirs), himself, and even his favourite cat 'Sambo'.[4] It is unlikely that this pampered puss stayed in the bad books for long, however. When Thoms' Kirkwall landlady visited Charlotte Square, 'Sambo' was sporting a splendid new ribbon to mark the occasion of his birthday.[5]

Another visitor, Mrs Muir of the Shetland hosiery firm, was intrigued by the system of fines and asked Thoms' domestic servants about it. They said they took it as a joke. It was his way of teaching them to be particular and tidy, but they also delighted in pointing out his breaches of the rules so that he would fine himself. His then housekeeper, Mrs McCallum, said Thoms was very kind, which meant that they overlooked things like the fines or any crossness on his part.[6]

It seems, indeed, to have been a fairly happy household, and a small one: usually a housekeeper and two maids. The staff, whose evidence we have, all spoke of the Sheriff having been a good master before his decline into illness. He was generous to them and they were well-fed. Some of them stayed for a long number of years. Those who completed seven years' service received a present of a silk gown. He looked after their interests, provided them with a kitchen library, and even had sweet williams planted in the garden 'as sweethearts' for them. All this helped make his pernicketiness and occasional volatility bearable.[7]

From what we have already seen of Thoms' character, it should come as no surprise that he was pernickety in the running of his household. In every aspect of it he took a detailed interest. He was determined to demonstrate to the world that a bachelor could run a home as well as any lady could. Not only that, but he set himself up as an expert in matters that were usually considered to be the exclusive province of the female sex. His lecture on darning has already been mentioned. With it he coupled general remarks on housekeeping.[8] He lectured his Kirkwall landlady on cooking,[9] and instructed the Avoch minister's cook on keeping the water in which she had boiled his tripe (a favourite dish) to use as stock.[10] A Kirkwall lady, who had known him since she was a child, said of Thoms:

> He was to my mind a faddist on certain subjects such as housekeeping, darning etc., but I attributed that to him being a bachelor and not having a lady to take charge of his house.

If the Sheriff had been a married man I should have considered him eccentric but being a bachelor I consider that he simply made a hobby or fad of matters which as a married man he would have had no business to trouble about.[11]

If any dish the Sheriff encountered when dining out caught his fancy, he would take the menu home and have his housekeeper make it.[12] At his own dinners, his guests would be served such things as tripe fried in batter or boiled Orkney goose.[13] Some of the dishes were given strange names. 'Potage tempting' was one.[14] He was particularly fond of soups, and had some made from fruit. According to a former housekeeper, the apple soup she was required to prepare was made from very good stock.[15] Helen Fleming, however, the girl who had found Thoms monotonous, was equally unimpressed with his culinary tastes. 'He had soups made of sour apples and oranges,' she said.[16]

Thoms liked a good dinner. He also liked his drink and was a 'great smoker' to boot. In fact, for some time he refused to visit his brother because the latter had banned him from smoking in the house. According to a Caithness acquaintance of Thoms, he:

> . . . could take a good drink but I never saw him drunk and in the house he behaved in every way as I would expect a gentleman to.[17]

He certainly seems to have enjoyed convivial company. An early friend in Kirkwall was Captain John Baikie, octogenarian veteran of Nelson's navy and usually good for a salty yarn or two after dinner.[18] More nautical tales were no doubt shared when Thoms used to visit Captain Sutherland on board his ship in Lerwick harbour of an evening,[19] while Sheriff James Robertson records finding him in Kirkwall 'smoking and imbibing' with a Captain Geddes and the Papa Westray laird Thomas Traill of Holland.[20] Although nowhere is there any suggestion of Thoms having been a drunkard, his consumption was no doubt frowned upon in those increasingly abstemious times. At home, according to one of his former maids, he would take his favourite tipple, whisky,

James Robertson, Sheriff-substitute at Kirkwall at the time of Thoms' appointment. He found his new superior 'a nice jolly fellow'. (Orkney Library Photographic Archive)

not just in the evenings but through the day as well. She mentioned three times he would take it: at meals, when he had visitors, and in between.[21]

As part of Thoms' daily routine, before he became an invalid, he would go down every evening to the kitchen to discuss his dinner and his next day's breakfast with his housekeeper. When there, he took the opportunity to inspect that everything was in order. A stickler for cleanliness and tidiness, he had a particular hatred of dust, even clambering up on the dresser with a magnifying glass in search of it.[22] To aid his inspections, he had that same item of furniture fitted with glass ends so that he could see that the dishes were clean and dust free.[23] The cheese dish, too, had a specially-made clear glass cover so it would be obvious if 'mites' were helping themselves to the Stilton.[24] To make sure his maids were cleaning properly, he would make chalk marks on the floor and see if they disappeared.[25] According to his household rules, the pantry had to be kept 'like paradise'. When Thoms surprised one of the maids entertaining her young man there, she said it could not be paradise without an Adam.[26]

The Sheriff's taste for specially-made furniture was not confined to the kitchen. Possibly the most unusual such item was found in his spare bedroom. It was a large mahogany bed with a projecting top containing a looking glass. Thus anyone lying in the bed could see himself in the mirror above his head.[27] It was an object of amusement to his cousin when, as a dinner-party guest, she laid her cloak on the bed,[28] and provided equal entertainment when mentioned during the will case. As for what its function may have been, the jury received no guidance from witness, counsel or judge.

Throughout 13 Charlotte Square there were odd little touches which reflected the personality of its owner. All round the house there were Shetland knitted Tam o' Shanters and mufflers to ward off draughts. In the library lay bundles of photos of Thoms ready for distribution to visitors (and staff too – each servant had been given at least three pictures of her master). These photographs showed the Sheriff in various poses and uniforms, including wearing his masonic regalia.[29] He was also pictured sitting on a donkey.[30] In the dining room were a pair of

Orkney Museum artefacts associated with Thoms: the silver trowel with which he laid the foundation stone of Stromness Masonic Hall in 1889; his Royal Caledonian Curling Club medal; and a birch approved by the Sheriff for use on juvenile offenders in Orkney. (Picture: David Mackie).

silver spoon-warmers shaped like buoys, his 'spoony buoys' he called them,[31] while on a drawing-room table lay a duster printed with the words:

When servants' hands have done their best,
The Master's hand must do the rest.[32]

Thoms was determined to have the house just as he wanted it. The whole building, not just the pantry, was to be like paradise: his idea of paradise. Illness would bring more than a touch of purgatory.

Thoms' doctor of about twenty years, James O. Affleck, MD of Heriot Row, certified the causes of his death as chronic gout and general debility.[33] This was accurate so far as it went, but fell short of total candour, for Thoms also suffered from what his nephews' and nieces' written pleadings simply referred to as 'a malignant disease'.[34] This coy lack of specification continued throughout most of the jury trial. The disease was variously alluded to as 'something else that was the matter with him',[35] 'a very nauseous disease',[36] and:

> that other disease, which we don't mention, but you quite understand how things are?[37]

On the few occasions it was mentioned by name, the press did not report it. It was, in fact, syphilis.[38]

That Thoms suffered from syphilis casts a new and slightly lurid light over what we are discussing. The fact that it is a sexually-transmitted disease raises questions about his character and habits. Its potential effects upon the brain add an extra dimension to the issue of his mental capacity.

In examining the latter question, an important matter to be determined is to what extent his symptoms were the product of syphilis, and to what extent they were the product of gout. That he suffered from both diseases made him doubly unfortunate, but probably not unique. Shakespeare has Falstaff say:

> A pox of this gout! or, a gout of this pox! for the one or the other plays the rogue with my great toe.[39]

For centuries, both venereal disease and gout have been a source of humour for those not afflicted with them. This has been particularly true of gout, since it is a more socially acceptable and less deadly ailment. Its association with rich living no doubt contributed to the humour, and the figure of the port-soaked irascible old colonel nursing his bandaged gouty foot became a comic stereotype. For the sufferer, however, neither gout nor syphilis is remotely funny.

Gout is caused by an excess of uric acid in the blood. This crystallises in the joints of the extremities, particularly the big toe and the knees, causing swelling, excruciating pain and immobility. One sufferer described the pain of an attack as 'like walking on my eyeballs', and another as:

> sometimes the gnawing of a dog, and sometimes a weight and constriction

of the parts affected, which become so exquisitely painful as not to endure the weight of the clothes nor the shaking of the room from a person's walking briskly therein.[40]

In the light of this, one can appreciate the dry understatement of one of the witnesses in the Thoms case:

> The advance of gout generally does not sweeten the temper or improve the spirits.[41]

Gout remains incurable, although modern drugs have made the attacks more treatable. In Thoms' day the usual treatment was colchicum,[42] and he took large doses of it; so much, indeed, that one of his friends thought it harmed him.[43]

If gout is bad, syphilis is worse, and well deserves its description as 'loathsome' and 'nauseous'. Although mild in its initial stages, when not treated with modern drugs, it advances to symptoms of quite horrifying unpleasantness. Thoms was unfortunate to have laboured under its effects just before medical science made a series of important breakthroughs in its diagnosis and treatment. In the very year of his will case, 1905, the cause of the disease was discovered: the parasitic organism *treponema pallidum* (also called *spirochaeta pallida*). In 1908, Wassermann described his test for the presence of the disease, and then, in 1910, Ehrlich produced his famous 'magic bullet', salvarsan, as a cure.[44]

It was all too late for Thoms. In the absence of a cure, he just had to let the disease take its course, alleviating the symptoms as best he could. There were, of course, some drugs available for this purpose. When the diagnosis was first, tentatively, made in his case, he was prescribed the then usual treatment of iodide of potassium, but took it only once.[45] It might not have been much more palliative than waistcoat-pocket camphor had proved prophylactic.

Although syphilis may be transmitted by several means other than sexually, including kissing, smoking the same pipe, and even, it has been reported, sharing glass-blowing equipment, the typical form of contracting the disease is by sexual connection. We do not, of course, have any information as to how or from whom Thoms caught it, but there is no reason to suppose that he caught it any differently from most other sufferers. We may be reduced to speculation, but there is enough knowledge of Thoms and his circumstances to confine the speculation within relatively narrow parameters of probability.

Thoms was, of course, a bachelor, and was very conscious of the fact, too. Indeed, from the way in which so many of his eccentricities and humorous conceits focused on his single status, one cannot help suspecting that it rather bothered him. Apart from his self-proclaimed expertise at household management, and the tales of his rejections and his fissured heart, he also held himself out as a

'Professor of Flirtation', offering lessons on the topic to young ladies.[46] He even offered them to the nurse who had looked after him during his illnesses of 1891 and later, a revelation which, when she made it from the witness box, provoked some rather ungallant laughter in court.[47] Thoms had summed up his attitude at a banquet celebrating yet another stone-laying ceremony, this time that of the new Thurso bridge in 1887. In replying to a toast, he:

> illustrated the principle of his judicial and social action to be one of love to all mankind, and specially to the ladies. (Applause).[48]

How justified Thoms' pose as a ladies' man was is difficult to judge. It may have been a way of coping with his painful lack of success: self-mockery in pointing out his nine failures, combined with braggadocio about having had the nine opportunities in the first place. Whether these nine incidents actually happened is unknown, but even to be spurned once must have been a bitter experience for a man of Thoms' conceit. That Thoms was thought likely to be seeking a wife may be surmised from an interview that the Rev. John Mackenzie Gibson had with him. Mackenzie Gibson himself had not married till the age of 54.[49] His account preserves intact an authentic slice of late Victorian dialogue on such a delicate matter:

> In consequence of a rumour I had heard, I called upon him one day – I cannot give the date – and I said, 'Have you had any news?' He said, 'No, have you?' I said, 'Yes, I have heard extraordinary news concerning you.' 'Me?' he said, 'What is it?' I said, 'It is a rumour you are married.' 'Me married!' he said. 'Yes,' I said, 'that is the current rumour.'
> He did not say anything for a moment, and I said, 'Is it true, Thoms? It is very shabby of you going away and getting married privately without telling me.' He said, 'It is not true.' I said, 'Do you authorise me to contradict it?' and he said, 'Certainly, contradict it'; and he added, 'God help the woman that would marry me!'[50]

There is another possibility which should perhaps be addressed. It is that all this talk of the ladies was not so much designed to deal with his lack of success in that quarter, as to conceal a lack of inclination: that, in other words, the Vice-Admiral may have caught his loathsome dose in pursuit of one of the less-celebrated aspects of naval tradition. Tempting, and fashionable, as such a speculation may be, it is also, at least on the evidence we have, a speculation too far. It

A portrait of Vice-Admiral Thoms donated to Kirkwall Town Council in 1918 and hung for some years in the Town Hall before being discarded and damaged. (Orkney Museum/David Mackie).

would take more to 'out' Sheriff Thoms as homosexual than a camp love of dressing up and a fondness for his mother. A little too much can be read into bachelorhood.

More likely, from what we know, is that Thoms' attitude was that of slightly frustrated heterosexuality. Thoms was not only a bachelor but a respectable one. Such creatures were not, in his time, expected to indulge in the sin of fornication. Sexual activity was to be kept within the sanctified bounds of Christian marriage. That at least was the theory. The practice was somewhat different. Admittedly, the opportunity for sexual dalliance with the chaperoned spinsters of Thoms' own class was very circumscribed, but opportunities among the women of lower classes were more extensive.

Some of these liaisons were exploitative. The wicked squire of 'She was poor but she was honest' was not just a cliché. In rural areas there were indeed lairds and factors who used their position to take advantage of the daughters and wives of the tenantry. In Orkney, the most notorious example was Fiscal Macrae's father-in-law, Robert Scarth of Binscarth.[51] There were, too, in both town and country, some masters who preyed on their female servants. One such, it is said, was Galloway, the Lerwick Fiscal. He got rather more than he bargained for one night, however. The story goes that he slipped into his maid's bed only to find it occupied by his wife. The resourceful Mrs Galloway, in order to teach her husband a lesson, had given the girl the night off.

It is dangerous to generalise in this area. There were no doubt women who were happy to be 'exploited', and found advantage in being the mistress of an important man. Some, indeed, were supported along with the almost inevitable children.[52] Thoms, though, would not necessarily have had to pull rank to relieve his frustrations, or rely on finding a woman willing and able to conduct an illicit affair, for in Edinburgh what he sought was available for ready cash.

Prostitutes were, of course, with their numerous sexual partners, a common source of venereal disease, and it seems highly probable that this is how Thoms contracted his. Although never openly condoned, it was long accepted that many young middle-class men would gain their early sexual experience from such women; at least it was accepted by many middle-class men. Nor were older clients a rarity. In 1871, there were said to be about eighty-five brothels in Edinburgh, catering for all classes and occupations of men. Rose Street was a centre of the trade.[53] Indeed, only a few years ago an old building there revealed its louche past during renovations, when escape hatches were discovered leading to a neighbouring attic. These were intended to ensure a swift exit for patrons in the event of a police raid. A pleasing symmetry is brought to mind: the enforcers of the law burst in at the bottom while its practitioners scramble out at the top.

There is, moreover, a piece of real evidence to link Thoms to such establishments. Beds with mirrors above them were, it seems, a feature of better-class brothels in the nineteenth century.[54] That may well be where he got the idea. It certainly chimes with the mischievous humour of some of his bequests. In Shaw's cross-examination of the Rev. John Mackenzie Gibson we find this exchange:

> (Q.) You told us about the bed with the mirror in the top. Where is it now? – (A.) I have it now. (Laughter)[55]

Thoms had told Mackenzie Gibson many years before that he would leave him the bed, but instead gave it to him, presumably when he left Charlotte Square. Mackenzie Gibson's wife did not want to take it, but her husband insisted lest they offend the Sheriff.[56]

The progress of syphilis is usually divided into three stages: primary, secondary and tertiary, although the divisions are not always clear in each case. In addition, some of the late tertiary symptoms are sometimes termed quaternary or parasyphilis. The first stage occurs some two to three weeks after infection, and usually consists of a single hard sore or 'chancre' which commences as a painless small red papule, enlarges to the size of a pea, and then ruptures to form a small ulcer. It appears at the site of the infection, typically the genitalia (unfortunate glass-blowers get it on the tonsils), and the lymphatic glands in the area also swell up. While the primary stage is localised, the secondary stage is a period of general infection, usually commencing some five to six weeks after the primary chancre and lasting about two years, but with no definite limit. Its principal manifestations are a long-drawn fever, rashes of various types lasting weeks or months at a time, sore throat, mucous patches, swelling of the mucous membranes, general enlargement of the lymphatic glands, hair loss, anaemia and often headache and insomnia. It can also affect the bones, eyes, kidneys, nails, spinal cord, joints and testes. If this were not bad enough, the sufferer then had to look forward to the onset of tertiary syphilis, which occurred usually between two and ten years after the initial infection, but could happen later still, and lasted for the rest of the patient's life.

The tertiary stages were often accompanied by fever, but their main characteristic was the formation of 'gummata'. These tumours swelled up rapidly, enlarged, softened, ruptured and discharged their contents, leaving a deep ulcer and commonly a foul discharge. Scarcely any of the body's tissues or organs was immune, with gummata being particularly common in the skin, mucous membranes, subcutaneous tissue and muscles. The nasal cartilage, the palate and the tongue were often affected, leading to destruction of the tissue, perforation of the palate and, in the worst cases, destruction of the entire structure of the nose. Finally, in the late tertiary stages, the disease attacked the spinal column and the brain, causing locomotor ataxia (unco-ordinated movements and lurching gait) and ultimately the condition known as general paralysis of the insane.[57]

It was a dreadful price to pay for a fleeting moment of pleasure, but Thoms, like the Burray youth he lectured, had evidently not counted the cost before he commenced operations. The Burray youth got off lightly by comparison. Moreover, the cost Thoms would likely have to pay would probably have been apparent to him almost as soon as the first ominous papule appeared on his person. The effects of syphilis, though not as well understood as they would be after 1905, were still well-enough known in Thoms' time. Indeed, some fathers took their adolescent sons to syphilitic wards to see the patients, some with their faces eaten away by the disease, as a warning against the consequences of immorality.[58] Thoms would not have been human if the thought of what awaited him some ten, fifteen or twenty years down the line had not had some effect on his behaviour. Irascibility and impatience are only to be expected in such circumstances; that, and a desire to do what he wanted while he still had the chance.

Of course, there is one thing which Thoms may have desired but felt his condition precluded him from doing even while his health held up. Even if he was willing to risk passing his infection to a sexual partner, there were further potential consequences. It was well known, even in his time, that syphilis could produce severe congenital defects in the offspring of the infected.[59] To Thoms, so fond of children, the prospect of inflicting such suffering on them would surely have been an appalling one. A certain poignancy may therefore be discerned in his continued bachelorhood and his delight in the young, just visible through the heavy humour in which he cloaked them.

When, in the nineties, the inevitable breakdown in Thoms' health occurred, the first major change it produced in his lifestyle was the necessity of having a male servant to attend to him. This change was not easy for either Thoms, his existing staff, or indeed the male servant. Although the manservant was often described as such, or as a valet, his duties were largely those of a nurse or attendant. His job thus straddled awkwardly the contradictory roles of servant under the control of a master, and nurse in charge of a patient. This awkwardness was at the root of much that came out in evidence in the will case.

At first, Thoms was in no doubt who was to be in control of whom. The men who came to work for him were treated 'rather roughly',[60] spoken to 'pretty sharply',[61] and 'bullied fearfully'.[62] Not surprisingly, they did not as a rule stay very long. Between 1893 and 1895 at least six menservants passed through the doors of 13 Charlotte Square in fairly short order. The first was Thomas Gibson, the man who had been sent to Caithness to nurse Thoms and bring him home after his collapse at Stemster. He lasted about two or three weeks after they got back to Edinburgh. 'Melancholy and religious', he enraged the Sheriff by proposing to read the Bible to him.[63] One of his replacements read a book that Thoms found more congenial, at least until the man dropped it on his gouty foot. He was not actually dismissed for this, but took such offence at the volley of foul language it provoked from his master that he resigned.[64] Another valet, who was in fact sacked, paid the price for finding an effective way of escaping his master's sharp tongue. Thoms, by then, could stand unaided but could not walk without assistance, so one day on a busy pavement the attendant just walked away and left him.[65] Finally, there was the manservant who learned in memorable fashion just how painful a gout sufferer finds unexpected motion. When he bumped against the Sheriff's bed, his patient threw a boot at him.[66]

Whenever Thoms fell out with one of his valets, or vice versa, he would send for Nurse Margaret Morrison to fill the gap till he got a new one. When she had nursed him through his serious illness of 1891, Thoms had dubbed her his 'life preserver', and he called upon her services several times thereafter.[67] In October, 1895, she was fulfilling the role of attendant as well as nursing him after one of the operations on his jaw when he asked her to find him another male servant. She suggested Adam Melrose.[68] Melrose came highly recommended. Then aged about 51, he was trained as a gentleman's servant and had had a varied number of engagements, including being butler at Monzie Castle and several of what he called 'surgical cases'.[69] He had attended Sir William Forrest of Comiston until his death, and was so highly thought of that Forrest's son paid him a year's salary afterwards.[70] Nor should a more difficult patient have held many terrors for him, since he had also spent some time in the south of England looking after a well-to-do inebriate.[71]

Nevertheless, Melrose almost went the same way as all the others, and that after only one week in the job. It was a Sunday morning, and Nurse Morrison had just come in from church when Melrose told her:

I am going away. I am not going to stay with a thing of [a] man like that.

Thoms' cousin Mrs Watt also came in, and both she and Nurse Morrison went up to Thoms to get him to apologise to Melrose and have him stay on. From then on, in Nurse Morrison's view, Melrose had the upper hand on his master. Whatever the case, the Sheriff at least began to grasp some of the realities of his position as an invalid.[72]

Melrose did not just have Thoms' dictatorial behaviour to deal with. As Dr Affleck put it, 'this was a very nauseous affair.'[73] Thoms' sores, which Melrose had to dress twice a day, were on his chest, his back, his legs, hips and heels, between his toes and on his head, and all produced a foul discharge, as did his nose and mouth. Since he had to lift Thoms, the discharge also ended up on Melrose, on his clothes, collar and even on his face, particularly when lifting his master in and out of bed or on and off the stool. This last task was a particularly irksome one, given Thoms' obsession with regularity. He took Hunyadi Janos mineral water every morning to aid his digestion, and if it did not produce the desired effect immediately after breakfast, Melrose was faced with a tedious succession of liftings-on, waitings, and liftings-off throughout the remainder of the day. If none of these met with success, the Sheriff would resort to his old faithful Gregory's mixture before retiring, thus ensuring that Melrose's sleep would be disturbed in the small hours.[74]

In his eight years of service to Thoms, Melrose never got a holiday, and was on call practically twenty-four hours a day. The one time he arranged for Nurse Morrison to stand in for him so he could have the holiday that Thoms had promised him, in 1897, he made the mistake of arranging it first and only then telling the Sheriff. Thoms refused to allow it.[75] Accompanying Thoms on his own holidays was certainly no holiday for his valet. In 1901, their Gullane landlady complained of having to lie down because of the offensive smells, so Melrose agreed to clean up the Sheriff's room himself. The previous year, at Moffat, a carpet had to be replaced, so bad was the discharge from Thoms' sores. On this occasion, Melrose, who claimed to be sick every morning because of the stench, suffered a particularly bad fit of retching. In 1896, Thoms and Melrose spent ten weeks at the Strathpeffer Hotel, during which the manageress told Melrose that Thoms' condition the previous year had been so offensive that she had been afraid some of the other guests would leave. Outside servants had to be brought in to clean the room as her own staff refused to enter it, and the whole room had to be painted and papered to get rid of the smell. The smell, if this is true, was presumably from the oral and nasal discharges, the sores on the skin not yet having broken out.[76]

For his pains, Melrose was paid the fairly high salary of £9:2s a month.[77] In addition, he received occasional small presents, plus a new suit of clothes every year to replace that soiled in his work.[78] His daughter was given a child's Orkney chair.[79] Yet however well paid Melrose was, there can be no doubt that some of his duties were stomach-turning. It was a point, too, which he was keen to emphasise, even perhaps to overstate. The reason for the emphasis was that he had found the work a little difficult to cope with; or rather he had found a way of coping with it that was itself to prove a little difficult. He had taken to drink.

At what point Melrose first began to hit the bottle is unknown. Neither is it particularly clear how often he did so, though it seems he was given to binges rather than to continual tippling. According to Isabella Dougall, the housekeeper, he was 'very often' the worse of drink.[80] Even then, his drinking did not usually prevent him from discharging his duties, although it did at times expose the Sheriff to somewhat rougher handling than was altogether appropriate. Melrose would lead his master along rather faster than the latter was able to walk, ignoring his cries of 'Wait now, wait now';[81] he would speak disrespectfully to him: 'Come away, you auld rascal, or I'll screw the nose off you'[82] or 'You auld devil, can you no' stand steady?';[83] sometimes he even swore at him.[84] When Mrs Dougall complained to Thoms about the 'offensive and nasty' language that Melrose was using in the kitchen in front of her and the other servants, Thoms replied, 'I have a great deal of that to put up with myself.'[85]

If drink sometimes made Melrose behave as if he had the upper hand on his master, it in turn, before long, began to get the upper hand on him. One day, in around March of 1897, Thoms rang for Mrs Dougall and asked her to help him through from his bedroom to the drawing room. It was about midday. 'That fellow has gone and got drunk,' said the Sheriff. Mrs Dougall replied that Melrose was scarcely ever anything else but 'in the blues'.[86] He certainly was when he sobered up and found himself dismissed and a new man in his place. Luckily for Melrose, however, the new man did not care for the job. This may have been, as Mrs Dougall alleged, due to Melrose not leaving the house after his dismissal but hanging around feeling sorry for himself and trying to get his job back. According to her, Hay, the new servant, called Melrose 'a damned sneak'.[87] In the witness box, Hay told a different story. His reason for leaving was that he was unwilling to clean the Sheriff's boots, answer the door and polish the silver; he was a certificated invalid attendant and masseur, not a general manservant. He left after two days, having suggested to the Sheriff that he give Melrose another chance, and Melrose, sober, contrite, and on the spot, was reinstated.[88] Thoms said to Nurse Morrison:

> What can I do? If I don't keep him on he will starve, and he has promised to do better.[89]

Unfortunately, Melrose did not do much better at all. His intemperate habits returned, and on several occasions he drank until he fell over. One time he fell his length in the street and arrived in the kitchen covered from head to foot in mud. In an effort to make him half-ways presentable, Mrs Dougall, and the housemaid Margaret Bullions, washed his face for him and scrubbed his clothes.[90] Another evening – at Easter 1899 – Thoms had sent Melrose out to get some Easter eggs. Having seized the chance to stop off *en route* for a little refreshment and more, Melrose returned too full to eat his supper. Instead, he left to go upstairs, carrying the Sheriff's eggs with him. Later, when the maidservants came to go to bed, the eggs were lying in a mess at the foot of the stairs, and so was Melrose.[91]

One evening in September the same year, Thoms was rather lucky not to share the fate of the eggs. Melrose, as usual, had the task of helping him to his bedroom and putting him to bed, but had on this particular evening taken so much alcohol that he could hardly walk himself. It was not so much a case of the blind leading the blind as the legless bearing the legless. Still, somehow or other, and with much stumbling and commotion, the unsteady pair got to the foot of the Sheriff's bed, but then it seemed they would get no further. Only when Thoms said that he would have to call for one of the female servants to help him was Melrose roused to a final effort. With one last heave, he just managed to fling the Sheriff onto the bed before collapsing dead drunk on the floor. Mrs Dougall, eavesdropping on the stairs, heard a great noise and went up to investigate. It was a bizarre tableau that met her eyes. There they lay, master and servant alike, one as helpless as the other. While the servant was crumpled in alcoholic oblivion on the floor, the master lay a few feet away on the bed, wide awake and still fully clothed, but with all the mobility of an overturned old tortoise.

Neither man could have put in a very good night. Although Mrs Dougall made Thoms as comfortable as she could, he insisted on lying where he was. In the morning, the housekeeper brought up hot water, plus a cup of tea for Melrose, who by then was sitting on the end of the bed with a rather dazed look about him. Said the stiffly recumbent figure further up: 'There now, Melrose, Mrs Dougall returns good for evil.'[92]

It may have been during the same binge – it was certainly during the same month – that the Rev. John Mackenzie Gibson called at Charlotte Square on a Sunday afternoon to see his old friend. He was a little surprised when the front door was opened to him not by Melrose but by Margaret Bullions, the housemaid. On coming down from seeing the Sheriff he asked her where Melrose was, and received the startling reply that he was lying dead drunk in the Sheriff's bed. Mackenzie Gibson was not for believing it, but was told to see for himself. Sure enough, that is where he found his friend's valet, not unconscious but very drunk. What Mackenzie Gibson said – 'Dear me, what's the meaning of this?' - is what one might expect from a retired Minister of the Gospel. Less expected is what he almost did:

My first impulse was to seize hold of him and drag him out of the bed.

But he did not act on this impulse:

I began to reflect that perhaps I had no right to do so without the Sheriff's permission, and that it would be as well not to make a disturbance.

He resolved instead to speak to Thoms about it the next day.

Before doing so, Mackenzie Gibson called on Dr Affleck to let him know what had been going on. The doctor proved almost as concerned as the minister, and undertook to find a replacement for Melrose within a few hours should Thoms dismiss him. Both Mackenzie Gibson and Affleck separately recommended this course of action to Thoms, the former urging him to consider how dangerous it was to have a man who might let him fall and break an arm or leg; but Thoms was having none of it. He would keep Melrose on. 'He suits me,' he said, and that was that.[93]

Thoms' refusal to sack Melrose in 1899 was cited in the will case as an example of the ascendancy that the servant had allegedly acquired over his master. It was even said that Thoms was frightened of him. Yet there were weighty alternative reasons for keeping Melrose on. The trouble Thoms had originally in finding an attendant who was prepared to put up with him should not be discounted. The thought of similar problems, and of then having to become accustomed to a stranger performing such intimate duties, may have weighed heavily on the thoughts of an elderly invalid. Melrose by then had been in Thoms' service for nearly four years, and the latter had got used to him. He had also clearly grown to like him. The maid Bullions said that, when sober, Melrose was kind to his master,[94] while even Mrs Dougall conceded that he got on well with the Sheriff.[95]

The same could not be said of relations between Melrose and Mrs Dougall or the other female servants. They, too, tried to engineer the dismissal of Melrose in 1899, presumably after the involvement of Mackenzie Gibson and Affleck already described. Mrs Dougall and Bullions ushered Alfred Thoms into the dining room one day to express their concerns,[96] and he then spoke to Affleck, Mackenzie Gibson and to Thoms' solicitor Wood, but found that there was no prospect of his uncle being persuaded.[97] Yet although this marked a new low-point in relations between Melrose and the female servants, these had always been uneasy. The Trustee's counsel put it to Mrs Dougall in cross-examination that she resented having any manservant in the house.[98] Melrose said that Thoms himself had told him that Dougall was jealous of everyone that was likely to suit him.[99]

It is not hard to see why this should have been. We come back to Thoms wanting someone to combine the duties of medical attendant with those of general manservant. When Thoms was fit and well, the housekeeper had been mistress of everything that went on downstairs, answerable only to the master. This simple dynamic was upset by the arrival of a man to attend to Thoms, particularly in the case of Melrose, who had previously been employed as a butler and was therefore used to being top dog in the servants' hall. There was now someone else encroaching on what had hitherto been Mrs Dougall's province, and that someone else had the ear of the Sheriff – and every other part of him – almost twenty-four hours a day. It was a recipe for trouble.

It is possible, too, that the mere presence of a male servant in the house, no matter what he did or did not do, produced a subtle change in Thoms' behaviour towards the female servants. He may have been less inclined to be indulgent, more inclined to play to his male audience. An incident in Kirkwall recalled by Mrs Grant, the Superintendent's wife, shows something similar. Her precognition gives a perceptive account of her dealings with Thoms from the day in 1871 when 'a gentleman, very smart and well-dressed and a fine-looking man' marched unannounced into her kitchen, introduced himself as the Sheriff, asked what the matter was with her little boy who was then teething, and recommended she give him plenty of castor oil; to the day, about a quarter of a century later, when she encountered him crippling out of the County Buildings on two sticks and he asked her if she knew where he could get himself a new pair of legs. In between, he had been in the habit of inspecting the police station sometimes twice or thrice a year, always without warning and often when on his way to see Macrae or his widow at Crantit or Mellis or Cowper at Glaitness. These were nerve-racking occasions for the Grants, but one in particular stood out in Mrs Grant's memory. On this inspection, the Sheriff was accompanied by his substitute, Mellis, and the Sheriff Clerk, Bruce. In one of the cells Thoms noticed a cobweb, and asked Mrs Grant if she did not see what the mice had been doing. This, she said, put her a bit out, but when he went on to find fault with several other things, she bade him good day and left him and the others to complete the inspection by themselves. She felt sure that Thoms would never have found any fault if he had been on his own. Although she and her husband stood rather in awe of him, and he made it clear that he expected to be treated with the respect due to his position, he was nonetheless always very 'homely' with them and their children. No doubt, on this occasion, he was showing off his efficiency, as well as making sport of her, for the benefit of Mellis and Bruce: three proud men, grim hindsight might suggest, each concealing any sign of weakness from the others. Mrs Grant believed Thoms realised he had upset her, because the next day he returned with Mellis and was as nice as could be. After that, she never had a cross word from him, and she said she stood rather less in awe of him, too.[100]

Whether or not the presence of another man in the house produced a change in Thoms' behaviour towards the female servants, it certainly produced a reaction in them. The first sign of this came long before Melrose was employed, when the housemaid, Bullions, was required to wash some of the then manservant's clothing. She objected, and Mrs Dougall spoke to Thoms about it on her behalf. He then called for her and explained that if she did not do it he would have to look for someone else.[101] Bullions' objection seems a rather petty one, but this was the sort of situation where pettiness thrives and dignity is forever being huffily stood upon. The reaction of the female servants to an interloper on their territory was scarcely more rational than Sambo's would have been; and once their birse was up, Melrose was just the man to keep it there.

It is against this background of below-stairs antagonisms at 13 Charlotte Square that some of the allegations in the will case require to be viewed, in particular those stating that Thoms laboured under a delusion of his own poverty and that Melrose had acquired a controlling influence over him. On the former question, Falstaff once more has some potentially apposite words:

> A man can no more separate age and covetousness than he can part young limbs and lechery; but the gout galls the one, and the pox pinches the other.[102]

Yet, despite his gout, it was not a yearning for more money which Thoms was alleged to have displayed, but an unwarranted desire to hold on to as much as possible of what he already had. Mackenzie Gibson said that in former days Thoms had been very liberal, but latterly had become 'rather close-fisted'.[103] Although this was undoubtedly true in some respects, it seems Thoms had always been rather careful with his money. It may have been a characteristic linked to his finicky tendency to get worked up about trifles. His sometime amanuensis recalled that small mistakes irritated him more than large ones.[104] At any rate, according to Nurse Morrison, even when she first nursed him, she found that he had a 'sort of mania for small economies' which increased over the years to something like miserliness.[105] As far back as the early eighties, or before, it was said that he entered into a correspondence with Her Majesty's Postmaster General on the vexed question of whether, in sending a telegram from Thurso Post Office, he had been properly charged for '*et cetera*' as two words.[106] Similarly, years later, in 1897, he sent a postcard to the Orkney Sheriff Clerk demanding he forward him a sum of money that he had earlier short remitted him. The amount was a halfpenny.[107]

Thoms had a dislike, too, of being 'dunned' for charitable subscriptions. In 1900, Mackenzie Gibson's wife wrote asking him for a donation and received what her husband regarded as an unbecoming reply. Not only did he reprove her for misaddressing the letter (she had shortened Macthomas to 'M'T'), but derided the cause for which she was fundraising – sending chocolates to the Marines in South Africa – as 'nonsense'.[108] Thoms' cousin Mrs Smith received a similarly tart response about the same time when she sought a subscription for the Dean Church. Part of it was censored by the court shorthand writer who took down her evidence:

> I hate bazaars as I do the D____.[109]

Then there is the evidence of John Lessels, who had been Thoms' clerk and private secretary from 1885 to 1897. When he worked for Thoms he would see him for an hour or two almost every night, as well as on Monday mornings. He attended to the clerical work of the Sheriffdom and Thoms' correspondence, and kept his cash books, banked his money and paid his accounts. Thoms kept careful books of income and expenditure which had to be balanced every month, as well as an annual balance sheet of capital and income. He also discussed with Lessels any fresh investments that he was contemplating. But Lessels had other interests outside his work, as he explained in answer to Shaw's questioning:

> (Q.) You are a sergeant in the Volunteers? –
>
> (A.) Colour-sergeant, please. (Great Laughter)
>
> Mr. Shaw: I beg your pardon, Mr. Lessels.[110]

At the end of 1902, he was collecting for the Queen's Brigade Volunteer Bazaar and, despite his knowledge of his old employer's reluctance in these matters, ventured out to Cluny Drive to see if Thoms would make a donation. After exchanging news, and giving Thoms the latest gossip of Parliament House, he explained to him that he was actually on a begging expedition:

> I said, 'You are no doubt aware we are building our new headquarters of the Queen's Brigade and I will be very glad if I can get a donation from you.' He said, 'Oh, I am very sorry, but I have had to pay a call on Scottish American Mortgage Shares, and I cannot afford it.' I took a book of shilling raffle tickets out of my pocket and said, 'Will you take some tickets, then?' He said, 'Yes.' I said, 'How many?' He said, 'One.'

It had cost Lessels fourpence to collect a shilling.[111]

Miss Emily Irvine, Thoms' amanuensis from 1898 until his death, made a similarly optimistic request for a donation to a church charity, and with similar result. Thoms said that he was very much obliged to her for giving him the opportunity. Then he looked at her and they both laughed. It was a form of words she had probably written for him quite regularly.[112]

The pursuers attempted to show during the case that this dislike of being asked for money came on late in Thoms' life in tandem with his alleged insane delusion that he was poor, but the evidence showed that he never particularly liked being pursued for donations. Dr. Logie, for one, recalled Thoms refusing to give subscriptions years earlier on the stated grounds that he could not afford it.[113] Even when he was younger and in good health he could be as tight-fisted as he could be generous. It is clear, however, that in his declining years the acts of generosity largely faded away, leaving the parsimony intact and strengthened.

As Thoms' health had declined, Mackenzie Gibson had frequently urged him to give up the sheriffship, but was told he could not afford to lose the salary: some seven or eight hundred pounds a year.[114] In the event, despite the loss of the salary, his income actually increased after he resigned his post. In addition to a pension of about five hundred pounds,[115] in 1902, for example, rents, feu duties, dividends and interest brought his total earnings up to about £3,500.[116]

When a pound was a gold sovereign, this was a handsome figure for an annual income. It would take well over half a century of paper money and inflation to render it otherwise. Yet Thoms proved reluctant to incur new expenditure, and he cut back on what he was spending already. 'Retrenchment is the word,' he said.[117] When Mackenzie Gibson and Alfred each suggested that he get himself a low-set brougham or other carriage, he claimed he could not afford it.[118] Whilst cancelling his subscriptions to his clubs – the Highland in Inverness and the University in Edinburgh – as well as giving up his seat in St. Giles seem justifiable economies for someone increasingly housebound,[119] he also stopped regular charitable expenditure such as buying the sweets for the nurses' annual Christmas entertainment at the Royal Infirmary,[120] and became less generous with his servants. Mrs Dougall got a present of a silk gown as promised on completing seven years in Thoms' service in 1889, but did not get the ten pound note that was supposed to come after fourteen.[121] Bullions, who started working for Thoms in 1892, was also promised a silk dress after seven years but never received it.[122] Every Christmas, there was a staff dinner, also attended by Mrs Melrose and her daughter and two old servants who had used to act as waitresses. These last two had always been given ten shillings by Thoms at the dinner, but this, too, stopped.[123]

Perhaps his most bitterly-resented economies were in household expenditure. In 1897, he became concerned at the amounts he was having to spend in this area. He mentioned it to Melrose, who said he should look at the books.[124] Mrs Dougall believed Melrose was behind the whole thing.[125] Whatever the case, Lessels was called in to examine Mrs Dougall's books. He found that the expenditure on groceries, greengroceries and butcher meat, in particular, was much too high for the number of people in the house. Accordingly, Thoms had him censure Mrs Dougall and instruct her to reduce her accounts.[126] After that interview the housekeeper came back down to the kitchen crying, and she remained very angry about the whole affair.[127] The upshot, however, was that from the following month the grocery and other accounts were reduced by about half. This was initially achieved by a reduction in quantities, and then from later in the year by going to cheaper shops than the rather high-class ones that the household had previously patronised.[128] Thoms ordered her to leave one butcher and go to another, where she was to get the meat in the evening when it was cheaper. The supplies of food for the servants were cut back, and she said she even had to go to Rose Street for her vegetables.[129]

The household expenditure was not the only area in which Mrs Dougall fell foul of her master. He also became suspicious of her honesty, believing that she had made off with two piles of Shetland blankets and some other items.[130] Then, just before he left Charlotte Square, he thought she was going to purloin the silver-plate. After dinner one evening he told her to bring up to the drawing room the dishes he had been using at dinner. She sent up the earthenware dishes and he flew into a terrible rage, saying it was the silver dishes he wanted. When she took them up, he said she just wanted to dodge and keep the silver dishes. She replied:

> Oh, Sheriff Thoms, how can you say such a thing after all these years? You have always been the best and kindest of masters, but it is your man Melrose.[131]

Thoms' cousin, Mrs Smith, thought so little of these suspicions that she offered Mrs Dougall the position of cook in her own house.[132] His sister, Mrs Anderson, offered her a character reference.[133]

This suspicious side to Thoms' nature, like his closeness with money and his irascibility, was used by the pursuers in the will case as evidence of mental deterioration in his latter years. Yet, although all these aspects of his character undoubtedly grew more pronounced towards the end of his life, there is ample evidence that he always possessed them. Lessels, who had worked for him from 1885, said he was exceedingly difficult to please, very few could get on with him, and it was very trying to one's temper. Thoms had always been irritable, sharp and very peppery, and Lessels thought he had always been of a suspicious nature, too. In particular, he was suspicious of his officials in the north, who he suspected were not doing their duty or were lax, and he took strong dislikes to people, often abusing them violently in conversation with his clerk.[134] We have already seen corroboration of this in some of Thoms' behaviour as Sheriff.

Of most significance to the questions at issue in the will case is how this increased suspicious nature may have been exploited by Melrose. It is apparent that Melrose's stock stood high with Thoms, despite the valet's drunken behaviour, while that of Mrs Dougall had fallen. Yet, although Melrose had the Sheriff's favour, he was an isolated figure in the house. Dougall may have been less favoured, but she at least had the two maids to support her, which they did loyally. It is not surprising that Melrose, trapped between the Sheriff's constant demands upstairs and the frosty female fiefdom down below, should have taken refuge in the library with Lessels when he was working there.[135] Nor would it be surprising to learn that there was a lot of tale-bearing, jockeying for position, and attempted one-upmanship, between valet and housekeeper, with the valet usually coming out on top. Thoms refused to believe it, for example, when Mrs Dougall told him that instead of giving him Hunyadi Janos waters, Melrose had been refilling the bottles with Epsom Salts.[136] Perhaps Melrose just wanted a decent night's sleep.

It may be that Melrose was adept at planting the occasional seed of suspicion in Thoms' mind, tending it carefully in the hothouse conditions of the sick room, and watching it, in due course, bear fruit. Certainly this is along the lines of what the female staff, Nurse Morrison and Thoms' nephew thought, although they also went further in arguing that Melrose exercised direct control over the Sheriff. The purported evidence for this includes the manner already mentioned in which Melrose bossed Thoms around. Thoms did not answer back and was quite cowed, said Nurse Morrison.[137] After Melrose came, Thoms seemed to get ideas about his friends and relations. Nurse Morrison asked him if his cousin, Mrs Watt, had not been to see him. No she had not, he replied:

She is only gadding about. She only wants to get what I've got.[138]

Nurse Morrison herself soon came in for similar treatment. Melrose told Mrs Dougall, according to the latter, that he had opened the Sheriff's eyes about Nurse Morrison, that she only came for 'grub and drink'.[139] Then one time the nurse called, Thoms was 'very rude' to her, something he had never been before. The next time she called, in the autumn of 1899, Melrose answered the door and, when he saw who it was, said, 'The Sheriff does not want to see you.' She never saw him again.[140]

Thoms' relationship with his sister, Mrs Anderson, also deteriorated. According to Mrs Dougall, Melrose once read her a letter that Thoms had received from his sister and said he had told the Sheriff to write her back and tell her to mind her own affairs. Mrs Anderson, incidentally, was seen by Dougall as a potential ally in her feud with Melrose, for she threatened to write telling her how Melrose

26 Cluny Drive, Edinburgh. The suburban villa to which Thoms moved in his declining years. Whether to save money or prevent dampness, the walls were neither papered nor painted, but the plaster left bare with workmen's scribblings plainly visible.

had been behaving. Melrose threatened back, telling Dougall that she would suffer for it and he would turn the tables on her.[141] Thoms and his sister had been on very affectionate terms, and in the winter of 1902/3 she travelled up from her home in London to see him. She stayed some time in Edinburgh and called on him almost every day at Cluny Drive. Alfred said to him how that would be a great pleasure to them both, but was shocked when he replied with a splutter of rage, 'I have seen too much of her.' After that, he never heard his uncle say a kind word about her ever again.[142]

We have already seen how relations between Thoms and his nephew changed over the years. According to Dougall, Melrose said once that Mr Alfred came in as if the place was his own, but he would show him otherwise.[143] Bullions heard him say that Mr Alfred was only waiting for the Sheriff's death but, once again, he would show him otherwise.[144] To Nurse Morrison he apparently said he would see the Sheriff made a proper and just will.[145] On other occasions he would rail generally about Thoms' friends and relations and how they were looking for his death and what they could get.[146] On one occasion, he took Mrs Smith into the library at 13 Charlotte Square and began:

> . . . abusing everybody all round, right and left, giving a sort of just general blow-up.

This was directed mainly at the relatives. While Melrose was ranting, Mrs Smith noticed a glass of whisky and water secreted under one of the chairs.[147]

It is a little difficult to judge what weight to give to these allegations. The accuracy with which the witnesses reported them and the interpretation they gave to them may both be called into question. Melrose frequently said it was he who was keeping Thoms alive. Some of the above could be interpreted as a touching protectiveness towards his master, coupled with a desire to spite the relatives by deferring their windfalls by as long as possible. It should be realised, too, that most of these incidents happened when Melrose was under the influence. He may well, it is true, have been attempting to exert an influence over the Sheriff. On the other hand, it is arguable that he was simply reflecting views that Thoms already had, or exaggerating, while in his cups, the extent of his own importance and influence with his master, or simply letting off steam.

Another explanation is suggested by two of the more bizarre allegations. The first was made by both the housemaid, Margaret Bullions, and the under-housemaid and kitchen-maid, Elizabeth Coghill. Melrose sometimes read hymns to Thoms, among them 'One there is above all others well deserves the name of Friend.' Both Bullions and Coghill, the latter 'often', heard Melrose on coming to the end of the hymn say to Thoms, 'Yes, you have a friend.' And it was quite clear that he meant himself.[148] The other allegation is more damning. It is that once, when drunk in the kitchen, Melrose said he was going to put his daughter through a form of marriage with the Sheriff. Coghill, disgusted at his condition and his talk, rose and left the kitchen.[149]

Both these incidents certainly square with the pursuers' portrayal of Melrose as a manipulative scoundrel with base designs upon their uncle's fortune, but there is an alternative that deserves consideration. Melrose was stuck in Charlotte Square having to face a demanding master, unenviable duties, and the hostility of his fellow servants (even if this last was much of his own doing). There was no prospect of a holiday and little respite except the bottle. In such circumstances, the temptation to needle his servant-hall antagonists must have been a strong one. Quite probably the comment on the hymn was aimed not at Thoms but the maids. It, and the remark about marrying his daughter to Thoms, would have 'set their gas at a peep' quite efficiently. It was not just the stench from the Sheriff's sores which hung heavy in the atmosphere of 13 Charlotte Square.

Out at Cluny Drive the air was a good deal clearer, at least in a metaphorical sense. On leaving Charlotte Square, Thoms had dismissed Mrs Dougall, Bullions and Coghill. In their place he employed Melrose's wife as his housekeeper, plus a full-time general maid, and a washerwoman who came in two days a fortnight. Melrose and his daughter, Susan, completed the household, and latterly she, too, was paid a wage of sixteen shillings a month for running errands.[150] Away from the antagonisms of Charlotte Square, and under the watchful eye of his wife, Melrose kept himself sober. Indeed, he had signed a paper for the Sheriff pledging to remain so.[151] Mackenzie Gibson, who continued to visit Thoms about once a fortnight, never saw any further sign of drink on Melrose.[152] Dr Affleck made surprise visits to check that everything was in order, and invariably found that it was. In his view, a patient afflicted as Thoms was would ordinarily have been admitted to hospital, but the treatment he received at the hands of Melrose was as skilled and careful as the best infirmary treatment he could wish, and effectively saved him a great deal of suffering and prolonged his life.[153] Both Affleck and Mackenzie Gibson thought Melrose fully deserved his bequest.[154]

At Cluny Drive there was no question of going to low-class shops. Thoms was a member of 'the Store' (the Co-operative),[155] from which, said Melrose, you could furnish a house with everything. In addition, there was a box of mutton, eggs and chickens which came every fortnight from the north.[156] Economies and oddities were not entirely absent, however. Although Thoms had a coat of varnish on the skirtings and facings at Cluny Drive, the walls remained neither papered nor painted. He had some pictures hanging on the walls, but the workmen's scribblings were still plainly visible on the bare plaster all around.[157]

The daily routine as described by Melrose was very regular. Whatever had happened during the night, he had to go to Thoms at seven o' clock every morning. He then washed and dressed the Sheriff's head before breakfast. After breakfast was served and eaten – a boiled egg, bread and butter cut into fingers, and tea with a lemon – Melrose got him up and washed and dressed the other wounds on his body. An average of four or five hours a day was spent on this task, as it had to be done in the evening as well as the morning. Thoms got his letters and his newspaper as soon as they arrived, and was always interested in both. At eleven o' clock he had a glass of milk with the white of an egg in it, and a dessert-spoonful of brandy. Around noon his amanuensis might come, and then a cold lunch was served at one. This consisted of fowl, lamb or mutton, plovers' eggs, jellies, and a small whisky with a large potass. When lunch was removed, the whisky and potass was allowed to remain, but not much of it was drunk. When Thoms tried to drink it, the discharge from his mouth would go in the glass. His appetite, however, was, said Melrose, much improved after the move from Charlotte Square.

After lunch Thoms would have a rest. At Charlotte Square, if the weather was fine, he would go for a drive in the afternoon, but at Cluny Drive he contented himself with a turn in the garden. Melrose would wheel him out in the bath chair – concrete paths had been laid for the purpose – and then take him out of it and walk him about. There were chairs in different parts of the garden so that Thoms could sit down when convenient. At four he would have a cup of tea and would then read until dinner. He got four books a week from Douglas & Foulis and could read them without glasses.

Visitors came at all times, and Melrose was as glad to see them as Thoms was, because it was the only chance he got of a break. The visitors were quite varied and some came frequently, others once or twice. There were colleagues from the law, people from the north and those who knew Thoms from his other public activities, as well as other old friends and relations. They included an assortment of Sheriffs, the captain of the *Pharos*, Orkney landowner Sutherland Graeme of Graemeshall, and Sir John Batty Tuke, MD. The last of these combined his position as Medical Director of New Saughton Hall Asylum with being Conservative MP for Edinburgh and St Andrews Universities. One would have thought he could have given valuable evidence on Thoms' mental state, but he was not a witness in the case.

Dinner was at six, and as a gentleman dressed for dinner even if he was an invalid dining alone, Melrose had to get Thoms into his evening-wear. The meal itself consisted of good strong soup, followed by fish and a joint of meat. After dinner Melrose might read to the Sheriff, a task Mrs Melrose also sometimes performed. Thoms would correct any mispronunciation – 'quite kindly', said Melrose. He also liked music and sometimes had Susan Melrose play for him. She was a member of Edinburgh Choral Union but much disliked playing for the Sheriff owing to the smell. Through the week he liked old Scotch songs, but on Sunday evening it was pieces from *Messiah*. At nine, Thoms would have some cold jelly and about a dessert-spoonful of brandy in a glass of potass. Then the evening might end with Melrose having a hand of cards with his master, 'Catch the Ten' being the favoured game.

After ten o' clock Thoms was taken to his room and the laborious preparations for bed began. All the dressings were taken off, the sores cleaned, and fresh dressings put on. This took until about midnight, when the Sheriff was put to bed. During the night he had at his bedside biscuits, jelly and brandy and water. Melrose was, of course, always on call. Then at 7am the whole routine began again.[158]

Thus did Thoms pass the last few years of his life: thus and in meticulous preparation for its end. He made his will. He organised his funeral.[159] He even had his gravestone prepared and engraved, all but the final date.[160] And if he viewed his impending death clear-eyed and unflinching, he also had a shrewd appreciation of what would happen after he was gone. Mr Alfred would not spend much of his money, he told Melrose one day. Then he laughed to himself and said that there would be a great commotion among his relatives over his will.[161]

VI

The Will Attacked

For five days in February, 1905, the Thoms will case was the best show in Edinburgh. Even those who were unable to obtain a seat in the stalls could follow the unfolding drama in the pages of their newspaper, not just in Edinburgh but across Scotland. Only a scandalous society divorce might have surpassed it at the box office, for it had almost everything to appeal to a curious public. Members of the upper middle classes were washing their dirty linen in public, the well-off were losing some of their dignity in an attempt to become better-off, and the testator whose puckish spirit seemed to hover over the entire proceedings had been admittedly eccentric, possibly deranged, and unquestionably a sheriff. Thus the human frailty of those whom fate had elevated to positions of wealth, status and authority was being exposed to public view in all its lurid and hilarious detail. The public looked on in wonder and amusement.

Others seemed to be amused, too. Although the parties themselves probably were not, their lawyers gave every impression of enjoying themselves. At times the reports of the proceedings make the two leading KCs, Thomas Shaw and F. T. Cooper, sound like front-of-cloth comedians trying to upstage each other, with the Lord Justice-Clerk making regular interventions as if to show that he could still get a laugh or two himself. Yet there was a serious purpose underlying the humour which they never lost sight of, and the humour was exploited for that purpose as much as to provide light relief.

The burden of proof was on the pursuers, Alfred Thoms and his siblings; that is to say they had to prove their case to the satisfaction of the jury, or they lost. This task devolved on their counsel, Cooper, and his two juniors. Each witness they put in the box was questioned ('examined in chief') by one of them in an effort to draw out the evidence necessary to prove the case. Then Shaw or one of his colleagues would cross-examine for the defender to negate if possible the evidence that the witness had just given, at least in so far as it had been favourable to the pursuers' case. Then Cooper could re-examine to repair the damage. The same procedure was followed for the defender's witnesses, only the other way around. This all sounds very logical, and very dry. So it was, to some extent, but this was also a jury case, and with juries the impression created can be as important as logic. Here, then, is where the humour came in, and here, too, we can see that those counsel a century ago would have recognised the concept of a 'sound-bite', if not the term. Listen to Cooper in his examination of Nurse Morrison for example:

> (Q.) Outside of a madhouse have you ever met a more eccentric person than Mr Thoms? (A.) No, I don't think I have.[2]

We have already considered the possible advantages to the pursuers of commencing their case with the evidence of the Rev. John Mackenzie Gibson. Of course they would only secure these advantages if his evidence backed up their case. Mackenzie Gibson's evidence covered most things – the eccentricities that would be recited by most of the witnesses almost to the point of tedium, the tawse, the cracked heart, the gutta-percha and the rest; the decline into illness; the clan chieftainship; the behaviour of Melrose – but on the central question of Thoms' mental capacity he was disappointingly vague:

> (Q.) Along with the breakdown in his bodily condition, did you observe any deterioration in his mental condition? (A.) That is rather difficult to answer; he was not so alert as he had formerly been. (Q.) Did he become subject to moods? (A.) Sometimes he was not so pleasant; he seemed to be rather grumpy.[3]

He said that Thoms seemed to listen to him and seemed to take an interest in matters, but he had no direct method of testing his intellectual powers further than just casually. His only other observations were that Thoms latterly had some appearance of vacancy in his expression, that he was apparently very anxious about continuing to live, and that towards the end of his life he seemed to find difficulty in finding words to express his meaning, mumbling indistinctly.[4]

Shaw, in cross-examination, counteracted what little damage these comments may have done. He had Mackenzie Gibson concede that the mumbling could have been due to the condition in Thoms' mouth, that a desire to continue living was not a sign of mental deterioration (it was 'a pretty human weakness,' agreed the minister),[5] and:

> (Q.) You said he was grumphy [*sic*]. Is that a sign of deterioration of mind? (A.) – Hardly.

> The Lord Justice-Clerk – I hope not. (Laughter.)[6]

Otherwise Shaw's questioning was simply a matter of ensuring that the defender's interpretation of the various incidents described by the witness was put to him, and, in particular, to have him agree that Thoms' eccentricities had been a product of his cheery and humorous disposition and had existed years previously when Thoms held the high position of Sheriff, had been Mackenzie Gibson's best man, and had been undoubtedly, in the witness's opinion, in full possession of his faculties.

With the three female servants who gave evidence next, Cooper and Hunter perhaps wisely did not ask them specifically for their views of Thoms' mental condition, contenting themselves with bringing out the aspects of his behaviour from which, they hoped, mental deterioration could be inferred. These included, once again, the eccentricities, the irascibility, the illness, the suspicions, and the meanness. From the servants, too, of course, came most of the evidence of Melrose's alleged influence. There were examples of what had thrown Thoms into rages: Mrs Dougall making white sauce too thin;[7] Coghill not carving a chicken properly; the soup plates not being hot;[8] not getting his words out properly when he was trying to speak.[9] He would flare up quickly and then calm down equally fast.[10] In addition, there was evidence of his acquiring a vacant expression as his illness advanced, of his memory deteriorating, and of his being confused when he left Charlotte Square. He apparently never said good-bye, said he would call past every second day to see how they were getting on, and generally gave the impression that he was not leaving the house for good.[11]

In cross-examination, the servants conceded that the fines, sweet williams, etc, were Thoms' jocular way of telling them how he expected them to behave. They admitted, too, that each of them had received presents of furniture when the Sheriff left Charlotte Square.[12] The cross-examination of Mrs Dougall also brought out the investigation and restriction of her expenditure, although Shaw sensibly did not attempt to challenge her with Thoms' dubious suspicions about the blankets and other items. His aim, instead, was to undermine her testimony as being distorted by her bitter feelings towards Melrose and her jealousy at the presence of a manservant. This general line of attack was also followed in Clyde's cross-examination of Bullions, and Shaw's of Coghill. The latter, in particular, being the youngest (23 at the time of the jury trial) and most junior in position, was portrayed as merely following the lead of her two senior colleagues from whom most of her evidence had come second-hand: 'the clash of the kitchen', as Shaw more than once contemptuously termed it.[13] He suggested that all three servants had got together to discuss their evidence;[14] something neither he nor Clyde had put to the others, nor led any evidence of themselves. Although that allegation was denied, Shaw's tactics were quite effective:

(Q.) You knew what Dougall's opinion of Melrose was, and it was a very low one? (A.) Yes; it was, and so was mine. (Q.) You belong to the Dougall party? (A.) Of course I do.[15]

93

Nurse Morrison generally supported the evidence of the servants and was, of course, particularly able to speak to Thoms' physical deterioration and the employment and subsequent conduct of Melrose. She described how Thoms became melancholy and suspicious, how he did not laugh the way he used to do, how his memory failed and how he got enraged at trifles.[16] She also said how, in former years, if anyone left legacies to churches he would laugh and say, 'Oh, I suppose that is for a name to themselves.'[17] As she herself said later in the context of his protestations of poverty:

> He said a lot of things, but you could not be certain that he meant them or not.[18]

That aspect of his nature proved rather more difficult for the pursuers than the defenders.

Nurse Morrison's evidence concluded the first day's proceedings. Shaw and his colleagues probably went home that Saturday lunchtime a little happier than Cooper and his. When the court reassembled on the Monday morning, the first witness did not really do anything to strengthen the pursuers' case. He was Thomas Gibson, the attendant who had taken Thoms down from Caithness in 1893 but had not seen him since. He said Thoms had traces of blood poisoning about him due to syphilis - the first witness to mention the disease either by name or obliquely – but did not say much else other than that Thoms was the most eccentric man he ever attended, he was difficult to work for, irritable and easily angered, did not let Gibson go out to get fresh air, and instead of following his doctor's orders to avoid liquor, drank too much of it. Shaw dismissed his evidence succinctly:

> (Q.) – Do you know why you were brought here?
>
> Witness. – No.
>
> Mr. Shaw. – Nor do I. (Laughter.)[19]

The next witness was of more substance. He was Alfred Patrick Macthomas Thoms.

One can only speculate as to the thoughts and feelings of first Alfred, then his brother and sisters, as they put themselves through the ordeal of giving evidence that day. Of hopes or misgivings, disagreement or united determination we know nothing. Yet there was one matter that surely weighed upon them: their mother had died eight days before. She had been suffering from cancer, and had been staying with her sons in Edinburgh when she died.[20] In accordance with the conventions of the time, her children would still have been wearing mourning when they appeared in court.

As the principal pursuer, Alfred Thoms was a crucial witness, and how his evidence was received was vitally important. Cooper accordingly took him carefully and at length through his dealings with Thoms over the years and the ups and downs in their relationship, as well as the various features of his late uncle's character that had already been gone over extensively by the other witnesses. In the course of this, Alfred showed an occasional tendency to use slightly overstated language, a tendency which would become more obvious when he was put under pressure in cross-examination. He began by describing his encounters with Thoms during his childhood, when he found him very kind-hearted but very eccentric. He and his brother and sisters called their uncle 'the funny man' because of the very odd things he did, such as producing the tawse:

> He said that if we were good, it would help to keep us good, and if we were not good, it would make us good. In any event, we were to get a thrashing, especially the boys; my sisters got off sometimes.[21]

After going through his contact with Thoms while he was a student, he described how, on his arrival in Edinburgh to attend the law classes in 1896, he was 'much shocked' at the change in his uncle's appearance. There he sat, broken in health, unable to walk, wrapped in rug and overcoat with a cap on his head that slipped occasionally to reveal the sores beneath. He was, thought Alfred, keeping up his spirits with an effort. Now and then, when Alfred did not understand something he had said, he drummed his hands on the table and his face became highly coloured. He became confused, too, forgetting the names of Alfred's younger sisters or mixing one of them up with an aunt of the same name.[22]

When Alfred returned to Edinburgh in the autumn of 1902, after his knee problems, he found that Thoms was even worse than before. He looked 'terribly ill', and his face had lost even the remains of his former cheery look, being instead 'dull and vacuous'. He would rouse himself for a moment with a great apparent effort, then relapse again. He was very much bowed, with his head sunk on his breast presenting only its crown to the visitor. His right arm was too stiff to put out to shake hands, his hand deadly cold, a reddy-blue colour and with no grasp in it. He could speak no more than two or three words at a time.[23]

Alfred outlined his dealings with his uncle about the will, the alleged delusions, and all the other matters to which he could speak from his own direct knowledge. He could not say much about Melrose from his own observations except that he had often smelt drink on him and that, although always civil in his presence, he had a distinct tone of authority with the Sheriff. Alfred confirmed, however, that when Bullions and Dougall had ushered him into the dining room that day in 1899, it was to say how Melrose intended to have the Sheriff disinherit his 'gaping' relations and 'scoop every penny the old man had' for himself.[24]

It took some time for Alfred Thoms to get through Cooper's questioning, but the real ordeal was yet to come. When Shaw rose to cross-examine him, the

Frank Towers Cooper KC, leading counsel for the Thoms siblings in contesting the Sheriff's will.

tyro WS found himself facing one of the leaders of the Scots bar, and Shaw was not about to pull any punches.

Shaw began by having Alfred confirm that it was he who was responsible for bringing the action. Then he had him spell out precisely what he was trying to achieve in bringing it. Alfred wanted to claim his rights under the will of 1893 and the subsequent codicils, apart from those in favour of Melrose which had been obtained allegedly through Melrose's influence, up to that of 19th June, 1902:

(Q.) May I take it accordingly from you that in your judgement your Uncle George was fit to make testamentary settlements up to that date? (A.) Yes. (Q.) So that your attack upon his testamentary power is something which occurred between 19th June, 1902, and the date of his death, notably March, 1903, when he made the last will? (A.) Or rather perhaps the outcome of what had been going on for years; the delusions had hold of him before that. (Q.) But your attack upon his testamentary power to make a will, apart from Melrose's influence, affects the period subsequent to the last holograph codicil of 19th June, 1902, which you are not reducing? (A.) I don't think these delusions took full possession of his mind and affected him adversely to me until the autumn of 1902. That is proved by his writings. (Q.) So that this is a case in which testamentary power is being tried applicable to the period from August, 1902, onwards? (A.) Yes – well, no, in so far as the former writings shew the effect of undue influence we seek to reduce them.

Alfred was obviously a little ill at ease already. The Lord Justice-Clerk intervened to have him clarify that, apart from questions of influence, up to the autumn of 1902 he thought his uncle had capacity to make a will. It was an important point. Most of what the court was hearing about Thoms and his behaviour related to a period when, according to Alfred, he was still sane.[25]

Shaw then moved on to the implications of Alfred's action. Sheriff Thoms was survived by his full sister, Mrs Anderson. If all his wills were reduced, she would receive a substantial share of his estate, but by relying on the 1893 will, that share would go largely to Alfred instead. And Mrs Anderson was not, for some reason, one of Alfred's witnesses, as he attempted to explain when Shaw challenged him on the point:

Mrs. Anderson was very unwilling to give testimony, as it was about her own brother. We are not to have her testimony. There is a barrier. Messrs. Melville and Lindesay are her agents. (Q.) You think we should have brought her? (A.) I believe you did ask her. (Q.) Is it not the fact that Mrs. Anderson declined to have anything to do with an attack upon her brother's will? (A.) She said she would do nothing to defend such a monstrous will. (Q.) If that be the case, why didn't you have her here? (A.) Out of regard for her feelings. (Q.) Here is his only living sister, and she gets nothing; can you give any explanation why the lady has not been

Thomas Shaw, KC, MP, senior counsel for Thoms' Trustee in the defence of the Sheriff's will.

examined as your witness? (A.) She wrote me saying that in any case she would not touch a penny of my uncle's money; she did not wish to. (Q.) She knew, of course, that you were getting it all; that you were wanting to get it all? (A.) She knew that I was residuary legatee under the will of 1893.[26]

This exchange shed no light on whether Mrs Anderson considered her brother sane, but from the defenders' point of view it did some advantageous things. It highlighted that Alfred was acting to benefit himself and it hinted at disagreements in the family. The former point was rubbed in when Shaw then drew attention to the fact that Alfred's action, if successful, would deprive his own brother of a yearly income of some £500 for life. Alfred said Harry had, entirely of his own accord as a fair-minded man, declined to keep it, and there was no arrangement between them. This passage of cross-examination also showed that Alfred was trying to give as good as he got in his exchanges with Shaw – a tactic which easily gives an unpleasant appearance of arrogance as well as increasing the chances of saying something foolish.

Something of the sort occurred when Shaw moved on to Alfred's delay in getting down to professional practice. Alfred was attempting to justify his long absence during his knee troubles:

I went to Ilfracombe, and then I went to London to see Mr. Watson Cheyne, and attended a gymnasium for my knee there. I was at different places. I was at Brighton, and stayed at the Grand Hotel. I was at Bournemouth – just those dead-and-alive places. (Q.) That is the nature of your evidence

– that Brighton is a dead-and-alive place? (A.) It was dead-and-alive to me, because I had to live a maimed life there.[27]

This was not perhaps the wisest use of hyperbole in the circumstances.

Then came a spot of professional embarrassment for the young lawyer. When in his will Thoms referred to his representing the Chiefs of the Clan Macthomas of Glenshee in the male line, he added, 'See Scots Acts 1587 Caput 59 and 1594, Caput 37.' Alfred was not impressed:

> The Scots Acts did not support his claim to be chief of the clan Macthomas of Glenshee. (Q.) Didn't you know that the reference to the Scots Acts is to shew that the Macthomases of Glenshee were an old-established Scotch family, well known to the law? (A.) Not well known to the law. I have looked at these Acts.[28] (Q.) Didn't you find that they confirmed the view that there was a clan Macthomas of Glenshee as far back as the year 1587? (A.) Really, I am not prepared to say. I read them over, and I know that they did not confirm his claim to be chief of the clan Macthomas. (Q.) But they confirm this, that there were Macthomases of Glenshee? (A.) They may be so [*sic*]. (Q.) Don't you think that is something? (A.) I don't think there is much in his claim. (Q.) Do you seriously say that it is an evidence of delusions in your uncle's mind when he refers to the statutes under which the clan that he has claimed to belong to is recognised by Parliament? (A.) He refers to that in support of his claim to be The Macthomas. (Q.) Isn't it in support of his claim to belong to an old clan, that there was an old clan? (A.) It would not be much support to the claim. It was another name from his own. It may be that Macthomas was spelt with a small 't' in the Acts of Parliament. (Q.) So that there is no delusion even there? (A.) It was a trifle in any case.[29]

Shaw then quoted from the will of 1893, where Thoms had left £5,000 for bursaries for Edinburgh University to be called the Macthomas Thoms bursaries, named after:

> the clan to which our family belonged, the Macthomases of Glenshee. See Scots Acts.

In the light of this, did Alfred still say it was a delusion that his uncle suffered under? -

> (A.) He had a delusion then that he was a Macthomas, but it did not influence him in making his will. (Q.) But he was still under delusions in 1893? (A.) He was already. (Q.) In fact, the delusion left him sane when he was giving you the property, but made him mad when it was going past you?

- the defenders' case in a nutshell. Alfred's answer laid himself open to a burst of questioning that left him floundering a little:

> (A.) A delusion does not invalidate a will unless it influences the will. At that time it did not influence the will. (Q.) In this present case you think it has influenced the will in 1903? (A.) His other delusions did, the delusion that he was poor did. (Q.) Had that delusion, in your judgement, anything whatever to do with the disposal of his estate? (A.) I think it is in accordance with that former delusion; he was very, very keen about the family – extra keen. (Q.) It is the same delusion in 1893, and you say it did not affect that will; does the same delusion in 1903 affect that will? (A.) I mention that delusion as an instance of his mental weakness. [30]

Next discussed was the alleged delusion that Thoms' relatives desired his death:

> There was no cause of difference between us in 1899 when my uncle said, 'Do you wish to kill me?' He never repeated that or anything like that in subsequent years. (Q.) That being so, how do you want to reduce the 1903 will, when you have admitted his testamentary capacity up to the autumn of 1902, and this delusion was in 1899? (A.) I have no interest to challenge his testamentary capacity before that. I cannot challenge a document that I have no interest to challenge. I think that the delusion had already entered his mind in 1899, and was growing then. I think for the moment I reassured him. [31]

After this, Alfred's disapproval of his uncle's move to Cluny Drive was ascribed to mercenary motives; the rationale behind the unpapered walls was explored (anxiety about damp walls, suggested Shaw; a belief he couldn't afford the papering, responded Alfred); and the fact brought out that when Alfred's father had died in 1897 he had left an estate worth £60,000:

> (Q.) You don't think that the reasonableness had ever struck him that you were well enough provided for elsewhere? (A.) I remained his heir until June, 1902, and it was only when he was in the very last stages of helplessness and depended on the person attending him, that he disinherited me.

Shaw then returned to Alfred's tardiness in getting down to earning a living for himself. [32]

One of the most potentially embarrassing matters for Alfred was his behaviour on the night that his uncle died. He did, after all, rush around trying to facilitate his uncle's apparent desire to change his will. The implications of this were not lost on Shaw, nor did he neglect to bring them to the attention of the jury:

> (Q.) In October, 1903, were you of opinion that your uncle was able to

make a will? (A.) I did not stop to think about it…..I thought it was right to go and let Mr. Babington and Mr. Wood know, and Mr. Wood said that it was quite right. (Q.) Did you intimate to them that your uncle was not able to make a will? (A.) I did not use these words, but I told them both about the delusions.[33]

Dr Affleck was then consulted at Wood's suggestion, said Alfred. Alfred neither approved nor disapproved of this course, he said.

(Q.) Do you say you took no steps to facilitate the making of the will? (A.) I went to Mr. Wood. (Q.) Did you not, in order to get a will out of your uncle, take a notarial docquet with you? (A.) I took with me a form of notarial docquet…(Q.) Would you be any party to taking a document from any person notarially unless you were of opinion that they were fit to execute it by understanding it? (A.) No, I should not. (Q.) May I take it that when you prepared this docquet to be executed by your uncle, that was done upon the footing that at all events it was perfectly possible he could understand the document he was signing? (A.) I told his agents the facts, but made no suggestions. I had cut the form of the docquet out of the Parliament House book. (Q.) Why did you do that if, in your opinion, your uncle was not able to make a will? (A.) I knew something about his will. (Q.) Why did you do that if, in your judgement, he could not give directions about making a will? (A.) I did not stop to think about it. I have heard that sometimes people who have been under delusions or insane for years have lucid intervals just before they died. (Q.) So that it was in the hope of a lucid interval which would bring the estate into your net? (A.) It was my uncle's real wish. I wanted my uncle's true will. If I had got the property, it would have been in accordance with my uncle's true will. I was his heir for twenty years until he became utterly broken down.[34]

Alfred's views on Melrose were the next point of Shaw's attack. He succeeded in bringing out that most of what Alfred said of Melrose was hearsay obtained from the servants. He said, for instance, that Melrose had often been closeted with a 'legal friend' in pursuance of his schemes. This was evidently how Melrose's time in the library at Charlotte Square with Lessels was interpreted in the kitchen. Shaw pointed out that Melrose had not 'scooped every penny into his own net', but had got what Thoms' old friend Mackenzie Gibson felt he was fairly entitled to. Alfred did not agree that Melrose deserved it.[35]

Finally, Shaw referred to the voluminous business correspondence that Thoms conducted almost up to the time of his death. Alfred had not seen it. The court would, and it would not help Alfred's case in the least. In the meantime, though, Shaw concluded his cross-examination, and, after a short re-examination from

Cooper to emphasise some of the more favourable points of his evidence, Alfred was able to resume his seat in the court.[36]

The evidence of Harry Thoms, who took the stand next, was much shorter than his elder brother's. Harry had only once seen his Uncle George between 1892 and his death, and that was on a Sunday afternoon in May, 1903. It seems he had been too busy working, at one time in a bank in Dundee,[37] and for a time as a 'manufacturer' in Peebles. Perhaps this concern for earning a living helps explain the comparative favour his uncle showed him in his will. At any rate, Thoms heard from Alfred that Harry would be spending the weekend in Edinburgh, so asked to see him. When Harry arrived he would, he said, have hardly recognised his uncle, the change in him was so great. His face, which used to be pretty well filled-out, was shrunken. Harry did not say

The wedding of the Sheriff's nephew Harry (centre, rear) to Amy Surridge, Coggeshall, Essex, October 1904. Alfred Thoms is standing at the extreme right with his sister Emily immediately behind him. Their sister Edith is believed to be either standing extreme left or seated centre. (Picture courtesy Andrew MacThomas of Finegand and Brian Turnbull).

anything about finding Thoms mentally weak, but spoke of how indistinct and hard to make out his speech was. His evidence-in-chief concluded with his confirming that he was surprised at the terms of his uncle's will, and he concurred with his brother in seeking to reduce it.

Clyde's cross-examination was notable for two things. First, he brought out from the witness that he had not been baptised Henry James Macthomas Thoms, but had assumed the name 'Macthomas' on reading his uncle's will, in order to comply with the condition for inheriting under it. He was surprised that he had received more than his brother, but leaving his brother out of the question, he did not see anything unreasonable about the bequest. Second, Clyde asked him if he had made any arrangement or agreement with his brother about dividing the advantages if the will was successfully reduced. After a pregnant pause, Harry answered that no, he had made no arrangement with him. The pause was Clyde's opening:

(Q.) Tell me why you have been so long in giving me a negative answer,

101

if you have no agreement or understanding with your brother on the subject? (A.) The present surroundings are unusual to me; it is the first time I have been in the witness-box. (Q.) Have you had conversations or communications with your brother about what is going to be done between you and him about this estate, if you get your way? (A.) No, there is no definite arrangement. (Q.) Is there any arrangement of any kind? (A.) No; I don't think I can say there is. (Q.) Is there any understanding between you of any kind on the subject? (A.) No; I don't think I can say so. (Q.) Won't you frankly tell us what there is between your brother and you about this matter? (A.) I agreed to join him in the action. (Q.) On terms? (A.) There were no terms about what is going to happen.[38]

Cooper rose to Harry's sardonic aid:

(Q.) There is a family hope and expectation – (Laughter) – that your brother will do something for the members of the family?

(A.) If he is reasonable he may give us a share.[39]

Alfred and Harry's three sisters then gave evidence. They were Mrs Grace Hallowes, who was married to a Derbyshire clergyman, Emily Thoms and Edith Thoms. Their testimony was not lengthy, and they were spared searching cross-examination. Mostly they spoke of their encounters with their uncle in his declining years. Mrs Hallowes mentioned the presents she had received from him. In her childhood he came with two bottles: one for her and one for her brothers. Hers contained eau de cologne; theirs castor oil. On her twenty-first birthday she received ten pounds. On her twenty-fifth her uncle gave her a diamond and ruby ring. Later, however, when she married, he only gave her five pounds. She did not regard it as an adequate present in the circumstances, particularly as she believed herself his favourite niece. This was about the time he left Charlotte Square. He said he was leaving it because he was poor and could not afford to stay there on 'dry nuts'. As his health deteriorated, his speech became bad and he often could not find a word in which to express his meaning. 'I cannot remember words now,' he said. His thoughts became muddled and, she said, he got the names of his relations mixed up. His hands were bluish and cold to the touch, he seemed to have bad circulation and used a small carriage hot water bottle to keep his feet warm.[40]

The other two sisters mentioned similar things illustrative of their uncle's physical and mental decline. By the time they visited him for the last time, in January, 1903, he was, they said, unable to recognise them at first, eventually saying, 'Oh, you are Tom's bairns!' This rather contrasted with the welcome he had given Emily Thoms five years earlier when, after she had, as usual, shaken him by the hand and kissed him, he asked her 'in a most kind way' for another kiss. She said she would give him another when she left. He said, 'But I want one now.' She kissed him again and asked him why he had wanted her to do so. He replied, 'Because you remind me so much of your dear father.' Emily had a less pleasant glimpse of her uncle's emotions on a visit in November, 1902. In it we see his volatility, but also the dangers and limitations of relying too much on one witness's evidence. What happened, according to Emily, was that she 'passed the most simple remark about the weather' and he flew into a rage. She remarked that it was a cold day, but her Uncle George, despite his being swathed in shawls with gloves on his hands, a cap on his head, a muffler around his throat and a hot water pad at his feet, harangued her that it was not cold and that she had no right to say that it was. The evidence of her sister Edith, who was also present, provides the missing detail that explains the outburst. What Emily had asked was if he did not find Cluny Drive colder than Charlotte Square.[41]

After the Thoms siblings had finished their evidence, the stand was taken by a number of witnesses whose acquaintance with the late Sheriff had been rather less intimate. First was William McCombie Smith, who briefly explained his dealings with Thoms over the clan book and confirmed that he had been unable to find any evidence to prove Thoms' descent from the chiefs of Clan Macthomas other than Thoms' own family tradition. In cross-examination, he stated that he always looked upon Thoms as a great joker, that he never had the slightest suspicion that there was anything wrong with his mind, and that, on the contrary, he always thought him a 'very shrewd, level-headed fellow'.[42] After Smith came Robert Blackadder, a Dundee civil engineer and architect who had known Thoms since 1867 and had from 1883 acted as surveyor in the feuing of The Crescent. According to him, Thoms' behaviour was generally prudent and steady through most of the time he knew him, although he had wanted to do one or two things to the property that Blackadder regarded as stupid. In the late nineties, however, as his health deteriorated, he became increasingly irritable and suspicious, and seemed to have difficulty keeping to the business in hand without being diverted on to trifles. In the end Blackadder stopped having direct communication with him. He said Thoms seemed to think that he was attending to the feuars' interests as well as his own. Cross-examined by Shaw, Blackadder confirmed that Thoms had gifted five acres of land to the town of Dundee in 1896, a gift worth several thousand pounds.[43] He also said that right down to the end he treated the Sheriff as perfectly able to do business.[44] Blackadder was followed into the box by the solicitors Murray and Grierson, whose evidence has already been considered.

After this the jury received a welcome break from Thoms' ailments and oddities. The pursuers instead turned their attentions to St Magnus Cathedral, the building he had sought to benefit. In doing so they hoped to attack the will from within, for if they could show that its main provision was an irrational one, the reason of the man who made it was much easier to challenge.

The provision in question stated that the Provost and Magistrates of Kirkwall should apply the residue of Thoms' estate for the restoration and repair of the cathedral. It did not go into specifics, except in providing for the memorial window and suggesting T. S. Peace, architect, Kirkwall, or Hippolyte J. Blanc, RSA, Edinburgh, as persons to advise on the details of the restoration, which should include:

> . . . *inter alia* the removal of the galleries, like the Restoration of Saint Giles cathedral Edinburgh.

Following the Reformation, congregations in St Magnus had come to use only the eastern part of the building, the choir and presbytery, for public worship. This was partitioned from the nave and transepts by a wooden screen. Within there were rows of pews, galleries slung between pillars, whitewashed walls and plain glass, but without there just lay:

> . . . the ashes of the mighty dead while around stand their memorials in sad and solemn array well fitted to repress every feeling of levity and check every thoughtless wanderer.[45]

There had been other ashes there, too. At the turn of the eighteenth century the Town Guard had burnt great fires in the nave to warm their drunken revels.[46] Although the ashes were cleaned out, the damage done by the fires was still visible on the pillars in 1905.

The building had not been totally neglected. In particular, there had been quite major repairs and renovations in the mid-nineteenth century when the Commissioners for Her Majesty's Woods, Forests and Land Revenues erroneously assumed ownership and evicted the congregation. Between 1847 and 1849 some £3,000 was spent on, amongst other things, re-roofing, rebuilding of wallheads and parapets, restoring the floor level of the nave and repaving it, rebuilding the east window, and generally cleaning and repairing stonework. Then, after the legal wranglings over ownership had been settled in favour of the Town Council, the council and the heritors had the south transept gable and rose window rebuilt between 1854 and 1856, and the choir fitted out once more for use by the congregation. A new partition, new pews and new galleries were put in, and this is how the building remained in Thoms' time.[47] To fund ongoing maintenance and repairs there was the interest on a bequest of £1,000 made by Gilbert Meason or Mason in 1808, and in 1894 Francis Taylor also left a thousand pounds to be expended on the fabric. Before spending the Taylor bequest, the town council obtained a report from Hippolyte J. Blanc on the condition of the building.[48]

It was the pursuers' contention that little else was required. To support that contention they secured the services of two witnesses who were both eminent architects, both expert on ecclesiastical buildings and both called Ross. Alexander Ross of Inverness and Thomas Ross of Edinburgh spent five days, from 16th to 20th January, 1905, inspecting the cathedral, and they gave their findings to the court on 6th February. Alexander Ross, then aged 70, stated that he had been in practice as an architect for over fifty years, with an extensive practice building churches and castles. He had built Skibo Castle for Mr Andrew Carnegie, and Inverness cathedral. He had restored several castles and churches, and had made church architecture his special study. He was familiar with the most important cathedrals in Britain and on the Continent, and he had inspected many of them during their restoration. As for St Magnus, he was of the view that the condition of the fabric was very good. The structure did not require anything to keep it in good order, and if decayed stonework were to be cut out and replaced, it might not in any way be an improvement. It would take away the antiquarian interest. There were, admittedly, things that could be done to advantage in the interior. He thought the screen, pews and galleries should be removed and the church arranged somewhat as St Giles had been, with the pulpit under the tower. To carry out these alterations, and such work as he did consider necessary to put the building in a thorough state of repair, would cost, he estimated, £4,250.

Two views by Tom Kent of the pre-restoration nave and transepts, a place of dampness and decay where the roof timbers were so rotten in places that the wood could be pinched out in handfuls. (Orkney Library Photographic Archive).

Cross-examined by Shaw, he confirmed that he understood restoration to mean restoring a building to its original architectural features:

> (Q.) Do you represent you can restore this cathedral to anything like its original condition for £4,200? (A.) I think so; it is in very good order.

The only portions of carving he considered for restoration were those at the west doorway:

> . . . but it struck me as a very grave question from an antiquarian and ecclesiological point of view whether it would be wise to touch it. I think it would cost about £700 to restore the west doorway and the south doorway. The north doorway did not seem to me to require restoration. (Q.) Is it not defaced very much? (A.) Yes, but not sufficient to require renewal.

He examined the roof very carefully and it seemed to be watertight, but he allowed £100 to £200 for pointing it as a contingency. He was aware that the nave piers up to a height of about six feet were, in Shaw's words, 'not only defaced but destroyed by fire', but he thought it best to leave them as they were. The buttresses were in very good order and only pointing was required:

> (Q.) And your idea of restoration is to leave an 800-years-old work

Two Tom Kent views of the pre-restoration choir and presbytery, white-washed and filled with pews and galleries for use in public worship. (Orkney Library Photographic Archive).

defaced, or restore it by pointing? (A.) To restore it where necessary, but where it is good there is no need to restore. (Q.) Supposing I said, 'There is £40,000 or £50,000; I want the cathedral of Kirkwall restored, to be an ornament to the north and a monument to me,' I suppose you could do it nicely? (A.) No doubt, but it would be no longer St. Magnus if I were to spend a large sum of money upon it.[49]

Thomas Ross had been in practice for over forty years and was senior partner of the firm of MacGibbon and Ross. Joint author with the late David MacGibbon of *The Castellated and Domestic Architecture of Scotland* and a similar work on Scottish ecclesiastical architecture, he told the court that he had seen and measured every important ecclesiastical building in Scotland. He had erected the ladies' retiring room at St Giles on the instructions of Sheriff Thoms, was the architect for the restoration of Iona cathedral, and had restored a portion of Beaulieu Castle and St Kentigern's, Lanark. He confirmed his agreement with his namesake's views on St Magnus Cathedral.

Clyde's cross-examination concentrated on comparisons with the restorations of Iona and Dunblane cathedrals, and their costs. Ross said nobody knew what the total cost of restoring Iona would be. They had already spent four or five thousand pounds upon it. That was in roofing the choir and transept, laying a floor and glazing the windows. The nave had not been touched. The restoration of Dunblane cathedral had cost upwards of £20,000. This was because there was a lot of very elaborate carving on the stonework which required to be taken out and replaced. They did not propose to do this at St Magnus. Clyde asked him then if he regarded the restoration of Dunblane as a mistake. No, he said, he did not.

> (Q.) What is the difference between the deteriorated or defaced carved work on St. Magnus and the deteriorated carved work or tracery at Dunblane that should make a difference in the treatment St. Magnus receives? (A.) Round the west doorway of St. Magnus there is very elaborate carving, and that carving is entirely gone beyond recall. You cannot restore unless you take down the doorway and put up a new one, and then you destroy the whole antiquity of the thing.

After Ross, under re-examination, had mentioned other differences that increased the costs at Iona and Dunblane, mainly the need of new roofs, the Lord Justice-Clerk made an intervention that was probably of more assistance to the defenders than the pursuers. He asked Ross if there were many things done in the way of restoration by architects, and also by people in spite of architects, that he as an architect would disapprove of. Yes, he agreed, there were.[50]

When Thomas Ross had finished his evidence, the court turned back to the character of Sheriff Thoms, and heard from some more members of his family. These ones were not present in court. Instead, their evidence had been taken on commission and was now laboriously read out to the jury by junior counsel for the pursuers. Two of them, Thoms' cousin Mrs Helen Fleming and her daughter, also Helen, were then residing at the Hotel Beau Site in Rome, and they were required to answer a series of questions or 'interrogatories' prepared in advance by the parties' representatives. Their answers did not add much that was new. Much more interesting, and entertaining, was the evidence of Thoms' cousin Mrs Smith, who was confined to her house in Edinburgh by an attack of iritis. To take her evidence, the commissioner attended at her house with the parties' counsel, a clerk and a shorthand writer, and she was put on oath and questioned as if she were in open court.

Her evidence suggests that Thoms was not the only member of the family with a touch of contrariness about him. Mrs Smith, it seems, did not view cousin Alfred's court action with much favour. Certainly the pursuers' counsel had a hard time drawing her out to give the evidence he was expecting:

> (Q.) Was he in any way unusual in his manner? (A.) Never different, that I saw. (Q.) Was he in the habit, when he came about your house, of saying or doing any things that seemed to you peculiar? (Q.) Never. (Q.) Did he ever do anything odd when he came to your house? (A.) Not more odd than he always did. There was no change that I ever noticed. (Q.) Was he always, so long as you knew him, somewhat odd in his manners? (A.) He tried to be different from other people. (Q.) Did that lead him into sometimes saying and doing some eccentric things? (A.) Not that I would have remarked. (Q.) You had got accustomed to him? (A.) Perfectly.[51]

When she did begin to detail the oddities of her cousin's behaviour, she showed a marked reluctance to condemn them. Even when describing how his condition had caused him to choke on a whisky and soda at her house, she insisted that it was 'quite a manageable choke.'[52] As for his household management, she understood his was 'just the perfection of a kitchen', though she was never in it. She thought his code of rules was excellent. He handed copies of them out and she knew of ladies who had them yet. She, herself, adopted his idea of making chalk marks on the floor to test the servants' cleaning, and seriously considered getting herself a glass-ended dresser. The cat was fined, Thoms told her, when the servants had blamed it for breakages.

This, said Mrs Smith, was done as a joke. Some of his other humour she did not quite understand. Once, when she and her sister were young girls, Thoms introduced them to other guests at his house as 'Perpigena' and 'Agenoria', one being the name of a sewing machine the two of them had been discussing.[53]

When her younger sister got married before her, her cousin presented the still-spinster elder sister with a pair of green stockings:

> (Q.) There is some superstition that if a younger sister gets married first the elder should get a pair of green garters? (A.) I never heard of going beyond garters; but I got stockings, and the price was on them.[54]

She wore them nonetheless. Then, when she did get married, her husband's present from the Sheriff was pink kid gloves – three dozen pairs of them. This was, she said, a bit of fun she never understood. Perhaps it was her cousin's sly comment on how he felt she needed to be handled.

Mrs Smith's evidence did not greatly benefit the pursuers. True, she was critical of Thoms in places. The business of the clan chiefship she dismissed as 'a foolish fad' and she thought nothing more of it.[55] She also recalled a remark of his that he held his property 'in trust', but in cross-examination said this was one of his defences against being asked for charitable subscriptions. Asked by the defender's counsel if, at the time of the kid gloves, it ever occurred to her that her cousin was weak in intellect, she replied, 'Never, never.'[56] Nor did she notice any change in his mental condition thereafter: 'I never did – never.'[57] The role that Thoms had adopted, she said, was to be different from other people and to amuse whatever company he was in, and he stuck to it faithfully.[58]

When the evidence on commission had been read, another member of the Fleming family gave evidence in person. Robert Fleming had the advantage of being a medical doctor. So, when he said that in his opinion Thoms had not been fit to make a will, that should have carried some weight with the jury. However, he had several disadvantages too: he had not seen Thoms for two years before his will was made, he never transacted any business with him, he knew nothing of how the will was prepared, in fact he knew nothing of the will at all. By the end of his cross-examination, these disadvantages had been well underlined for the benefit of the jury.[59]

After an accountant had given brief evidence on Thoms' finances, the pursuers brought their case to a close with the evidence of two expert medical witnesses. The first of these was Dr Alexander Bruce, a Fellow of the Royal College of Physicians in Edinburgh. His testimony was mainly to the effect that Thoms' physical ailments would have weakened his mental powers, and any person who had the control and care of him would have been in a position to exercise a very powerful influence over his mind. The effect of this evidence, however, was limited, in that Bruce had only read a transcript of Saturday's evidence plus the precognitions of the pursuers' witnesses, and based his opinions on these and a number of assumptions put to him in the box by Cooper. He had not, of course, heard the defender's witnesses or even seen their precognitions. So Shaw was able to point out that he was giving an opinion having heard only one side of the case. He then asked Bruce's opinion of Thoms' mental state in the light of the eccentricities of the tawse, the household rules, the cat, and the rest. When Bruce replied that he would not put any legal matters of his own into the hands of a man whom he knew to conduct himself so absurdly, and that if he was told that this absurd conduct had lasted for a quarter of a century, he would have inferred that the man had not had very strong mental powers to begin with, Shaw was able to highlight that Thoms had held the high office of Sheriff at that time and had even been offered promotion. He then had the witness concede the advantage Thoms' own medical attendant, Dr Affleck, might have in giving an opinion on his patient's condition, before moving on to the question of the Sheriff's business correspondence. Bruce had read it.

> (Q.) Will you tell me whether you can find any signs of mental decay in these letters and, if so, where do you find them? (A.) If I recollect rightly, there was one letter where he seemed to confuse between the credit and the debit side of his accounts.[60]

Under re-examination by Cooper, Bruce reiterated that Thoms in his later years would not have had the power to resist influence – 'He was entirely helpless.' – and that just because someone remains capable of transacting ordinary business does not mean that they are not seriously mentally affected. However, the Lord Justice-Clerk then intervened:

> (Q.) Are there any letters that you have come across in which Mr. Thoms did not intelligently answer the letters that reached him? (A.) I don't remember any. (Q.) No letter impressed you as a letter that misunderstood what was addressed to him or was not perfectly intelligible to the person whom he addressed, as regards the sense of the letter? (A.) I don't recollect anything of that kind.[61]

If the potentially negative effect of Dr Bruce's evidence had been quite successfully countered, the defence found the pursuers' second expert medical witness an altogether tougher proposition. David Yellowlees had been for twenty-seven years head of the Gartnavel Asylum in Glasgow, and was a consulting physician there still. As such, he was probably an experienced expert witness. At any rate, there was a wonderfully po-faced certitude about much of his evidence. He began with Thoms' eccentric behaviour:

> I know about the eccentricity and am prepared to discount it as arising simply from a want of common sense.[62]

In Yellowlees' theory, Thoms was always very eccentric. His eccentric fancy and family pride had always been very strongly marked and, said Yellowlees, an eccentric man is more liable to become insane than one who is not eccentric. One way in which this could happen was the way in which the 'Highland Chief business', even though it was very likely only affectation at first, took hold of

Thoms so that he actually came to believe it. Then there were the perverted feelings towards his nephew, which had arisen from Alfred's enforced absence, and began gradually to operate upon Thoms' conduct:

> He began to distrust him, then to dislike him, and at last he disinherited him.[63]

These perverted feelings made Thoms, in details, an insane man, though he might yet be perfectly acute and intelligent in business matters:

> I have known many men emphatically insane and yet exceedingly acute in matters relating to business and capable of giving clear advice.[64]

The witness thought the 1903 will was determined by this man's perverted feelings and was the outcome and result of them. Moreover, he did not think he fully appreciated the consequences of what he was doing, because it was 'absurd' to leave such a large sum to Kirkwall.

Syphilis, according to Yellowlees, produced a mental disturbance which rendered a man 'moody, irritable and suspicious', with the result that he was apt to take dislikes and was ready to act upon them. In addition, the mental effects of the disease, combined with Thoms' general condition, rendered him very amenable to influence. This, of course, was an important part of the pursuers' case, but it was also one considerably undermined by the evidence of Thoms' persistent stubbornness. Here Cooper tried, not altogether successfully, to shore it up:

> (Q.) You might find him very stubborn in one direction, and very facile in another? (A.) Possibly, but he was too weak, too helpless to be stubborn. He was utterly and completely helpless, and utterly and completely in the power of his attendant, so far as I can gather.[65]

Yellowlees evidently did not have much room for half measures. Asked what he inferred from Thoms' having made eight codicils within five months and four days, he replied that he inferred he was a man of unstable mind. No reasonable man, he said, would do such a thing unless in extraordinary changes of circumstances. He then concluded his evidence-in-chief with the opinion that a man's medical

Professor David Yellowlees, expert medical witness for the Thoms siblings. Of the Sheriff's relationship with his nephew he said: 'He began to distrust him, then to dislike him, and at last he disinherited him.'

attendant could quite well visit him without having proper opportunities to observe his mental condition:

> You might come upon a man who was thoroughly mad, and as long as you did not touch upon the immediate subject of his madness, he will seem perfectly sane; that is a matter of daily occurrence.[66]

Although generally trenchant in supporting the pursuers' case, in one important respect Yellowlees contradicted it. He said that he did not think Thoms believed himself poor, as he had been investing money up until within six months of his death. Shaw chose this as the point with which to start his cross-examination, and had Yellowlees spell out for the jury's benefit that he did not believe Thoms was under any delusion on the matter. Then, after having Yellowlees reiterate that the eccentricity was of no importance other than indicating a want of commonsense which might lead Thoms on to a second stage, Shaw challenged his reasons for holding that the second stage had been reached:

> (Q.) Am I right in saying that because Mr. Thoms left his money to another object instead of leaving it to his nephew, therefore his feelings must have been perverted? (A.) No; I don't say that. (Q.) Can you give me any other reason for your opinion than that? (A.) The will shews that his feelings were perverted. (Q.) In respect that he left his money past his nephew? (A.) Yes; I think that was the result of perverted, morbid feeling. (A.) You were led to that by the fact that he did it? (A.) Yes, and the further fact that he had no reason for doing it.[67]

Shaw suggested the reason that between the 1893 will and the 1903 one Alfred had succeeded to a pretty considerable fortune from his father, but the witness did not attach much weight to that. Then came the 'absurdity' of leaving money to Kirkwall cathedral:

> (Q.) If you were told first that Kirkwall thinks this a noble bequest, and [it] will be splendidly executed, and second that Sheriff Thoms had for years dwelt upon that topic with delight, do these facts which I ask you to assume have any influence in inducing you to recall your term 'absurdity'? (A.) That is a mere assumption because in his previous will he made no such bequest. I still think the bequest absurd from what I know of Kirkwall cathedral.

Whether on questions of mental health or church architecture, this witness's opinions were equally unshakeable:

> Mr. Shaw – We will leave you to digest the word 'absurdity'.

> The Witness – As I have not eaten it, I cannot digest it. (Laughter.)[68]

In the remainder of the cross-examination Shaw and Yellowlees continued to spar on the question of what evidence the will contained of mental perversity. Although Yellowlees did not advance anything other than the bequest past Alfred, he did make the point that such a provision was 'altogether foreign to a man of so much family pride.' Shaw concluded by exploring the significance of Thoms' lack of headaches in determining whether his syphilis had affected his brain. Yellowlees said that although headaches were a symptom of this, their absence was of no real significance.[69]

In re-examination, Cooper drew out two significant points. First, despite Alfred's inheritance from his father, as late as June, 1902, Thoms had left him further estate. This, to Yellowlees, indicated an entire change of feeling on the part of the testator between then and the will of March, 1903. Second, as additional evidence of perversity of feeling, Cooper reminded the witness of Thoms' gibe about leaving his curling stones to his nephews 'to make men of them'. Perhaps, though, Cooper should not have revisited the basis for Yellowlees' views on St Magnus Cathedral, for the reply he got was:

> I have never been at Kirkwall, but I know about the cathedral there very well.[70]

When the pursuers closed their case it was half past six on Monday evening.[71] Although the day's proceedings would only have started about ten or eleven, and there had been a good deal of amusement along the way, it was still a long and tiring day whether for judge and jury, parties and counsel, solicitors and clerks, or press and public. The packed courtroom, with its hard seats, its stale air growing ever staler as the afternoon wore on, and the glare of the new-fangled electric lighting,[72] was not the most congenial place to be confined with relentless tales of illness and oddity. To escape into the cool February evening was probably rather a relief.

113

VII

The Will Defended

On Tuesday morning there was a change of emphasis. The pursuers had finished their case and it was now the defenders' turn to answer it. In cross-examining the pursuers' witnesses, Shaw and Clyde had not just challenged their evidence, but laid a solid foundation on which to build the case for the defenders. Although, it must be said, they were aided by some inherent weaknesses on the opposing side, those weaknesses had still required to be exposed, and they had done it skilfully. Now counsel's task was to follow up any advantage they had obtained. They could not afford to be complacent, for however well things appeared to be going, there was no predicting what view the jury would take. There was a lot of work to be done yet.

James Avon Clyde KC. In Shaw and Clyde, Thoms' Trustee had secured the services of two of the ablest counsel at the Scots bar.

Conscious of this uncertainty, the defenders tempted Alfred with an offer of settlement before starting to lead their witnesses. What exactly they offered is unknown, but it is unlikely to have been overly generous; just something worth sparing from their bequest in order to make certain of the remainder. Perhaps it was outright ownership of Aberlemno, which Kirkwall was not due to receive until the end of Alfred's liferent, anyway. Whatever it was, Alfred rejected the offer and the jury trial continued.[1]

Clyde made the opening speech. In addressing the jury, he gave them their first clear view of how the defenders were to approach their task, and set the tone for what was to come. The pursuers' case, he said, was based on the tittle-tattle of the servants' hall and resolved itself into 'an attack with no scruple, no consideration, and no quarter' upon the Sheriff's servant, Adam Melrose. To say that there was anything unnatural or perverted in a bachelor leaving his money to a public object, instead of to nephews and nieces who had fifty or sixty thousand pounds of their own, was 'astonishing'. Thoms was fond of playing the 'funny man', and Clyde was:

> . . . afraid he wore his jokes about tawse, sweet williams, fines, Sambo the cat, rather thin, that his laughing waistcoat became rather threadbare, and that his little bits of gutta-percha became too dry to fill up cracks either in his own heart or in the hearts of ladies to whom he may have delivered lectures on flirtation. . .

but it was not because of his posing as a funny man that a man's will was to be reduced.[2] And as for Thoms' mental and physical condition:

> . . . was it not to be reckoned to the credit of Mr Thoms' mental power and force of will that, having to hear what they had heard, he was able none the less to keep intact his patience, his fortitude and his courage to the end?[3]

While the pursuers' first witness had been the respectable figure of a clergyman, the defenders matched him with a doctor, and not just any doctor, either. James Ormiston Affleck was 64 years of age and at the top of his profession. He was a Fellow of the College of Physicians, a consulting physician at the Royal Infirmary and a former assistant to the Professor of Medical Jurisprudence in Edinburgh University.[4] He thus had the qualifications one would often find in an expert witness allied to twenty years' experience as Thoms' medical adviser. Thoms had chosen well. Affleck's reputation may be gauged from the fact that he was in constant demand from his own professional colleagues when they themselves were ill. It was said of him that he both felt and conveyed genuine sympathy for suffering and anxiety, and:

> . . . although he never treated a serious case with an optimism he did not feel, he always, no matter how bad things looked, had some message of hope or comfort for the patient, while his resourcefulness in treatment helped him to relieve much suffering.[5]

Like Sheriff Thoms, Affleck was a bachelor, but there the similarity between patient and doctor ended, for the latter was reserved to the point of shyness, with no taste for ceremony or the social whirl. His habitually grave demeanour was, however, belied by what his obituarist called 'an innate goodness…that could not be hidden'.[6] This was a useful combination in a medical witness.

His patient, he told the court, had suffered mostly from chronic gout, the disabling effects of which he proceeded to explain. Some five years before the Sheriff's death, sores broke out on his body due to syphilis, but there was no lesion to either the brain or spinal cord. He could state that quite affirmatively. Such lesions show up in the urine and he had tested regularly for them. Nor did Thoms suffer from headaches, so far as he was aware. He had visited Thoms on average once or twice a month, but when the need arose he was called in more frequently. He last saw him two days before his death. In all the time he knew Thoms he never had occasion to have any suspicion as to his mind going or being affected. The first he heard of it was when this case arose. He would have said at the relevant time that Thoms was of sound mind and capable of making a will, and that was his opinion emphatically still. He praised Melrose's care of Thoms, and he outlined his knowledge of Melrose's drunken episode, of how Melrose had promised not to behave like that again, and of how he had kept faithfully to that promise. There was no truth in the idea that Melrose had excluded people from the Sheriff's presence. Nor was there anything to suggest that Melrose was taking advantage of his position to influence his patient. Thoms was about the last man, he thought, who could be unduly influenced. The bequest to Melrose was most appropriate. Nor was Affleck altogether surprised at the residue being left to restore St Magnus Cathedral, given Thoms' interest in his sheriffdom and his involvement in the restoration of St Giles. And as for Yellowlees' opinions:

> (Q.) We were told by a gentleman of your profession that there was some disease of the mind from perverted feeling. What do you say to that? (A.) I never saw any evidence of that. Apart from the fact that he changed his mind, there is nothing in that, so far as I am aware. I think that up to the time of his death he was perfectly capable and fit to change his mind intelligently in all respects.[7]

Affleck recollected Thoms' solicitor, Mr Wood, WS, calling on him in the spring of 1903 to ask him his opinion on his patient's testamentary capacity, which he gave. He also recalled Mr Alfred Thoms calling on him on the night of 25th October, 1903, accompanied by Mr Wood. Affleck understood he wanted to know whether Sheriff Thoms was in a fit state to make some communication to them intelligently. His power to make any testamentary writing was not discussed. Affleck said he thought his ability to communicate doubtful from the physical state he was in, but that it would do no harm to try him. Even then, he said, he was in no doubt as to Thoms' mental capacity, but his patient

Sir James Ormiston Affleck, Thoms' doctor and a leader of his profession. (Royal College of Physicians of Edinburgh).

was suffering the failure of the physical powers that accompanies the last days of life. In his later years, Thoms' articulation was not very good, owing to the condition in his jaw and his increased enfeeblement, but those who saw him regularly had no difficulty making him out. Affleck confirmed that he had seen Thoms' last will, and his view was that Thoms had been able quite well to understand its terms and purport both at the time it was made and up till the later days of his life.[8]

Cooper cross-examined Affleck at considerable length and in assiduous detail, but without making any obvious impact. Although transcripts of court evidence are a poor means of ascertaining the manner in which testimony was given, it is fairly clear from the written record that Affleck's responses remained as measured, unruffled and persuasive in response to Cooper as they had been to Shaw.

After having Affleck once more go over Thoms' long physical decline, Cooper dwelt on the shortness of the doctor's visits to his patient and tried to show that the conversation had been one-sided enough that Affleck would not have been aware of Thoms' true mental state. He spent considerable time on the topic of Melrose, and sought to lead the witness from praise of Melrose for keeping Thoms alive to drawing a connection between that and the alleged influence over the Sheriff:

> (Q.) I suppose that if a person was clinging to life, or very anxious to keep on living, and believed that another person was the person who had to keep him alive, the person to keep him alive would have considerable influence over him? (A.) Oh, no doubt he might have considerable influence over him. (Q.) If the person whom a patient thought would preserve him in life had also complete control over his movements, might not the person – the preserver of the life – have a very great influence indeed over the patient? (A.) He might have, but in the case of the Sheriff he had a very strong individuality himself and a strong will.[9]

The witness acknowledged that he had recommended Thoms to resign his Sheriffship, but that was merely because of his physical condition. He had never heard that his continuing to hold the Sheriffship had become a public scandal. Around the time Thoms resigned, he told Affleck that he would have to retrench, but this was said in a 'sort of playful manner'. The doctor would not agree with Cooper that Wood's asking his opinion of Thoms' testamentary capacity suggested that there was some doubt about it. In his view:

> . . . the impression always conveyed to me was that there was a marked contrast between the state of extreme physical enfeeblement in which the Sheriff was and his mental clearness…He comprehended at once, and answered promptly, and shewed no mental confusion.[10]

The description of Cooper as alert, resourceful and persistent is borne out in the way he seized on the smallest opening to try to advance his clients' case. The uncharitable might call it clutching at straws, as when he brought Affleck back to his reaction on hearing of the cathedral bequest:

> (Q.) How were you surprised? (A.) I said I was not surprised. (Q.) You said you were not altogether surprised? (A.) No, I was not surprised at all.[11]

Something similar can be seen in the evidence of the next witness, Dr Alexander Black, a 'friendly neighbour' of Affleck's who had looked after his patients for him in the latter's absence in Spain in the spring of 1903.[12] While Black supported Affleck's opinion of Thoms' mental state, it became obvious that he did not know the patient's full medical history and, in particular, that he suffered from syphilis. He described Thoms' sores as probably gouty, but hinted that there might be some other cause. Cooper tried to have him commit himself to the wrong opinion:

> (Q.) Having examined him several times, is it your evidence that the sores upon his body were the result of gout?

But Black was not caught out:

> (A.) Well, I can hardly explain. There are certain ailments that in the course of time may be hidden, and what we call tertiary symptoms may develop, but in these cases it is an extremely difficult point, and in any case it does not require any variety of treatment.[13]

If medical evidence of Thoms' mental fitness was an essential plank in the defenders' case, no less important was the need to demonstrate the manner in which his last will had been instructed, prepared, approved and signed. From the evidence of the next three witnesses, Thoms' solicitor John Philp Wood, WS, Professor of Conveyancing at Edinburgh University from 1892 to 1900, and two of his colleagues, plus that of Thoms' amanuensis, Miss Irvine, who gave evidence on Wednesday, the jury was able to follow the whole process from beginning to end.

It was about the beginning of 1903 that Thoms told Miss Irvine that he would require her to attend several more hours during the week as he wished to make a new will.[14] Evidently with this in mind, he had obtained the packet containing his testamentary writings from Wood in December, 1902. These had already passed backwards and forwards between Wood's office and Thoms' house several times in the preceding year.[15] Miss Irvine's first task was to take home a draft of Thoms' 1893 will and transcribe from it certain passages that he had marked. When she returned with these, he dictated further paragraphs to her from notes and previous codicils which he held in his hand as he dictated. He then told her the order in which the various passages were to be fitted together. In this way, slowly and deliberately, the first full draft of the will was prepared. Several alterations were made as he went along. However, with the minor exception of the addition of a second named architect to advise on the details of the restoration, the cathedral bequest remained the same from when Thoms first dictated it. When the draft was completed, he asked his amanuensis to add up all the pecuniary legacies and the capital value of all his stocks, and then to subtract the former from the latter so he could see the approximate value of what would go to Kirkwall. The whole process had taken about five weeks.[16]

Thoms sent the completed draft to Wood on 17th February, 1903. Wood acknowledged it the following day, and then the day after that wrote again, stating that he had now 'gone carefully over the draft of the very careful will which you have prepared' and would call on Thoms to discuss it in the next two days. There was only one point in the will with regard to which he had reservations. The point was a technical legal one, but his reservations on it were to result in the one major change made between the first draft and the version that was eventually signed.

John Philp Wood WS, Thoms' solicitor and personal friend and, in the words of the Lord Justice-Clerk, 'a man above suspicion in every way.'

Although Wood, cautious conveyancer that he was, was reluctant to admit it under cross-examination, it is quite clear that Thoms originally intended to leave Alfred and Harry the full ownership of Aberlemno and The Crescent and not just the liferent use of them. This is confirmed by the way Miss Irvine calculated the value of the residuary bequest to Kirkwall without including the values of those two properties. However, the original bequests were to be subject to the condition of adopting the name 'Macthomas', and gave detailed provision as to who would receive the properties if this condition was not adhered to. It was this latter provision which gave Wood concern. He doubted its effectiveness, and suggested as an alternative that Thoms instruct his Trustee to convey the properties to Alfred and Harry in a deed of strict entail, a device by which a specific line of succession could be laid down. Wood had given similar advice to Thoms in 1897 when the latter had included the same condition in a codicil. Thoms had rejected the advice then, and this time, after meeting Wood to discuss it, he likewise refused to accept his alternative wording. Instead, he instructed Wood to change the bequests to liferents.

The practical consequences of this for Alfred and Harry were that they would enjoy the income from these properties without having the ability to sell them. Yet their rights of disposal would also have been severely restricted if Wood's suggestion of an entail had been taken. The most significant aspect of the change to a liferent was what was to happen after Alfred and Harry had died. Instead of falling to their respective families, the properties would go to Kirkwall.

This, too, gave Wood concern, but not for any legal reason. After being instructed on 21st February, 1903, to make the changes to liferents, Wood produced a clean draft of the whole will and sent it to his client on the 24th. Thoms replied on 9th March, returning the draft with some further amendments, some in his own handwriting and some in that of Miss Irvine. Wood then arranged to visit Thoms on the 11th, and it was at this further meeting that he raised his latest concerns. He told Thoms that he did not approve of family properties being left to relatives merely in liferent, while the fee (that is ownership) was left outside the family. Thoms listened to his objection, understood perfectly what he meant, said Wood, but refused to change the provision. Instead, he instructed Wood to engross the will for signature, adding that Wood could not be a witness as he was leaving him a legacy.[17]

Thus it was that one of Wood's partners, Joseph Inglis, WS, and their clerk, William Yeaman, attended at 26 Cluny Drive at 3 o' clock in the afternoon of 16th March, 1903, to have Thoms sign his will. Melrose showed them into the dining room to wait while he announced them to the Sheriff. He then took them up to the drawing room, announced Mr Inglis' name and withdrew, closing the door behind him. The same procedure had been followed on Wood's visits.[18] Thoms was sitting near the gas fire, a table in front of him with a library book, a paper and pencil upon it. He shook Inglis by the hand, a little stiffly, and told both men to sit down. He directed Yeaman to sit in a chair in front of him and, after Inglis had said he had brought what Thoms expected, Thoms told Yeaman to read the will to him. While Yeaman did so, Inglis observed that Thoms seemed to follow every clause of the will and, indeed, jotted something down on his sheet of paper while listening. When the reading was finished, Thoms said:

> You have designed Mr Blanc wrongly; he is not an A.R.A., he is an R.S.A.[19]

The letters after the architect's name having been corrected, Thoms signed the will with no particular difficulty beyond what might be expected of an old man with stiff hands, and Inglis and Yeaman signed as witnesses. Thoms then told them to complete the testing clause (giving the details of signature) and keep the principal will in their office at 110 George Street, while letting him have a copy to keep by him. Both Inglis and Yeaman confirmed to the court that in the half to three-quarters of an hour that their interview had lasted, everything that Thoms had said had been intelligible and perfectly sensible to their minds. They had no doubt that Thoms perfectly understood the will and appreciated what he was signing.[20]

Wood, too, was more than satisfied on this point, stating that Thoms knew every line of his will. In this respect, his late client had in fact been exceptional:

> I never received more definite instructions for any deed. I have prepared a good many wills in the last generation, and I certainly never saw one give more the hand of the testator himself.[21]

It is hard to disagree. Yet the solicitor had not only had his misgivings about the will's terms so far as respecting Alfred and Harry, but had also foreseen the possibility of their mounting a challenge to it. This is why, before meeting Thoms to express these misgivings, he called upon Dr Affleck to ascertain the doctor's view of Thoms' mental capacity. He did so, he said, not because he doubted Thoms' fitness, but in order to have his own view that Thoms was indeed perfectly fit to make a will confirmed by the doctor.[22]

Wood, who was aged 57 at the time of the will case, had known Thoms all his life, for the latter had served his Bar apprenticeship in Wood's father's office. Ever after Thoms had been very kind and friendly to him, or as Wood put it:

> I don't think he lost an opportunity of doing me a good turn.[23]

This included putting business arising from Thoms' family trusts his way, and also his own private legal work. But he did not instruct Wood exclusively. He instead kept his business 'in compartments', employing a different set of lawyers for each area of work. Thoms' whole correspondence with these firms from 1897 up until his death was printed up by the defence and produced in court. Counsel took Wood through it for the benefit of the jury. There was the correspondence with his own firm of Melville and Lindesay, which concluded with a copy of the Sheriff's will being sent to him on 19th March, 1903. Then there were letters passing to and from the Forfar firm that managed the estate of Aberlemno, the Dundee firm that managed the feuing of the Crescent property, and the Edinburgh firm – not Wood's – that acted in the sale of 13 Charlotte Square, not to mention a lengthy correspondence with Thoms' stockbroker. All these showed Thoms taking an interest in the minutiae of his various business interests right up to and past the date of execution of his will. On 20th April, 1903, for example, he writes to his stockbroker:

> I have another £1,000 to invest at Whitsunday. I suppose the best investment is bank stock. I have the whole of the Scotch banks with the exception of the Union and the other small banks. Failing that, I can take the balance in Coats' shares.[24]

A large number of the letters were in Thoms' own handwriting.

Thoms instructed Wood to act for him in the purchase of Cluny Drive in 1898, and there was considerable correspondence when Thoms got into dispute with the builder, but it was Wood's involvement with his client's wills which received the lion's share of the court's attention. When he confirmed that there were a long series of both complete wills and codicils by Thoms dating right back to 1856, Shaw had him address Yellowlees' point:

> (Q.) …is it your experience that testators very frequently indulge in the practice of making numerous codicils to their testamentary settlements within a very short period of time? (A.) It is a well-known form of amusement. (Q.) Sometimes they do it themselves and sometimes they employ their law agents to do it? (A.) To the profit of the law agents.[25]

Shaw also had him speak to some of Thoms' correspondence to which he had not been a party. This was a letter of April, 1886, from the then Lord Advocate, John Blair Balfour,[26] offering Thoms promotion to the Sheriffdom of Ross and Cromarty. Despite the prospect of a higher salary, Thoms replied that he preferred to remain in his 'Island Kingdom' and see the completion of certain schemes in which he had taken an interest.[27]

Wood was a friend of Thoms as well as his solicitor and made regular social calls on the Sheriff. At these they would discuss the news of Parliament House, or mutual acquaintances in Caithness, or the books they had been reading. Some time after the will had been signed, Thoms wrote Wood asking him to come and see the book that his zoologist brother-in-law, Dr Anderson, had written on the mammalia of Egypt, which Wood did. The last visit he paid to the Sheriff was about four or five days before he died. Thoms knew him perfectly, but Wood could see that he was dying. Before taking his leave, Wood shook his old friend by the hand and bade him good-bye.[28]

Wood was also on friendly terms with Alfred Thoms, which put him in rather a difficult position, given his knowledge of the will. This was particularly true when Thoms tried to get Alfred to commence practice in Dundee. Wood 'most urgently pressed upon him that he should try and meet his uncle's wish', but did not, he said, disclose the terms of Thoms' will; well not quite:

> I was very friendly to Mr. Alfred Thoms, and I went as far as I dared. I tried to make the suggestion that it was of importance in his own interests that he should go to Dundee.[29]

This friendship probably influenced Wood's views on the liferent, as well as giving Alfred his inkling of his uncle's testamentary intentions. What it did not do was prevent Wood stating categorically in the witness box that Alfred had never, during all the running around on the night of his uncle's death, suggested to him that Thoms was incapable of making a will.[30]

After Wood and his colleagues had finished giving evidence, the jury had heard five of the defenders' witnesses, and Tuesday was wearing on. Thus far, the witnesses had all been professional men and, even if not used to giving evidence, would have known pretty much what to expect and what in turn was expected of them. Counsel would have had few doubts of how they would perform on the stand. It is unlikely that the same could have been said of the next witness, for sixth into the box was Adam Melrose.

Judge, jury and public gallery had heard quite a lot about Melrose in the preceding days, and not much of it complimentary. Melrose had heard it, too, for as a party to the action he was entitled to sit in court instead of being sequestered with the other witnesses. Perhaps there was a question as to whether he should give evidence at all. If so, it was unlikely to have been pondered over for long. A failure to put him up to answer the charges made against him might not have looked good. Moreover, in a question of Thoms' mental capacity, the evidence of the man who had been by his side almost constantly for the last eight years of his life could not really be dispensed with. Still, he did present an easier target for attack than the previous witnesses and Cooper was not blind to that. It is noticeable that, while Shaw's examination-in-chief of Melrose takes up six and a half closely-printed pages of transcript, Cooper's cross-examination fills twelve.

It was quite predictable that Melrose's drinking would feature prominently in cross-examination, so Shaw had his witness give his own version of events early on. After briefly outlining his qualifications and experience and the circumstances of his engagement by Thoms, Melrose described the unpleasant nature of his duties:

> (Q.) At first, I believe, you had great difficulty with yourself in resolving whether to stay on or not? (A.) I did not like him at first. It often made me sick and fainting. There was a frightful odour. I had very often to get up through the night with him. When I felt sick and faint I took a little stimulant. (Q.) And I believe in 1899 you were very bad? (A.) I was very faint and sick one day, and I took a little stimulant. There was an inquiry about it. Dr. Affleck came, and Sheriff Thoms and I had a dust-out about it. (Q.) And I believe you were very sorry? (A.) I am always sorry when I do anything wrong.[31]

This was not quite the full and frank acknowledgement that might have impressed the jury. A persistent reluctance to admit the undeniable, often combined with the pious attitude of the reformed drunk, was to be a recurring feature of Melrose's evidence, particularly under cross-examination. Shaw, for his part, moved on to draw out the important point, namely, that Melrose had promised to remain sober and had done so. After that, he had Melrose run through his eight years without a holiday, the jealousy of the female servants and the fall-out about the household accounts, before obtaining an emphatic denial of having given the Sheriff Epsom Salts in place of Hunyadi Janos – Melrose said he had mixed salts for himself. Then the daily routine at Cluny Drive was gone through in detail, followed by how six weeks before Thoms' death Melrose noticed he was failing and reported it to his sister, Mrs Anderson. He said he got a nurse on 18th October and reported by postcard to Mrs Anderson, Mrs Smith, Mr Alfred Thoms and, he thought, Mr Lessels. Here Shaw asked him if he disliked Alfred Thoms:

> I am happy to say I dislike no one.

Nor did he try to turn the Sheriff against his nephew. The first he knew that he had acquired an ascendancy over his master was when he read it in the papers. Thoms' testamentary writings had been kept in an unlocked bag where anyone might have had access to them, but Melrose had only read those parts that Thoms had instructed him to read. This was when the Sheriff got tired of reading himself. He used to read his testamentary writings so often, Melrose said, it was as usual as seeing him read the newspapers. As for his final will, Melrose said he had had no involvement in its preparation and knew nothing of its contents except parts Thoms had read to him after it had been signed.

Other allegations Melrose denied included the suggestion that it was his idea that the Sheriff leave Charlotte Square; quite the contrary, he claimed. Nor did Thoms become moody and morose towards the end of his life. He remained fond of making jokey remarks. Melrose said he never had the slightest doubt as to his master's mental capacity. He thought him rather sharper than the average of men and never knew a gentleman more methodical. He was the first to remember everything. In conclusion, Shaw put one of Alfred's allegations to him:

> (Q.) Did you hear Mr. Alfred Thoms say that notwithstanding all that account you have given of those eight years' services you were a careless and neglectful servant? (A.) I heard him say so. (Q.) What have you to say in regard to that? (A.) Well, I forgive him for it. (Laughter) It is absolutely unfounded. It is not in my nature to be careless.[32]

If there was more than a touch of sardonic humour lurking in Melrose's stated forgiveness, this became more pronounced as Cooper's cross-examination increased the witness's discomfiture. Melrose had already expressed his irritation to Shaw at the injustice of the allegations being brought up against him after he had sacrificed himself for eight years to do Mr Thoms good,[33] and Cooper's efforts did nothing to soothe him. The drinking was his first point of attack, and Melrose's mantra, 'I was sick and faint and took a little stimulant', became less convincing with each repetition. Yet it was not all one-sided. When Cooper made play of the bottle of whisky (or *aqua* as it was entered in the cash book) consumed every three days when Thoms and Melrose were at Moffat in 1899, the servant gave the explanation that a glass was laid out for Thoms in the forenoon, with his lunch, after his afternoon drive, at dinner, and at nine in the evening, but the glasses were sipped at without being finished. Asked why then such consumption did not show up in the cash book at Charlotte Square, Melrose had the answer that there it was entered in the separate book for household expenses.[34]

His account of the time that the Rev. John Mackenzie Gibson found him drunk in the Sheriff's bed was altogether less convincing:

> I saw Mr. Gibson. As soon as he went downstairs, I went and complained to Sheriff Thoms about Mr. Gibson coming into the room and spying on me…I told Sheriff Thoms that Mr. Gibson came into his room and looked at me while I was sleeping in his bed, and I asked him what he meant by it. (Q.) What did you object to? (A.) I can surely take a rest without being treated in that way. I was not drunk at the time. I was sober. (Q.) If you were sober, how did you come to be sleeping in the Sheriff's bed? (A.) Because anyone who is disturbed during the night sleeps when and where they can. (Q.) Did you drop down in the Sheriff's bed through sheer fatigue? (A.) I lay down deliberately. (Q.) Why did you not go to your own room? (A.) I was so used to his room that it was about the same. (Q.) Were you used to sleeping in your master's bed? (A.) No, not usually. (Q.) That was an exceptional occurrence, then? (A.) Well it happened that day. (Q.) What did Mr. Thoms say when you grumbled about Mr. Gibson spying on you? (A.) He told me what Mr. Gibson said. (Q.) Did you contradict Mr. Gibson? (A.) He saw for himself that it was not true. He saw that I was sober. (Q.) How long after Mr. Gibson had seen you in the Sheriff's bed did you go to the Sheriff? (A.) Just as soon as he went out of the house. I do not think it would be a few minutes. (Q.) Did you hear anything about the proposal at this time to send in another man in place of you? (A.) There was another man got. (Q.) At that time? (A.) Oh no, it happened before that – well, I beg your pardon, I am really not sure. (Q.) How did you know that Gibson had complained? (A.) Well, I heard him. (Q.) When you were lying in the Sheriff's bed? (A.) Yes. I heard him complaining in the drawing-room. I then went to the Sheriff and told him I was not drunk, and Sheriff Thoms told me what Mr. Gibson had said. It ended there.[35]

This, of course, flatly contradicts Mackenzie Gibson's evidence that he went away and only spoke to Thoms about it the next day. All the same, it is perhaps understandable that Melrose's recollection of events was a little hazy. Feeling sick and faint can play havoc with the memory.

Of particular interest to Cooper was the series of codicils granted by Thoms in favour of Melrose and his family between 1896 and 1900. Several of these had been signed at Moffat:

> (Q.) Can you explain to us how it comes about that three, if not four, of the codicils giving benefits to you are made at Moffat when you were alone with Mr. Thoms? (A.) Just simply because he chose to do it.[36]

Their provisions, too, seemed to strike Cooper as suspicious. That of 26th December, 1897, provided that, if the bequests to Melrose fell, Thoms' trustee should ensure that Melrose's daughter was never allowed to want. Cooper drew from the witness that at that time Thoms had seen Susan only once, if at all. Again, when on 10th October, 1898, a codicil allowed Melrose and his family twelve months to remove from the Sheriff's house and fifty pounds to pay the expense of removal, the valet's wife and children were not living there. It was, however, in the autumn of that year that Thoms bought the Cluny Drive house, and it may well already have been in his contemplation to instal Melrose's wife as housekeeper. According to Melrose, the delay in moving to Cluny Drive was due to Thoms wanting the house to be perfectly dry.[37]

The first codicil with a provision in Melrose's favour was dated 7th December, 1896, and awarded him an annuity of £100 sterling to be paid half-yearly. Melrose said Lessels read this to him at the time. Thoms himself read him that of 26th December the following year, and Melrose said he also read him the one concerning the removal. Cooper was trying to show that Melrose had read it for himself without the Sheriff's knowledge:

> Yes, he read that to me. I cannot tell when he did it. (Q.) I tell you the date was 10th October, 1898? (A.) Still, I cannot tell you when he did it. I cannot tell whether it was in Charlotte Square that he read it to me. (Q.) What was the occasion of his reading to you that codicil? (A.) Well, I don't know that there was anything particular. (Q.) Were you at the time talking about his settlements or not? (A.) Oh no, we never talked about his settlements. It must have been the case that Sheriff Thoms read this codicil to me while we were talking about other matters. (Q.) He just broke off in the middle of a conversation to read this codicil to you? (A.) I can't remember. (Q.) And you don't remember where it was read? (A.) I do not; perhaps I would be drunk.[38]

This was not a sincere admission. Melrose then denied any knowledge of a codicil executed at Moffat in 1899 granting him and his wife a liferent lease of

26 Cluny Drive. It referred to Melrose as 'my friend and valet'. His explanation for that was a little unexpected:

That is a common thing. You often see on a tombstone 'an old friend of the family' (Laughter.).[39]

In the remainder of his cross-examination, Melrose denied having spoken ill of Thoms' relations, he denied having opened the Sheriff's letters unless asked to do so, and he denied speaking to his master disrespectfully and dragging him along:

To allow you to understand, in helping him along I had to keep him up, and that would give the appearance of dragging him. If I did not do that, he would have gone back. Not only would he have gone back, but so would I, and then we would have been both drunk.[40]

He also shed some interesting light on Alfred's attitude towards him. After the death but before the funeral, he said, Alfred called and told him:

Melrose, if you have got everything and I nothing, thank you all the same for your kindness to my uncle.

Orkney Bench and Bar 1898: Standing, left to right, D. J. Robertson, W. P. Drever, William Cowper, S. B. Armour (Sheriff-substitute), A. Buchanan, J. A. S. Brown, J. S, Copland, J. Begg. Seated, left to right, T. H. Liddle, T. W. Ranken, W. J. Heddle, W. D. Firth, M. L. Howman, T. P. Low. (Orkney Library Photographic Archive).

He repeated this twice. Later Alfred said his uncle had told him that Melrose had done him a lot of good. Later still, Alfred called and told Melrose that his uncle had accused him of trying to murder him, and he asked Melrose if he could say anything. Melrose replied that if it could help him he could say that his uncle had a peculiar temper and was full of fikes and fads, but no more. Taken with Melrose's statement elsewhere that Alfred had told him that his court action would not affect him, only Kirkwall, it seems that Alfred may have been angling for his support in the action on the understanding that Melrose would keep his bequests. If so it did not work. All it did was cause poor Melrose even more discomfiture at the hands of Cooper:

> (Q.) It was your view that he was full of fikes and fads? (A.) Well, I have got no view in the matter. (Q.) You apparently had told Mr. Alfred Thoms that his uncle was full of fikes and fads? (A.) That was everybody's opinion. (Q.) And they were sometimes very extreme, weren't they? (A.) They were amusing sometimes.[41]

By the end of the cross-examination, Melrose was showing distinct signs of weariness. When Cooper asked about the hymn-reading incidents, Melrose replied:

> I never suggested to him that I was the friend; he often called me his friend, though, and if you allow me to say so, I wish he was alive to-day. After serving him for eight years, night and day, this is very harsh treatment.

Cooper concluded by referring to Melrose being 'fortunate' when he was able to give up his house at Dalry Road and get his wife and daughter into Cluny Drive:

> (A.) Unfortunate. Sheriff Thoms gave us one day to make up our minds whether we would go with him or not. (Q.) And you had the great misfortune of not keeping on 62 Dalry Road? (A.) It would have been far better.[42]

What to make of Adam Melrose is not altogether easy. In re-examination, Shaw referred him to a letter he had written to Thoms' Moffat landlady in February, 1904. In it Melrose had stated:

> I am happy to say he did not suffer much, but had a general break up. He was in his right mind up to the end of his life. I cannot tell how much I miss him. Had it killed myself, I would have kept him alive if it could have been done.

Asked by Shaw if it was absolutely true, Melrose replied that he would take his oath upon it.[43] Although it would be temptingly easy to dismiss this as

129

self-serving overstatement, its sentiments had at least a foundation of genuine feeling. For a more balanced view, however, we need to look to the precognition Melrose gave before he was sent into the cauldron of the courtroom. When not provoked to overstated self-justification, Melrose said something with a distinct ring of truth to it:

> I got to pity Sheriff Thoms and to bear with him and to like him. His case was so deplorable that it would have moved anyone. We still continued to have our tiffs and bickerings but altho' I came to like him I never felt that my place was a fixture and I had always the feeling that I would be sacked at any moment.[44]

For eight long years, twenty-four hours a day, Melrose had been responsible for Thoms' care and well-being. Whether they were getting on well with one another for the time being or not, each was the central and ever-present figure in the life of the other. It was only to be expected that an emotional bond should exist between them, and that on Thoms' death Melrose should experience complex feelings of loss and release.

That Melrose had his faults, there is no doubt, and his evasions and unconvincing denials may not have created the best of impressions in the witness box. Yet it cannot be said with much conviction that his performance there was that of the scheming villain portrayed in the pursuers' pleadings. Paradoxically, the greater success Cooper had in wrong-footing Melrose and making him look stupid, the less likely it would have appeared that Melrose had been capable of getting around Thoms. Even supposing he had achieved it, he would have been a remarkably altruistic villain to go to all that trouble to benefit Kirkwall cathedral, while obtaining for himself only what his master's doctor, lawyer and oldest friend all considered no more than he deserved.

After Melrose, there were two more witnesses on the Tuesday afternoon. James Hay, the attendant engaged to replace him, had the briefest of involvements in the case and accordingly a similarly brief appearance in the box. He was followed by John Lessels, whose involvement was more substantial. Some of his evidence has already been outlined. In addition, he was emphatic on the strength and quality of Thoms' mental abilities. It was 'utterly absurd', he said, to say that he would have been easily influenced. While his physical health deteriorated, his mind, Lessels found, remained alert and he stayed cheerful and open to a joke. Some of the most interesting parts of Lessels' testimony, however, concerned the witness's relations with Melrose.

Lessels had a high opinion of Melrose. He considered him 'a very faithful servant, and in every way an excellent man.' Considering the problems Thoms had had with his previous attendants, Lessels was anxious that he should not lose the services of Melrose. Thus, when the latter, not long after starting work for Thoms, gave up his situation, it was Lessels who suggested a wage increase, suggested the amount, got Thoms to agree to it and persuaded Melrose to stay:

> The Sheriff agreed to every word I said about Melrose being a capable man. It was a great thing to get flattery from the Sheriff, because he was so particular.[45]

Lessels said Melrose never forgot himself: he knew his place with the Sheriff and Lessels and was always most respectful. Nor did Lessels ever see any signs of Melrose having any undue influence or control over Thoms:

> The man is not born that could have done that.[46]

Lessels admitted telling Melrose about the first codicil in his favour, and that he did so without the knowledge of the Sheriff. This, too, was to induce Melrose to stay on.[47] Cooper took him up on the point:

> (Q.) Did you regard yourself as the confidential clerk of Mr. Thoms? (A.) Yes, I was in a way. (Q.) Then how did you go away within a day or two and tell Melrose about the Sheriff's testamentary writings? (A.) I quite recognised at the time that it was a breach of confidence on my part, but it was purely in the interest of the Sheriff that I did it.

Cooper then suggested that Lessels and Melrose were very friendly and used to spend a lot of time together in the library at Charlotte Square. Lessels said he took an interest in Melrose for the sake of the Sheriff to keep him in the Sheriff's employment, that was all. Melrose would come and sit in the library when Lessels was working there, and Lessels would listen to him when he said how the Sheriff was and described any difficulties he was having with him. Lessels tried to smooth things over between them. Asked if he still took an interest in Melrose, he replied:

> So far, I take an interest in him, because I feel that I was the cause of his staying on in the Sheriff's service, and I would be very sorry if he was turned adrift at the age that he now is for the services that he had rendered.[48]

As he did with many of the witnesses, Cooper tried to prise out evidence of Thoms' alleged mental decline. In response, Lessels did say that the Sheriff's mind was not so vigorous latterly as it had been. By this, he explained, he meant he became tired easily in company, became indifferent and rather wanted the visitor to go away. Hoping for helpful elaboration of this point, Cooper asked if Lessels knew of Thoms ever instigating a topic of conversation himself instead of following that of his visitor. Lessels replied:

> Yes, when he wanted to abuse anyone.[49]

Lessels' successor, Miss Emily Irvine, followed him into the witness box first thing on Wednesday morning. In response to Clyde's questioning, she told the court that she was the daughter of the late Rev. Walter Irvine, who had been minister of the Parish Church of Kilconquhar in Fife and a friend of Thoms since boyhood. Thoms used to visit the Kilconquhar Manse once or twice a year, staying for anything up to a week at a time, and Miss Irvine and her brother used to look forward to seeing him owing to the kindness he showed them. In June or July of 1898 she became his amanuensis. In all her meetings with him, whether before or after that, he always behaved towards her, she said, 'most politely and in the most gentlemanly manner.' Clyde then put some words into her mouth:

(Q.) Did he all along behave not only as a gentleman, but as a perfectly rational gentleman? (A.) Very much so.[50]

As well as describing her involvement in the preparation of the Sheriff's will, Miss Irvine gave an account of her routine duties. She explained that after she became Thoms' amanuensis she attended at his house usually once or twice a week. She had to write all his letters to his dictation and keep the whole of his accounts of his income and household expenses. She would be in the house usually between eleven and one, though not all the time with him, and about three quarters of an hour to an hour were spent writing to his dictation. She read his letters to him, although he had generally opened them already, then as soon as she had finished reading each one he began dictating his reply. In this, he very rarely showed any hesitation or uncertainty. He composed his sentences 'most clearly'. Although his articulation became less clear latterly, this was because of the trouble in his mouth, and Miss Irvine said she had no trouble making him out when she listened carefully. Some days it was better than others. All letters she wrote were at his dictation except, perhaps, for one or two of a purely formal nature which she wrote for him in the last six weeks of his life to save him the trouble of speaking.

At the end of each month Miss Irvine attended to balance the household accounts. She also had to attend more frequently at certain times of year when dividends came in greater numbers than usual. She found Thoms had a wonderful recollection of when each dividend fell due. He dealt with all of them 'not only with intelligence but with minute exactness.' Right up to the end, she said, he corrected any mistakes, and it was remarkable that even small details were remembered by him to the last.[51]

On Melrose, she had similar views to those of her predecessor:

The impression I formed of him was that he was a superior style of man. He was very attentive and punctual, and prompt in going about things.

When I heard him say, 'Coming, sir,' he was putting on his coat and running upstairs.

She had no doubt, from what she saw of her master's condition, that Melrose's duties must have been most trying. Answering Clyde, she said yes, she had herself, when in the room with Thoms for a long period, felt 'a little sick or faint'. She then said how Thoms had pretended to be poor as a shield against collectors of subscriptions, how he had been disappointed in Alfred for not sticking to his work, but had not shown any signs of perverted feelings towards his relatives, and how he had frequently spoken about St Magnus Cathedral. Indeed, she said, he had shown an interest in other cathedrals such as Brechin, and sent for a book on Orkney's antiquities which he looked at often in the last year or two of his life.[52] After a cross-examination by Cooper that did not bring out anything of material consequence, Clyde returned for a brief re-examination which concluded with an exchange designed to put paid to Thoms' 'delusion' about his own poverty once and for all. Yes, said Miss Irvine, in connection with church matters she had often had occasion to ask people with money to give her a subscription; yes, she had frequently been met by the reply that the wealthy person in question had many calls, that the times at present were very bad and stocks standing low, and that they really could not afford to subscribe; and no, it had never occurred to her that there was anything wrong with these people's minds.[53]

VIII

More weight in the scales

Wednesday was the last day of evidence in the Thoms jury trial and it had a slightly different character to those that had gone before. Once Miss Irvine had left the stand, the witnesses, for the most part, had a less intimate connection with either Thoms or the case and their evidence tended to be briefer and more straightforward. This, and the continuing outbursts of humour, no doubt helped the day to pass more quickly, as counsel hurried to the close of the defenders' case, leaving the fifth and final day for closing speeches, judge's charge and verdict.

Several of Wednesday's witnesses were there because they had visited Thoms around the time that his will was signed or later, and all confirmed to the court that they had found him in full possession of his wits. Hay Shennan, former Sheriff-substitute in Lerwick, had kept in touch with his old superior and visited him in April, 1903. James Murdoch, another regular visitor, had spent 51 years in the service of the Northern Lighthouse Board, latterly as Secretary and General Manager. He also recalled how, on the Lighthouse cruises, Thoms would take the Commissioners to the cathedral and act as guide. When Cooper tried to make something of the Sheriff's insistence that the lighthouses be kept dust-free, the Lord Justice-Clerk helpfully intervened to have Murdoch confirm the importance of clean lenses in the lamps. George Fleming Mathers WS was a lawyer and distant relative of the Sheriff, who remained grateful to him for professional guidance at the start of his career without being blind to his idiosyncrasies:

> Even in those days he was a bit rough in his manner, but I never lost my respect for him till the end of his life.

Mathers was the only witness ever to hear Thoms admit to being unwell. On 10th October, 1903, the Sheriff replied to his enquiry after his health: 'I have a very sore mouth.' He was two weeks from death.

Humour featured strongly in the evidence of the first witness to follow Miss Irvine. Even had his testimony been deadly dull, there would have been something amusing in the mere fact of Andrew Jameson KC giving evidence in a Court of Session case, for he himself was a Court of Session judge. He had taken his seat on the bench with the judicial title of Lord Ardwall only the previous month, so from bar to bench to witness box he had performed three different courtroom roles in as many weeks. In the latest one, he found himself not just viewing both his old and new stations from a novel angle but seeing them filled by other acquaintances of the man whose will was under reduction. A witness who was a judge was facing a judge who could have been a witness and counsel who could have filled the one role as readily as they aspired to the other.

Lord Ardwall, of 'stocky figure, cherry-coloured face, a shock of white hair and flashing dark blue eyes'; he was one of the star witnesses of the case.

Ardwall is unlikely to have been daunted at the prospect of appearing in the witness box. Indeed, he seems to have relished it. His colleagues probably did, too, for Ardwall was a larger-than-life figure. His friend and biographer, the novelist John Buchan, described him as:

> . . . the last of the great 'characters' on the Scottish bench, and a figure who might have stepped out of a Raeburn canvas.[1]

One of his idiosyncrasies was to blend his own whisky in a large cask, and his hospitality was liberal, if a little hard-going at times.[2] Buchan's wife remembered him, in spite of his 'great kindness of heart', as:

> . . . a somewhat alarming host, with his stocky figure, cherry-coloured face, a shock of white hair and flashing dark blue eyes. He roared his remarks to his family and visitors in the voice of a bull.[3]

It is not surprising that he and Thoms should have been friends.

They had been so, Ardwall told the court, ever since Ardwall passed advocate in 1870. He had been the recipient of many kindnesses from the older man, including being taken into cases as junior counsel where Thoms was the senior. From 1886 he was a Sheriff himself and so became a colleague of Thoms on the Lighthouse Board, where he observed the latter's assiduity in the performance of his duties. Thoms, he said, was very fond of his Sheriffdom and everything that came from it. Shaw then raised the question of Thoms' humour:

> (Q.) May I describe him as a cheerful, humorous man? – (A.) Oh, very.

He thought himself, perhaps, a greater humorist than he really was. (Laughter.)[4]

This was a little rich coming from Lord Ardwall, at least if we are to judge from the two samples of his own judicial humour recorded in a surprisingly-thick volume entitled *Law and Laughter*. After narrating the one, in which Ardwall told a witness who had given his occupation as coal miner and his age as twenty: 'Ah, then you are a minor in more senses than one', the compilers of that collection of legal anecdotes felt moved to add: 'Whereat, no doubt, the Court laughed.'[5]

Ardwall's disparagement of his old friend's humour was, in fairness, fleeting. He went on to say that Thoms was very amusing company and always quite willing to be drawn on any of his favourite topics, on which he would give his views in very humorous language. After Thoms' lameness prevented him getting around much, Ardwall continued to visit him frequently at Charlotte Square, but he only made it out to see him once at Cluny Drive as it was, he said, 'an inconvenient place to get at'. At Charlotte Square, he said he found Thoms still had his interest in current events and was especially anxious to hear about his friends at Parliament House and what was going on and being said. Neither there nor at Cluny Drive did it ever occur to him that there was anything wrong with Thoms' mind. He did have his 'fads and cranks,' but he was just the same as he had always been. As to specific conversations, Ardwall could only remember one at Charlotte Square in any detail. That was when Sheriff Thoms had auctioned his wine because he could no longer drink it himself. He complained to Ardwall about the low price it had fetched. Ardwall replied that that was because Thoms had resealed all the bottles himself, so no-one could tell what was in them.

The visit to Cluny Drive was on a Sunday afternoon in either 1901 or 1902, Ardwall thought probably the former. He told the court that when shown up to Thoms' room, Thoms asked him if he would like some refreshment:

> The witness said he would be glad of a whisky and soda after his long walk. (Laughter.) The Sheriff ordered that for him, and some tea for himself, remarking that was what he was reduced to. (Laughter.)[6]

Conversation turned to Thoms' new house. He said how pleased he was with it, and drew Ardwall's attention to the nice view across to the woods and trees about Morningside and to Arthur's Seat. Ardwall, perhaps still recovering his breath, remarked that it was a bit out of the way for his friends, but Thoms replied that he was visited by the Rev. Mr Mackenzie Gibson and by Sir John Cheyne, another of his former colleagues.[7] He added that the air was better there than in town. Although Ardwall noted that he was physically weaker and that his voice was much more indistinct, it never entered his head that he was in any way mentally deteriorated. Although he was not in the sort of spirits he used to be, Thoms did still make some comical remarks even then.[8]

Asked by Shaw if he knew of Thoms' interest in architectural or archaeological subjects, Ardwall spoke of his well-known interest in St Giles. He also recalled his recommending him to visit St Magnus if he was ever in Kirkwall on the *Pharos*:

> I was not surprised at his residue going to its restoration, because he was a man who was rather vain; and then he took a great interest in the restoration of St. Giles', and took a great interest in his Sheriffship. I would not be a bit surprised if he took an interest in the restoration of St. Magnus cathedral. In that way he would gratify his two fads – the restoration of ancient churches, and devotion to the place which had the benefit of him as Sheriff. (Laughter.)[9]

At the end of the conversation at Cluny Drive, said Ardwall:

> I blamed myself for being so long in coming to see him, and he said – 'Don't let it be so long next time.' These were the last words I ever heard him utter.[10]

This concluded Shaw's examination-in-chief. His was the easy part. Cooper's task of cross-examination was, on the other hand, rather more daunting, but he launched himself at it with some bravado:

> (Q.) You have been a Sheriff yourself? (A.) I have had that honour. (Q.) And you are inclined to overlook the failings of the class? (A.) Oh, certainly, a fellow-feeling makes us wondrous kind. (Great laughter.)

Cooper himself had belonged to that class for less than a week.

> (Q.) Mr. Thoms was all along very eccentric, wasn't he? (A.) I should say eccentric, without the 'very'. (Q.) Didn't he do a lot of things which ordinary people would never dream of doing? (A.) Oh well, I don't know. He certainly did things that were peculiar to himself, and in that sense ordinary people would not think of doing them.

Ardwall gave the example of Thoms' showing his laughing waistcoat to the ladies on his golfing trip to Musselburgh.

> (Q.) Did you ever know of any other man, pretending to be sensible, having a laughing waistcoat? (A.) No, I never did; I don't suppose you pick them up readily. (Q.) Did you ever hear about him carrying gutta-percha in his pocket to mend ladies' broken hearts? (A.) No. The only gutta-percha he ever carried was golf balls. (Laughter.)

Asked if he had ever heard of his carrying tawse, Ardwall replied:

138

Oh yes. After I was married, and when my sons were very young, he used to bring them down and take them out and pretend to give them palmies with them, saying, 'This is what I have got to keep bad boys in order with.'

The 'bad boys', of course, included junior counsel for the defender.

(Q.) Did you ever know any person who carried tawse? (A.) My schoolmaster carried tawse. (Laughter.) (Q.) Was it not an eccentric thing on the part of a Sheriff?[11] (A.) Certainly, but he thought it a good joke. (Q.) Did you know he planted sweet williams in his garden as sweethearts for his maids? (A.) I never heard of that. (Q.) Did you ever hear of any sensible man doing such a thing? (A.) I don't know. I have planted sweet williams myself. (Laughter.) It is a pretty, old-fashioned flower. (Q.) Did you ever do it for the benefit of your maids? (A.) No. (Laughter.)

Ardwall said that all through the time he knew Thoms he had, till the end, this jovial and cheerful disposition, with some eccentricities, some of which he knew and some of which he was now hearing for the first time. Cooper asked him if he would have had a different opinion of Thoms' mental state if he had known at the time of these further eccentricities:

(A.) Oh, I think not, because they were just the sort of jokes that he liked to make, and he wished to be a sort of character and to be recognised as such – a sort of funny man. That was the role he chose to adopt for his own amusement. He did not object to being laughed at. On that occasion at Musselburgh he was perfectly delighted, and laughed at himself along with the rest of the company. (Q.) I don't suggest a nasty word, but he liked somewhat to play the buffoon? (A.) That is rather a strong word. You may use that word if you like. He did like to make sport of the company he was in for the time. (Q.) Would you ever have selected him to carry through business of your own? (A.) Well, I think he was a pretty shrewd business man, and in these cases in which he acted as my senior he made two excellent speeches to the jury, and on each occasion won his case.

Ardwall did at least concede that he would not have employed Thoms to make his will:

. . . because he would probably have made my will according to his own notions. (Laughter.)

Shaw, in re-examination, briefly had Ardwall confirm that Thoms possessed all these eccentricities when he still held the office of Sheriff, and company directorships and was a Commissioner for the Northern Lights. Then the Lord Justice-Clerk decided to ask his brother judge some questions of his own:

(Q.) As regards these eccentricities that have been mentioned and of which you know yourself, was it your opinion that they were deliberately intentional on his part, for the purpose of making fun, or the result of something he had no control of? (A.) I think they were intentional. He just rather wanted to pose as a funny man in some ways. He professed to be a great epicurean in many ways, and I think the gusset waistcoat was part of that, because he said it gave him much more pleasure in laughing.[12]

The Orkney Sheriff Clerk, Thomas W. Ranken, and his wife had visited Thoms in the spring of 1903. Long-time bachelor Ranken, aged 54, had just married 27-year-old Fanny, daughter of a late Lieutenant-Colonel Greenland of the 56th Regiment of Foot,[13] and on Sunday, 3rd May, took his new bride past to see the Sheriff on their way back to Orkney from honeymoon. By coincidence, this too, was the day that Harry Thoms had come to see the Sheriff. When the Rankens were announced he tried to take his leave, but his uncle told him that he had to see the bride.[14]

When the newly-weds were shown into the drawing-room, the Sheriff, who was sitting between the fire and the window, shook hands with them and offered them his congratulations. He then introduced them to Harry – 'My nephew, Mr Thoms.' – who left shortly afterwards. The Rankens, however, had tea and stayed for the best part of an hour. Mr Ranken told the court that he found the Sheriff to be physically very feeble but his mind was quite bright and clear. He noticed no deterioration in his mind from what it had been before, but had some difficulty picking up the last part of some of his sentences when he spoke. The room in which they were sitting had a considerable number of pictures in it, and Ranken asked if he could show one or two of them to his wife. As they looked at each picture, Thoms explained about it, who had painted it and so on. Some had inscriptions on them which Thoms quoted from memory as the Rankens viewed them. Unfortunately, Ranken's appreciation of his old boss's pictures was not an outstanding success. Thoms was astonished that he did not recognise the Orkney scenes shown in some of them.[15] The visitors next came to a picture of a church steeple with people floating about it. When Ranken said to his wife in a whisper that he thought it was rubbish, he discovered that whatever manifold ailments Thoms suffered from, deafness was not one of them. The Sheriff began to speak about the picture 'very particularly', before referring them to the key beside it which explained it more fully.[16]

After the picture-viewing had been concluded, the conversation turned to Kirkwall. Thoms asked for news of the people he knew there:

He asked how his old sweethearts were. (Q.) Was that done as a joke? (A.) Yes, in his usual style.

Ranken said that Thoms conversed not only as an ordinary rational man but as a 'perfectly polite gentleman', the perfectly polite gentleman he had always known, he said, especially in the company of ladies. He had his difficulty in articulation – he told Ranken, 'I am not much of a conversationalist now; but, thank God, I can write a little' – but there was nothing to suggest to Ranken that his mind was wrong or absent. He said the Sheriff was 'a very shrewd, sharp, intelligent man, especially about his own affairs' as well as strong-minded and obstinate. Ranken saw no sign that Melrose had acquired any ascendancy over his master. Indeed, he told Thoms more than once that he was glad to see he had got a good servant at last.[17]

Ranken's acquaintance with Thoms was a long one, dating back much further than his appointment as Sheriff Clerk, to a time before Mrs Ranken was even a soldierly twinkle. In this long acquaintance there was one incident that stuck in Ranken's memory and came back to him when he heard of Thoms' will. About twenty years previously, he told the court, he had met Thoms one day in the Broad Street of Kirkwall. The Sheriff was on his way to the cathedral, so both men went together. Once inside, Thoms stopped at the north transept and gazed all around for some time without speaking. Then he said:

What a grand old place this is. Why should they not restore it?

Ranken said it would take a very large sum to do so, but Thoms spoke of steps being taken to raise the money. He suggested that a box be placed at the

A pre-restoration view towards the crossing and North transept. Note the marks on the pillar caused by the 18th century town guards' bonfires, the mid-Victorian partition and stairway. (Orkney Library Photographic Archive).

141

door of the building to collect money from visitors. It seems that the Kirkwall authorities had not even taken this most basic of steps. Ranken did not see the point. He said:

What would that do? That would be a mere nothing.

Thoms asked if ten thousand pounds would do it. Ranken questioned if fifty would. He then told the Sheriff how he had, some years previously, spent two or three hours going around the cathedral with the eminent Scottish architect Dr Rowand Anderson. Anderson had said that there had originally been beautifully decorated stucco and gold internal arrangements. He pointed out the remains of some of the gold ornamental work, particularly in the arches. In the light of this, Ranken told Thoms that to restore St Magnus along the lines on which St Giles had been restored would be no restoration at all.[18]

Ranken was brought back to this conversation under cross-examination:

(Q.) Why do you hark back upon a twenty years' old conversation in order to make the statement that you are not surprised at Kirkwall cathedral getting £40,000 or £50,000? (A.) Because I was interested in the cathedral and a native of the place. (Q.) Your desire is to get as much for Kirkwall cathedral as possible? (A.) No. I want to see it restored, in the proper sense of the word. (Q.) Do you mean destroyed like St Giles'? (A.) I don't want to see it destroyed like St Giles…(Q.) Do you seriously say that, in your opinion, if you were wanting to rebuild any portion of the cathedral, it would be necessary to spend anything like £50,000? (A.) If it is to be restored to what it presumably was somewhere about the 12th or 13th century, in stucco and gold, it would require a very large sum. (Q.) Is that the sort of cathedral you would want to see? (A.) I want to see it as it was. (Q.) With modern gaudy colours? (A.) I don't mind so long as it is properly restored.[19]

As regards Thoms' behaviour on the bench, Ranken was not giving much away:

(Q.) Didn't his joking on the Bench lead to a considerable amount of indignation amongst the gentlemen who practised before him? (A.) Not at Kirkwall. (Q.) Is it your opinion that until he resigned Sheriff Thoms was in every way quite capable of discharging his duties as Sheriff? (A.) Mentally he was quite able to discharge his duties, but physically he was weak. (Q.) Was there any suggestion among the people of Kirkwall for some time that it would be a proper thing that he should resign? (A.) The people were sorry to see him so feeble on his feet. (Q.) Didn't he more than once act in an eccentric way on the Bench? (A.) I do not remember.[20]

Nor did he offer any support for the pursuers' accounts of Thoms' condition towards the end of his life. In fact, his evidence was very useful because he had seen Thoms at the same time as Harry Thoms had, and Clyde returned to this in re-examination:

> (Q.) His nephew, Mr. H. J. M. Thoms, says, 'I just made out a bit of a stray word as to what he meant'; is that correct or not from your observation? (A.) Perhaps the gentleman is deaf. I made out the Sheriff quite well. (Q.) That is not consistent with your observation of the man? (A.) No. (Q.) In like manner Mr. H. J. M. Thoms says, 'He would stutter and then get out a sound, and I had just to form my opinion what it was'; is that correct? (A.) I could understand him quite well.[21]

Fanny Ranken corroborated her husband's account of their visit to Cluny Drive and confirmed that she, as a stranger who had never met the Sheriff before, followed perfectly all that he said.[22]

Another representative of Kirkwall officialdom was William Cowper, the former Kirkwall Solicitor and Town Clerk, by then retired to London because of deafness. His function as a witness was to speak to the occasion on which Thoms had urged the Town Council to draw up a scheme of restoration and advertise across the world for subscriptions. This had occurred on a summer's day in 1893 when Thoms and Cowper were returning from a visit to the Kirkwall Burgh School, as Kirkwall Grammar School was then known. Some time earlier the headmaster, John McEwan, had mentioned to Cowper, who was also Clerk and Treasurer to the School Board, that he was badly off for two or three standard books for his senior pupils. These included a Greek lexicon[23] and a Latin dictionary. Instead of obtaining funds from the School Board or putting his hand in his own pocket, Cowper waited till the Sheriff arrived in town and mentioned the matter to him. Thoms looked on the matter very favourably, and asked Cowper to arrange for him to visit the school where, as Cowper put it in evidence, Thoms 'spoke a few words of advice and counsel to each class.'[24]

This was a rather bland description of how Thoms behaved when faced with an audience of children. McEwan, the headmaster, who did not give evidence, recalled that he asked Thoms if he would like to put a few questions to the various classes. In one, he made a girl stand up and said, 'Girl, spell 'boy'.' When the girl answered, 'B-O-Y', Thoms said, 'No!' and asked a few more pupils. When they all failed to give the answer he was looking for, he said with a twinkle:

> It's not *that* boy, but that red fellow out in the bay!

McEwan said that he made himself agreeable to the schoolchildren generally, and he formed the opinion that Thoms was very fond of children. He added:

> I should say that he was a very humorous and kindly man who took

sometimes a very odd or fantastic view of things but nevertheless very clear-headed.[25]

The jury did not hear these details. Instead, Cowper said how Thoms had asked McEwan what books he needed and then told him to order them from Edinburgh and send the account to him. On leaving the school, Cowper accompanied Thoms as far as the Watergate. As they passed the cathedral, Thoms said:

> Why do you Town Council [*sic*] allow that old and noble building to go to wreck and ruin?

Cowper replied that it was not exactly to wreck and ruin, but Thoms insisted that it was little less. When Cowper explained that there was Mason's Mortification of £1,000, the interest of which was expended on repairs, Thoms said that that might be the means of keeping it wind and watertight, but that was not what he meant. He then made his suggestion of a scheme of restoration and soliciting subscriptions, but Cowper doubted that it would raise sufficient funds. The conversation ended with Thoms urging that it was a subject well worthy of the consideration of the Town Council, and if at any time they should think of it, they could depend upon his hearty support.[26]

After Cowper came another Kirkwall witness. Richard Bailey, a one-time captain in the Royal Artillery, was now Colonel of the 1st Orkney Volunteer Artillery. He had first met Thoms shortly after arriving in Orkney in 1883, when the Sheriff had asked him to take an interest in Freemasonry in Kirkwall. Bailey's evidence did not do much beyond confirming Thoms' mental sharpness and his interest in the cathedral. The witness's statement that Thoms performed his duties as Provincial Grand Master carefully and punctiliously brought a swift warning from the bench:

Thoms in his regalia as Provincial Grand Master of Caithness, Orkney and Zetland. Possibly the latest surviving picture of him, it shows signs of his declining health and mobility. (Morton Lodge No 89, Lerwick).

> The Lord Justice-Clerk: It is impossible to know what they are.[27]

Clyde hastened to reassure his lordship that he had not been going remotely to enquire and would not go into the matter further. Forensic enquiry evidently had its limits. Perhaps the length of the proceedings was starting to try Macdonald's patience. When Bailey, under cross-examination, said that they were all very proud of the cathedral at Kirkwall, the Lord Justice-Clerk cut in:

It is the only lion they have. (Laughter.)[28]

The artillery officer was followed in quick succession first by another Writer to the Signet, then by a chartered accountant. The WS was John A. Forrest, who came to praise Melrose for his care of his father, Sir John.[29] The CA was William A. Wood, the Trustee appointed in Thoms' will and the first defender in the action. Apart from repudiating the suggestion that Thoms was mentally incapable or facile, Wood's evidence merely confirmed the value of Thoms' estate. The total estate, heritable and moveable, was valued at £82,542, from which, Wood estimated, Kirkwall would get in the end about £52,000, but that would not be until both the Thoms nephews and Melrose were dead. In the meantime, taking account of the liferents, he estimated the value of the fund available to Kirkwall to be about £40,000 to £42,000, of which about £33,000 was available immediately.[30]

It was now the turn of Kirkwall's counsel, McClure, to lead the evidence of his two witnesses, architects called to refute the testimony of Alexander and Thomas Ross. The first of these was Walter W. Robertson, then aged 59, former principal architect and surveyor for Scotland to Her Majesty's Office of Works (successors to the Woods and Forests). He had held that office for 27 years and, as such, had had responsibility for many of the old ecclesiastical buildings in the country. While these, of course, did not include St Magnus, he said that he knew the building well and had frequently visited it. His evident enthusiasm for it was clear from his evidence.

A.L. McClure, Advocate, who represented Kirkwall Town Council and led evidence on the condition of the cathedral.

He began by outlining the history of the cathedral and the story of its construction over the centuries:

It tells its own story to those who know how to read it, but it is all singularly congruous, and the building is homogenous. I say, speaking from an architectural point of view, there is not a more interesting building in the whole of Scotland.

For the case, Robertson had spent three days conducting a careful survey of its present condition. It was extremely weather-worn, he said, especially in its more ornate parts:

It has suffered from natural causes, from injudicious treatment, and from deliberate abuse.

The most ornate, and most weather-worn, parts were around the doors, particularly the three at the west end and the one in the south transept. Almost all the carved work had disappeared, but here and there were some stones that could give a clue to restore the remainder:

> My opinion is that unless some means are taken to restore these architectural features soon, the chance will soon be gone. At the present time I think it is perfectly possible to restore the cathedral to its original design and character. It would require care and very much attention on the part of those who superintended the work, and specially skilled workmen. There must be very few workmen in the country who could undertake the work, but it could be done now. In a little while I believe there will be nothing left as a guide. It would be distinctly an expensive restoration to carry out.

To highlight the difference between what St Magnus was, and what it might be, he referred, or was referred, to a footnote in Dr Story's work on the Church of Scotland:

> It is very sad to see, as the writer did in August 1886, the noble and well-preserved cathedral of St. Magnus, now visited every autumn by hundreds of tourists, and still used as a Parish Church, yet fitted up in such a tasteless manner, to the scandal of the Church of Scotland. A magnificent church it might easily be if the hideous galleries, pulpit, and modern fittings were swept away, and the interior treated like the nave of St. Giles' in Edinburgh.

Robertson thought that this had long been the view entertained by people skilled in ecclesiastical architecture as to the possibilities of St Magnus.

There were many more instances on the outside of the cathedral, he continued, where restoration was required, and it would be necessary to do a great deal of work inside as well. The pillars of the nave had been reduced in size at the bottom by the Town Guard's fires having been laid against them. The entrances to the transept chapels had been built up. One chapel was used for a heating apparatus and the flue, a round metal pipe, was taken out through the window and up the outside of the building. There was also a vestry where the same thing was done. He thought that, if opened up and properly restored, the chapels would be most beautiful things. Much interior stonework required to be renovated. Some of the capitals of the choir pillars had been hewn off in an inexplicable manner, perhaps in order to fit galleries. Outside, burials had raised the ground level, causing ingress of damp into the building. This needed to be dealt with, while inside the floors required to be dug out, and concrete and asphalt laid under a new floor to prevent dampness rising. The triforium needed to be cleaned up and its floor repaired. The roofs of the nave and nave aisles were very much decayed. Robertson said that once one got through the skin of the wood it could be pinched out in handfuls. He had put some in his portmanteau to bring to court, but it had gone to dust. The upper part of the roof was worm-eaten and the lower part decayed by damp. It was on the point of being dangerous, and the flag slates used could hardly be made watertight. The idea seemed to have been to remedy defects by just plastering on more lime, which was quite inadequate. Indeed, he thought the roof was far too heavy and should be replaced with a lead roof, which would be about a third of the weight. The roof, as it stood, had a sag in it of six or eight inches. At the west front he thought something should be done to make a suitable approach for such a building. He suggested lowering the ground and putting in a flight of steps.

McClure put some of Alexander Ross's statements to Robertson. As for Ross's assertion that he thought the cathedral could be restored for £4,200 because it was in very good order, he said:

> It is impossible to characterise it. I do not know exactly what the witness meant, he must have meant something very different from what I have talked about. Why, the roof I am talking about is £5,500, because I consider it essential to the restoration of the building and its preservation that it should have a good roof, and a roof which will not only be good, but will continue good...(Q.) What do you say to this, 'The roof is all good enough. I examined it very carefully, and it seemed to be watertight. I allow £100 or £200 for pointing on the roof as a contingency'? (A.) I say it is nonsense, and that one or two hundred pounds spent in pointing would probably make matters worse than they are.

On the assumption that Sheriff Thoms' bequest amounted to £42,000, Robertson thought that sufficient to do a great deal but not everything that he had recommended. He thought that amount a little more than half of what could judiciously be spent on the building. He and a colleague had priced the necessary work at about £69,000.[31]

Cooper began his cross-examination by referring Robertson to the thousand pounds' worth of work that had just been done on the cathedral with the Taylor bequest. Robertson agreed that the slating on the north side of the nave roof had been restored within the last two to three years, but doubted Cooper's assertion that the slating on the south side had been renewed with partly new sarking, felt and pointing. This was where he said he had picked out the timber in handfuls:

> (Q.) Do you suggest that the town have put new sarking upon decayed

147

timbers? (A.) They may have done so; that is one of the things that poor people have to do. I saw that the timbers were in a very advanced stage of decay. (Q.) Then it comes to this, that if that is so they have put new sarking on to decayed timbers? (A.) It may be; that is to say, if they have put sarking there. I can hardly suppose that the timber has suddenly decayed during a year or two. To put new sarking on to decayed timbers is not a thing that a person would do of choice, but if they had no money they would be compelled to do it. (Q.) Would any architect in his senses sanction the re-sarking on a roof where the timbers were decaying? (A.) I cannot be responsible for what all the architects would do.

Cooper was trying to get Robertson to criticise Blanc, who was to be the next witness for the town. He followed up these questions by putting several statements from Blanc's report to him, but the only differences between the two architects were fairly minor.[32]

Cooper had more success when he turned to Robertson's own words, for the witness had written a paper criticising the restoration of old buildings. It now gave Cooper a stick with which to beat him:

(Q.)…your opinion is that there should be restoration? (A.) Restoration in a conservative sense. I would not remove a thing that was good to remain, and told its own story. (Q.) Have you ever expressed this opinion – 'I plead, therefore, most earnestly for the careful preservation of our old buildings, and above all for their preservation from restoration'? (A.) I remember having said that. (Q.) Did you entertain the opinion you then expressed? (A.) Well, yes and no. I may explain in what circumstances these words were uttered. I was president of the Architectural Association, and I wanted something to stir the Association up, and I wrote a paper on the restoration of buildings in which I put everything in the most absolute and aggressive way, in order that I might provoke discussion. I attained my object, because we had three nights' discussion in one session on the subject, and the end of it was that when I demitted the chair I said I thought we had gained something, because it resulted in this, that every case had to be considered on its own merits, and whether the work of restoration involved greater preservation or greater destruction was the point that would settle the question. I expressed my opinion as a controversialist, and my whole report and estimate are framed on the principle of what I call conservative restoration.[33]

Cooper had several more passages to quote at Robertson, but the witness was quite able to hold his own:

Witness - I suppose you have had discussions in the Juridical Society, and would not like to be faced afterwards with the opinions you expressed there. (Laughter.) Mr Cooper – It is the most unpleasant thing in the world to be faced with your opinions. (Laughter.)

Witness – Not at all; I rather like it. (Applause and laughter.)[34]

Cooper read another passage:

Witness – You do me too much honour.

Mr Cooper – I cannot do you too much honour. (Laughter.)

Witness (bowing) – I thank you. (Laughter.)[35]

In one part of his paper, Robertson had said that he did not believe there was a single building restored within the first fifty or sixty years of that century which would not call forth an almost unanimous verdict to the effect that it had suffered great and irreparable injury in the process. In the very best, the work had falsified a historical document and taken the life and interest out of the edifice. When this was put to him by Cooper, Robertson responded:

I had several notable instances in my mind, and there is one across the street, because no one can say that the restoration of St. Giles' has not utterly destroyed the building and destroyed the record; but the leading principle in the present case would be to preserve the record.[36]

Robertson had quoted Ruskin with approval that:

The true meaning of restoration is destruction, the most total destruction that a building can suffer, a destruction out of which no remnants can be gathered . . .

and

. . . more has been gleaned out of desolated Nineveh than out of rebuilt Milan.

He responded to Cooper that this was very much 'an academic discussion'.[37] But Cooper had not finished yet. He quoted one of the most purple passages in the witness's paper:

We have come to consider the thing, and we may as well pronounce the baneful word 'restoration', which I have hesitated so long to introduce. This is the word which, like that inadvertently uttered at some magical scene of beauty and delight, may suddenly change the whole aspect of our gathering; this is the special danger to which I consider old buildings are exposed in this century, but which I delayed to name. It is indeed a word of evil omen, and we should have been very much richer this day if it had never been uttered, or if the ideas which it represents had never been applied to our ancient buildings . . . There is no doubt that . . . so-called restorations . . . have wrought more havoc and destruction among our old buildings than any other single cause, or it may well be than all other causes combined. If this is so, it becomes the duty of every one who realised it to raise his voice in warning and protest, and do all in his power against the continuance of such destruction.

Just to rub the point in, Cooper repeated the last sentence. Was this the witness's opinion?

(A.) I am astonished at my own eloquence. I ought to have been a member of the Bar, I think.[38] But I think you have overlooked that I referred to 'the present century'. We are now in a new century, and I hope we are learning something. That was the argument I advanced at that stage, but I told you I was rousing discussion, but we discussed it two or three nights, and then came to a decision that every case would need to be judged by its merits, and the question seriously considered whether destruction or preservation was the motive. I adhere to that. (Q.) Did you tell the Association that what you had said was all a joke. (A.) I think they understood that perfectly at the end of the three-days' discussion. Perhaps I should not say it was a joke.[39]

After this, Robertson said he did not agree with Dr Story's statement that St Magnus was 'well-preserved' and said he considered himself a far better judge than Dr Story. He then explained to Cooper how it would be possible to recreate some of the carved work from the evidence that was left:

. . . we have all heard of the naturalist who from a tooth could construct the whole quadruped, and an architect has something of that ability if he knows his business. (Q.) Is it your idea that the way this business is to be carried out is by picking up a tusk and creating an elephant from it? (A.) No, but I could shew you all over these photographs little bits which sufficiently indicate what work was there.

He had to agree that there had never been any asphalt under the floor, but said the reason for putting it in was that people nowadays did not like to sit with their feet on damp flags. Under re-examination, he confirmed that the purpose of his paper had been to protest against the ill-advised restoration of old buildings which involved the destruction of the proper and appropriate features of those buildings.[40]

Hippolyte J. Blanc confirmed Robertson's evidence on the state of the building. In his view, the cost of restoring the building would be marginally lower. He estimated it at £67,800. Cooper picked him up on the wording of his report to Kirkwall Town Council as to how Taylor's bequest should be spent, but Blanc explained that his recommendations were made on the basis of there only being a limited sum to spend:

(Q.) Since your report, has not a lot of work been done on this cathedral? (A.) Oh, very trifling – patching. (Q.) Don't you know that the Town Council spent considerably over £1,000 on restoration? (A.) A mere bagatelle with a building of that sort.[41]

The architectural experts having been dealt with, Shaw returned to examine the first of three medical experts called by the defender. He was John Glaister, Professor of Forensic Medicine in the University of Glasgow, whose standard textbook on Medical Jurisprudence and Toxicology was to run to numerous editions. He had been present in court and had heard all the evidence with the exception of that of Saturday, which he had read. He had also read the large print of documents containing letters to and from Sheriff Thoms. On this basis, he was ready to give his opinion as to Thoms' mental capacity and testamentary power.

Professor John Glaister, expert medical witness for the defence: 'A man may wear a peculiar shape of hat, but that does not indicate that the head below it is wrong.' (Glasgow University).

He began with the sheriff's physical condition. He told the court that he attached very great importance, as Dr Affleck did, to the gout. This had been mainly chronic, but sometimes of a sub-acute and acute character, and led to the impediment to locomotion that had been described. As for syphilis, which Glaister, following Shaw's lead, did not mention by name, he observed that it was very difficult to say how much the sores were due to it and how much to gout. He had seen no evidence of paralysis, apart from the transient shock that lasted for a day or two but did not seem to leave any lasting effects. Inability to move the lower limbs could result either from some paralytic condition or merely some physical condition, such as gout. It was thus very important to see if there was any lesion or injurious affection of the spinal cord. He was satisfied that there had not been, primarily from Dr Affleck's evidence that no signs had shown up in the patient's urine. He added that, in his experience, where syphilis led to superficial running sores, there was rarely internal damage to the nervous system. In fact there was:

> . . . no evidence put before me that would lead me to suppose that there was any involvement of the central nervous system of the brain of the testator.[42]

151

Turning to Thoms' mental state, Glaister said he attached great importance to the fact that the patient had retained his memory, for memory was one of the modes by which a person exhibits whether he has a healthy mind or not. Neither was there any loss of control of his emotions. Thoms was irascible, but had been so, it appeared, all his life. Glaister next referred to the print of documents:

> When one looks through this volume of letters and sees what this testator wrote and dealt with in that period of his life prior to and succeeding the date of the will, one has great difficulty in believing that he was not competent to write or dictate his will.[43]

Then, having quoted from several of the letters written in Thoms' characteristically concise and acute style, he added:

> All these things convince me that so far as the will power of the man was concerned, he was undoubtedly able to exercise it firmly and clearly. The volume of letters speaks eloquently on the subject of his power of intelligence in appreciating anything that was put before him.[44]

The particular evidence on the preparation of the will showed that he was quite alive to what he was doing:

> I don't know of such a case in my experience where there was so much care on the part of the testator and of his agents and of those who had to deal with the will, and in regard to the signature, to effect its accuracy. I think all the processes of deliberation seem to have been gone through most carefully.[45]

Glaister could see no evidence of facility. Nor did he attach any significance to Thoms' eccentricities. These had lasted throughout his life and were, thought Glaister, 'simply forms of elephantine humour on his part'. There was no delusion of poverty – 'If he said he was poor, he pretended it' – nor any other delusions:

> A delusion…is something which affects to a morbid extent the brain, the mind, and power. A delusion is a mental conception of a wrong character, of the inaccuracy of which the holder cannot be convinced. I do not see any evidence of that kind in this case.

Finally, Glaister confirmed that he could see no evidence of perverted feelings, either. He thought they were merely the natural solution that would suggest itself to a person whose expectations had been disappointed.[46]

Cooper probed Glaister's reasoning for ruling out paralysis. The witness confirmed that, if there was paralysis, there would not necessarily be any injury to the spinal cord. It might arise from the brain. However, in that case, the paralysis would be one-sided, which was not the case with Sheriff Thoms.

Glaister did admit, for what it was worth, that a layman seeing Thoms would naturally jump to the conclusion that his was a case of paralysis.

Cooper then asked if a man, insane in some respects, might still be capable of transacting business as a businessman:

> (A.) I mean to say that there are cases of monomania where a man is mad on one subject only, but may be able to conduct his business.

Wasn't it the case, he continued, in Glaister's frequent experience that many people found even in lunatic asylums appeared to be able to talk rationally on most subjects, but it was only when you touched upon a particular subject that you found anything wrong?

> (A.) In the case of monomaniacs, that is perfectly true.

And might you not go on for a very long time with a man without your discovering that he had some mental defect?

> (A.) If you were a comparative stranger to the individual and did not know him, undoubtedly you probably might go on for some time without knowing this particular weakness.

It was becoming apparent why Cooper had made a point in cross-examining the defender's witnesses on the short duration of their visits, the limited nature of their conversations, and to what extent they had instigated the topics of conversation themselves:

> (Q.) So that I suppose if a gentleman was living alone, and his friends came to visit him for ten minutes or a quarter of an hour perhaps once a month or so, they might go on for a very long time conversing with him without finding out there was anything the matter with his mind? (A.) I should say that was not totally improbable, but I should think it is highly improbable. The moment that the friend began to discuss the subject which was the weak point, then the floodgates are opened. There is no difficulty in knowing about the insanity then.[47]

Cooper moved on to the alleged delusions:

> (Q.) You know that he believed he was the head of a clan? (A.) I am afraid that is a very common delusion, if you put it like that.

A lengthy exchange followed on the foundations of Thoms' belief and the definition of delusion. Glaister was quite clear that Thoms' belief did not fall into that category:

> . . . but if you go into this, there is no subject upon which people are very often more wrongly idea'd than in regard to their ancestors. If you take any heraldic book you like, you will find everybody has got some

delusion – if you like to call it that – from their ancestors from whom they have sprung. It is not a delusion – I say certainly not.

He thought that to have such a belief in the absence of proof was not a delusion but vanity:

> . . . it is a piece of that vanity which many people have, to think they are descended from someone extraordinary or peculiar. (Q.) Doesn't that come very near to a delusion? (A.) I don't think so. (Q.) If you have got no proof of what you are claiming to be, and still going on declaring that you are, isn't that a delusion? (A.) No. You omit the latter part of my definition, that the man maintains his opinion in spite of accurate evidence to the contrary being put before him. It is not so in this case.[48]

Further questions on this line having had no greater success, Cooper left the clan business and asked Glaister about the delusion that Thoms' relatives desired his death. Glaister said only one witness, the pursuer Alfred Thoms, had mentioned it. When Cooper told him to assume that Mrs Dougall and Miss Coghill had also mentioned it, Glaister said, 'I have gone through the evidence and I cannot find it.' However, on the assumption that a man told several independent witnesses that he thought someone wished to kill him, and there was no foundation for that belief, Glaister agreed that that would be a delusion, although the lack of foundation would have to be proved. On the assumption that a man got it into his head that his relatives wanted his death so that they might be bettered by it, Glaister agreed that that might affect his testamentary writing. And on that assumption, he agreed that such a man who had left his money to relatives might change his will and leave it to someone else:

> (A.) On the assumed case certainly; anything might happen in an assumed case.[49]

Cooper turned to Thoms' eccentric behaviour:

> (Q.) I understand you to lay no stress upon the eccentricities that Mr. Thoms had? (A.) I do not think anybody else did, as far as I can gather from the evidence.

Undaunted, Cooper tried to elicit some basis for a connection between eccentricity and insanity:

> (Q.) Take a man with extravagant eccentricities, does not that indicate a certain instability in his mental condition to begin with? (A.) That must be tested by his capacity for his conduct in other relations of life before you can say yes or no. (Q.) Would you agree that if a man is eccentric to the extent of being extravagantly so, that is a kind of warning that the man is not quite a sane man? (A.) It does not necessarily follow at all.

A man may wear, for example, a peculiar shape of hat, but that does not indicate that the head below it is wrong. (Laughter.) (Q.) If he does half-a-dozen other things besides wearing a peculiar shape of hat, doesn't it suggest that the mind is not quite on the balance? (A.) I do not think it follows. (Q.) Not necessarily follows, but may it not suggest it? (A.) To a person who paid no attention it might.

Glaister's answers were starting to show signs of impatience. When Cooper asked him the significance of Thoms having made eighty-five testamentary writings, he replied that it indicated he was a lawyer and that he had leisure:

(Q.) Suppose he was not a lawyer, would not that indicate some instability of mind? (A.) I am not aware of it happening, except in the case of a lawyer. (Laughter.)

Cooper then suggested that Thoms displayed a loss of control of his emotions indicating mental instability when he threw his boots at the valet who jostled his bed, when he broke out about Alfred not attending to business, and when he asked for a second kiss from his niece because she resembled her dead father. To laughter in the court, Glaister said he had seen a boot thrown for less. If loss of temper indicated mental instability, then 'we are all unstable in our minds'. And as for the incident with Thoms' niece:

I do not think it is unnatural for an uncle to ask for a second kiss from his niece; I would even grant a third.[50]

Closing his cross-examination, Cooper asked Glaister to suppose there was a man of extravagant eccentricities, with a slight shock that might pass off, with certain delusions and a very weak physical condition. Was this not, he asked, the sort of man whose mind might be very easily undermined?

(A.) You are dealing with certain facts which are identical with this case, and certain facts which are not identical with this case, and I want to clearly understand whether this is an assumed case or this case. (Q.) Assume a man with extravagant eccentricities, assume a man who has had a slight shock that has passed away, assume a man who has certain delusions? (A.) If I assume delusions, the whole thing is given away. Assuming a man with delusions, you have got to enquire very carefully as to his testamentary powers. (Q.) If the jury should consider that Mr Thoms laboured under delusions? (A.) Then my evidence is of no value.[51]

As the alleged delusion of poverty had been torpedoed by Yellowlees, the pursuers' own expert witness, the only two delusions remaining to deal with were that of the clan chiefship and the one that Thoms' relatives desired his death. It was to the latter that Shaw returned in his re-examination of Glaister, particularly to emphasise the point that the only evidence for it before the court was from the pursuer Alfred Thoms himself. Even that, as Shaw demonstrated from the transcript of Alfred's evidence, boiled down to the 'cold way' Thoms spoke about them latterly and the one incident in which Thoms had asked Alfred if he wished to kill him. Shaw had Glaister confirm that he thought it not in the least likely that a man labouring under such a delusion would have allowed the person who he thought wished to kill him back into his presence, let alone go on adding bequests in his favour to his wills for some years afterwards:

> (Q.) Therefore this so-called delusion is a delusion on the part of Mr. Cooper? (Laughter.)

Glaister then confirmed that he gave great heed to the evidence of Thoms' own medical attendant, especially when he was someone of the high position of Dr Affleck, before concluding in trenchant form:

> I cannot give the least countenance to the suggestion that Sheriff Thoms is to be called a monomaniac; I do not think it is seriously asked that I should. That is a suppositional case that has been put to me. (Q.) The thing is nonsense? (A.) Without hesitation, I say so. As to his wanting to be connected with a clan, he may have been quite wrong, but still not under a delusion.[52]

The remaining two expert witnesses, Dr David Wallace of Edinburgh Royal Infirmary and Dr Alexander R. Urquhart of James Murray's Royal Asylum, Perth, both corroborated the testimony of Professor Glaister. Only Wallace's evidence was deemed to have sufficient additional content to be recorded. He was a lecturer in surgery at the Royal College and was in charge of the special department at the Royal Infirmary devoted to syphilitic diseases. He was also about to become the son-in-law of the Orcadian mental specialist Dr (later Sir) Thomas S. Clouston of Holodyke and the Morningside Asylum, though this particular qualification was not mentioned in court.[53]

Wallace stated that Thoms' external sores were 'most probably' the result of syphilis. In his view, that diminished very much indeed the presence of the internal effects of that disease. He could see no sign whatever of mental decay or deterioration in Thoms, nor any sign that he suffered from any morbid condition of his mental organs at all. He retained throughout his capacity to attend to business and was master of his own will. Indeed, he showed 'a certain streak of obstinacy and pertinacity'. Returning to syphilis, he thought it most important that there was no suggestion that Thoms was suffering from headache. Once the disease infects the membranes around the brain, headaches are one of the most common symptoms. Their absence confirmed the view he formed from the other evidence in the case, and the conclusion he derived was that Thoms had retained perfect mental capacity. Under cross-examination, he stated that he thought it almost impossible for the disease to infect the brain without causing headaches. He agreed that its affecting the brain made people suspicious and moody, but if he found someone suspicious and moody he would not infer that the disease had reached the brain. He agreed that obstinacy and pertinacity were sometimes present in people who were insane, but under re-examination agreed that these were just the people who could not be got around.[54]

Although Dr Urquhart was the last witness to give evidence for the defenders, Wednesday's proceedings did not finish when he stepped down from the witness box. Instead, there was a change of pace, as the evidence of four witnesses taken on commission was read, and the jury was taken back to Thoms' Orkney days. The four witnesses were all members of Thoms' social circle in Kirkwall. There was Andrew Gold, for 58 years the Earl of Zetland's factor in Orkney, then aged 85, and living in Merchiston; there was James S. S. Logie, MD, aged 84, and by then three years into a retirement that would last twenty; and there were the septuagenarians Mrs Elizabeth Lees or Peace, widow of Provost Thomas Peace, and Mrs Jean Heddle or Bruce, widow of the former Sheriff Clerk. None, needless to say, had ever suspected Sheriff Thoms of being mentally unsound.

Gold said that he had seen Thoms frequently on his visits to Orkney. The latter had called at Gold's house, they had shot together, and Gold had met him often in society in Kirkwall. He said Thoms had been very fond of children, he had liked to joke with and try to amuse Gold's own children, and they in turn had been very fond of him. They were not at all frightened of him. Although Gold said under cross-examination that he thought Thoms' bequest was:

> . . . a large amount to leave for restoring St Magnus – a very large amount.

the attempt by pursuers' counsel to have him elaborate merely elicited:

> Oh, you could spend any amount on St Magnus.[55]

Dr Logie's value as a witness was to confirm the conversation about the possible restoration of the cathedral in which Thoms had said that the day would come and the man would come. His medical opinion was less valuable, as he said he knew Thoms to be suffering from 'what is called creeping paralysis'. No doubt the words were the pursuers' counsel's, but Affleck had been at pains to point out not only that Thoms did not suffer from paralysis, but that 'creeping paralysis' was a term unknown in medical nomenclature.[56] Dr Logie did, however, make a statement that succinctly confirmed the defenders' position on Thoms' eccentricities:

> He made his eccentric jokes to amuse people. At other times, when he was not trying to amuse people, he was just like any other man.[57]

Mrs Peace had got to know Sheriff Thoms through her husband who, as well as being chief magistrate of Kirkwall, had been Master of the masonic lodge there. Thoms had been a frequent visitor at their house in Broad Street, and continued to call regularly after her husband died in 1892.[58] Latterly, he came in his chair, being wheeled by his servant into the room and then lifted into an armchair. Mrs Peace remembered one of the Sheriff's menservants being extra kind to him. She thought that was the last one. Conversation on these visits was generally about the cathedral. Thoms used to speak about getting the galleries and partitions taken away like at St Giles in Edinburgh. Mrs Peace remembered Thoms borrowing two old collection plates from the cathedral to get them copied in Edinburgh. Thoms presented one copy to St Giles where it is still on display.[59] When Mrs Peace had been in Edinburgh for an eye operation some time before 1892, Thoms had come to see her every second day. He had also presented her and her husband with a copy of the Macthomas clan book.[60] All the time she knew him he had talked nonsense in fun, speaking of his 'sweethearts'. He did sometimes talk seriously, but he was not often inclined to do so:

> I thought Sheriff Thoms prided himself on being a little peculiar. I never met any person just exactly like him…That was always his way, but he was very gentlemanly.

On one occasion her servant had met Thoms in his chair, and he had recognised her and bowed.[61]

When Mrs Bruce gave evidence she did not repeat, or rather was steered away from repeating, her comment about the young Thoms' inordinate conceit and vanity. She, too, had got to know the Sheriff well through her husband, and, likewise, his regular visits had continued after her husband's death. He always behaved in 'a most gentlemanly way', 'joked at a great rate' and made 'humorous and witty remarks'. As with Mrs Peace, he spoke on antiquarian topics. He was always asking if she was keeping the table in her dining room in good order, as it was a historical table. She also had a toddy rummer which had come out of the Earl's Palace at Kirkwall and which Thoms wanted to borrow to have copies made. She spoke of Thoms' fondness for children and how he put himself about to amuse them, and mentioned the incident with the penknife and the tongues. He always took a great interest in her daughter, and would bring her a packet of sweets every year, presenting them with the words, 'Here's your dose of poison, but it seems to be doing you no harm.' According to Mrs Bruce:

> When children were present he was always joking, but with myself he was quite serious. I have discussed business with him. I thought him a very sensible and good business man.

As she lived at the top of Dundas Crescent,[62] the then outskirts of Kirkwall,

Thoms visited her latterly in a phaeton. His manservant had to help him into the house, and Mrs Bruce had the mats lifted to stop him tripping. She thought his last valet was 'kind and gentle' towards him (her daughter thought the previous servant had planted Thoms down in a chair like a piece of goods[63]). On one occasion Thoms had sent his valet – which one is not recorded – out to gather mushrooms for her daughter. Mrs Bruce echoed all the other defenders' witnesses' comments on Thoms' mental strength and clear memory. Indeed, she said she was struck with 'the frailty of the man and the clearness of his mind'.[64]

IX

Madness or method?

Thursday, 9th February, 1905, was the fifth and final day of the Thoms' will case; the fifth and final act of a drama laced with comedy, not to say farce. Once more the main players, parties and counsel, assembled in the court. Once more the public crowded in to watch the performance. Curtain-up on such occasions is always much the same, however much actors and plot may change. The low murmur of a dozen conversations is broken by a shout from the macer as he leads the judge onto the bench. The sound of subdued voices gives sudden way to the long rumble of a whole room rising to its feet at once, then hush, a round of bowings and good-mornings between bench and bar, and finally more rumbles, creaks and coughs as they all sit down again. Everyone safely in their place, the case is called, a nod or word goes from judge to counsel, and the latter rises to begin.

Cooper it was, that Thursday, who rose first to address the jury. In style he was usually slow and deliberate, each point following on in orderly and logical fashion from the preceding, his voice now and again betraying a trace of his Yorkshire origins.[1] He could employ humour, too, and in this case the closing speeches were where both he and Shaw used it most. Indeed, the Lord Justice-Clerk commented on one particular instance in his charge to the jury. Both counsel, he said, had dismissed the matter of Thoms' eccentricities as ridiculous, but while Cooper had said it was perfectly ridiculous that any man behaving in such a way could be sane, Shaw had said it was perfectly ridiculous he could be anything other. Here, though, Shaw had the advantage. His task was essentially a

Thomas Shaw in later life as Lord Shaw of Dunfermline. In his memoirs he wrote a short chapter on the Thoms case called 'The strange will.'

161

negative one, and it is easier to laugh a case out of court than to laugh one in. Yet Cooper was not a man to let any perceived difficulty daunt him, for he was:

> . . . never seen to greater advantage than in uphill cases, which he fought with unfailing good humour and invincible courage.[2]

Cooper began by explaining the issues the jury had to decide and what the effect of the decisions open to them would be. There were really only two questions for them, he said, and one was entirely different from the other. The first was whether Mr Thoms had been of sound disposing mind at the time he executed his last will. The second assumed that he was of sound disposing mind, but asked whether he had been in such a condition of body and mind as to have been circumvented by Melrose. If they answered the first question in favour of the pursuers but not the second, the will would be cut down, but Melrose would still get his bequests in terms of the codicils to the earlier will. The principal effect of cutting down the last will would be that the residuary gift would go not to Kirkwall cathedral but to the Sheriff's heirs and relatives.

According to Cooper:

> The defenders laboured under two considerable difficulties. They had to admit that Sheriff Thoms was getting physically weaker year by year from 1893, if not from 1891, onwards. They had to admit that in the last years of his life he was so weak that he had to be treated like a child. They had to admit that he was unable to move about without assistance, and had to be attended to like a baby in arms. They had to admit that his whole physical constitution was gone, that he was covered with these terrible sores, and then they came to the jury saying that notwithstanding all this his mind remained good to the last. That did not sound very like common sense. A man could not suffer for years as this man did without its having a very considerable influence upon the state of his mind. Again, the defenders had to admit that the position was such that the opportunity was there if Melrose chose to take advantage of it. They had to admit that codicil after codicil was made in favour of the man who had the power to exercise influence, but they asked the jury not to infer that the influence was actually exercised when they admitted there was opportunity of exercising it.

He then ran through some of the evidence, to show the deterioration of Thoms' mind over the years. He pointed out that as far back as 1882 Thoms had executed a codicil making his nephew Alfred, then aged ten, his residuary legatee. Two years later he had bought the Charlotte Square property, and letters of his from the time show that he intended it as a house for one or other of his nephews if they came to Edinburgh. In 1891, however, Thoms had a serious illness and a slight shock, 'which must have affected his mind.' He

162

was looked after by Nurse Morrison, whom he regarded as his 'life preserver.' In 1893, he made the will which referred to being in at the 'general scramble at the resurrection':

What did they think of the state of mind of the man who wrote that?

The same will left Nurse Morrison £100, but it was significant of Thoms' state of mind that the legacy was not repeated in his subsequent testament. He had forgotten the great services that he had acknowledged she had rendered him. In November, 1895, said Cooper, Melrose came on the scene, and counsel went into the evidence of his drinking. Within a month of being found drunk in the Sheriff's bed, the Sheriff had left him an annuity of one hundred pounds: 'That showed an extraordinary state of mind.'

Next Cooper dealt with the eccentricities, and made great play with them:

And what did they think of a man who made rules covering 20 pages of printed matter for his servants, of one of Sheriff Thoms's position going down to such trivial and pettifogging details as that? What did they think of a man who set up an elaborate system of fining his servants, marking down pennies here and twopences there, and did not exact them? Was it not making a fool of the whole affair? (Laughter.) If he had exacted the fines, and given the money to the infirmary, there might have been some sort of reason in it,[3] but to go through that system in the way he did was perfectly ridiculous. He not only fined his servants, but he fined the cat. (Laughter.) What did they think of a man of 60 years of age going about marking down on a slate pennies and twopences against the poor cat? (Laughter.) Then there was the sweet william which he planted in his back garden, one piece for each of his maids to take the place of sweethearts. (Laughter.) What was the state of mind of a man like that? Then he went down to the kitchen and climbed on the dresser to see whether there was any dust, and opened the shutters of the window to find whether it had been dusted. They did not expect that of a rational mind. Again, there was his laughing waistcoat, and more absurd still, his flirtation waistcoat, in the pockets of which he put camphor to prevent matrimonial germs from infecting him. (Laughter.) Counsel thought the Sheriff would have been a much better man if the matrimonial germs had infected him. (Laughter.)

Then, having spoken of the Gregory's mixture, and the three dozen pairs of gloves, Cooper continued:

And, last of all, he had lamentations with young ladies about the broken state of his own and their hearts. They would remember that he carried about gutta-percha to seal up the cracks. Counsel suggested that the gutta-percha might have been applied to healing up cracks in the poor old man's head. (Laughter.)

The Lord Justice-Clerk – To cement the loose slates. (Laughter.)

Cooper dismissed Thoms' claim to be head of a clan as no less ridiculous than had he claimed to be the heir of Julius Caesar:

Frank Towers Cooper, KC earlier in his career. He was 'never seen to greater advantage than in uphill cases, which he fought with unfailing good humour and invincible courage.'

> Counsel then showed the jury a photograph, which, he explained, showed the Sheriff seated upon an ass. (Laughter.) He did not know whether it would be regarded as a case of like drawing to like, but it was symbolical of the man who was always wishing to appear in a way in which no sensible person would like to be seen.

In March, 1897, said Cooper, Melrose had got drunk, been dismissed, and then been reinstated. It was said that the servants conceived a spite against him, but it seemed rather that Melrose conceived a spite against the servants who had seen him drunk. Cooper listed the provisions in favour of Melrose that had been made in the various codicils:

> The Sheriff had learned his lesson that 'One there is above all others / Well deserves the name of friend.' Yet the 'friend and valet' of June was the drunken servant of September 1896…A sad part of the case was that in April 1900 that poor old man, a physical wreck, removed to Cluny Drive, where he had none of his old servants, but was under the control of Melrose & Co.

Cooper pointed out to the jury that in a codicil of 1899 Thoms had left a thousand pounds to Kirkwall, so even if the last will was reduced, Kirkwall would still get something. As for that last will, Cooper said it was 'inexplicable' that Wood, having instructions to make that will, should have gone to consult Dr Affleck as to the Sheriff's state of mind:

> The state of his mind was shown by the fact that he cut away his heirs, and took away a legacy of £1,000 to Miss Irvine, who had worked well for him, and gave a very large fortune to the restoration of St Magnus Cathedral, Kirkwall – a doubtful project. In the circumstances that could hardly be the will of a man of sound disposing mind. The Sheriff was under the delusion that he was a poor man, and that his relatives desired his death. Kirkwall cathedral, counsel pointed out, could be restored

in two ways. Mr W. W. Robertson told them it would cost £60,000 to restore it. On the other hand, it appeared that for about £3,000 Kirkwall cathedral could be put into the condition of a church somewhat like St Giles. What the jury were asked to do by the defenders was to decide that Kirkwall cathedral should get £50,000 or £60,000, which there could be no need for, and that the relatives of Sheriff Thoms should be left out in the cold. Was that just? Did they believe that Sheriff Thoms ever in his sane moments intended that such a state of things should happen?

Cooper asked the jury to give a verdict for the pursuers.[4]

Shaw's jury speech was quite different from Cooper's. His was not a detailed rebuttal of every allegation, but a bold and sweeping general attack on the pursuers' case with ridicule as its main weapon. He submitted that:

> . . . the pursuer had totally failed to make out any rational challenge of these deeds. He did not know how it struck the jury, but it rather appeared to him that they had been engaged for five days on a very fruitless search.

He took the wise precaution of sympathising with the jury:

> Five days was a considerable block out of a busy man's life, and it seemed to him regrettable, even apart from other considerations as to the exposure of family affairs, that they should have been engaged for five days hunting shadows.

But he gave them a cheeky warning against finding for the pursuers:

> That was what it came to. It was just chasing shadows, it was just suspicion and disappointed expectations, a trying to grasp here and there at something which would subject twelve countrymen of the pursuer to the observation for the remainder of their lives, that the pursuer wanted them to write themselves down in the category of that animal which was shown in the photograph. (Laughter.)

He continued:

> One was accustomed in cases of that kind to have a serious challenge founded upon serious grounds. Deeds of that kind were very sacred to the law. They were so sacred to the law as this, that they would never be overturned except upon demonstrative proof that the deceased's mind was unhinged. Therefore, they at once saw that were it not for the grotesque nature of the case itself they would be confronted with a very serious duty. It was very difficult to treat the case seriously, and the only serious aspect was that it was thought within the bounds of reason to present the case against that will to a Scottish jury.

There was flattery for the jury, if not for Shaw's opponents:

> He should have understood a jury in ignorant countries trying the case, but that a Scottish jury should have to adjudicate on that case, and that friends like Mr Hunter and Mr Cooper should be called upon to present it as serious baffled his comprehension. The ridiculous nature of the case reminded him of the remark of a theatrical person who once said to him that if they wanted to see a comedy in its most comical form they should put a heavy tragedian in the principal part. By imparting a heavy tragical air to the case they had had five days of real enjoyment.

Shaw then dealt briefly with Thoms' professional and public life. He referred to the correspondence with Lord Advocate Blair Balfour which showed that, notwithstanding Thoms' eccentricities, he was of sound, shrewd and intelligent mind. He referred also to Thoms' work on the various boards of which he had been a member:

> That was the public life of the man. It was the picture of a man active, acute, level-headed, and helpful in all his public duties. In private life he seemed to have been fond of the gun and fond of the game of golf. He had, however, a most terrible weakness – Mr Shaw hoped the jury would not think very badly of him for it – he loved a good dinner and a good glass of wine. (Laughter.) But, above all, in private life it was characteristic of the man that nothing could daunt his cheerful spirit. He was the gaiety of a party. He was the man to whom everybody looked to make things hum. With Thoms at the table they were sure of a jolly evening, and none the worse was he for that.

Shaw mentioned that Thoms had written a book on judicial factors; that one of his main tastes was antiquarian; that he was a Fellow of the Society of Antiquaries of Scotland; and that he loved ancient buildings. He was proud of his connection with St Giles cathedral, and another building he was interested in was Kirkwall cathedral:

> Above all – these being his tastes – it was interesting and rather beautiful to think of this man, debilitated by bodily disease, bearing up cheerfully and manfully, and showing an interest in others, a solicitude for their welfare, with kindly recollections of his past life, and cheerful demeanour to the world. Here and there a little ebullition of temper was shown if he was not properly attended to, but he was none the worse for that. A man was not much worth if he had not a little explosion now and again. (Laughter.)

After this, Shaw damned Alfred with the faintest of praise; or, more accurately, he damned him first, then praised him faintly:

The nephew seemed not to have shared any one of the tastes of his uncle, and Mr Shaw had not discerned in any part of the case any sense on the nephew's part of what might be called gaiety or humour. He was none the worse for that. The world required all kinds of people, and the very solemn view of life which the nephew took acted as a capital foil to the lighter view of affairs taken by the uncle.

Then, turning to Melrose's character, he stated that he was a man with one of the best records as a gentleman's servant he had ever come across.

Shaw next came to the nub of the case: the validity of Thoms' will and the alleged grounds of reduction. After mentioning the two bases on which the will was sought to be challenged, he continued:

> Sheriff Thoms had the right of every subject to make his own will. He had the right to change the provisions of his will. What was the nature of the evidence brought to show that the Sheriff was insane? He was said to be the subject of delusions. One of these was about the Clan Macthomas.

Here Shaw reached his most audacious. He said that:

> . . . he had thought that as Scotsmen we had some privileges left, and one of the privileges inalienable to every Highlander was to think that on sound investigation he was the head of his Clan. Everyone thought that except those who were too modest.

> The Lord Justice-Clerk – I hope you will exclude me. (Laughter.)

> Mr Shaw said he did so. The bench was superior to all human weakness. (Laughter.)

> The Lord Justice-Clerk – I may remember these words if you apply for a new trial. (Laughter.)

> Mr Shaw, continuing, asked what was all this about the Clan Macthomas. Many sane and rational gentlemen whom he had known thought they were heads of clans. One of the greatest clans was Clan Chattan, and in that clan were the Macphersons and the Mackintoshes and the Shaws – (laughter) – and on one occasion he was asked to determine whether the true head of that clan was Cluny Macpherson or the Mackintosh of Mackintosh, and his reply was that they were both younger branches of the original stock, which was the Shaws. (Loud laughter.)

According to Shaw's memoirs there was a roar from the court, after which the judge, gathering himself together, ordered immediate silence;[5] but the laughter was not suppressed for long. Shaw continued to address the jury:

> He did not know who was the real Macthomas. He might have a chance

of it himself – (laughter) – but at all events he declined to put that in the category of delusions going to the reduction of a will.

Coming to the end of his speech, Shaw turned to the subject of St Magnus Cathedral. He quoted from Dr Story's book, and also from Scott's *The Pirate*, to show the wide interest there was in the building. He then mentioned Thoms' comment to Logie on the subject of its restoration that the day would come and the man, and his other expressions of interest in restoring it:

> What was the use of rich old bachelors if they could not be drawn upon for money for high objects such as that? (Laughter.) He submitted there was no case for the jury. The Sheriff's will stood as a monument of his good sense, and it was prepared and executed with care and propriety. Mr Wood acted as a prudent man of business in getting his opinion of Sheriff Thoms' mental capacity confirmed by Dr Affleck. It was said that Melrose got the Sheriff to make his will, but it was a great shame that Melrose should be accused in face of the evidence of the witnesses, Dr Affleck testifying that the annuity and the life-rent of the house was no more than Melrose deserved, as he had prolonged the Sheriff's life in comparative comfort. He asked with confidence a verdict for the defenders.[6]

All that remained now before the jury retired to consider their verdict was for the Lord Justice-Clerk to deliver his charge. It was said of Macdonald that he had a great aptitude for dealing with juries,[7] and in the Thoms case his words were couched in an admirably clear and occasionally homely style, even if the charge itself was long and a little rambling. In jury cases it is always said that the judge is master of the law and the jury is master of the facts, but the judge, in his charge, deals of necessity with the evidence which has been led before him. Macdonald explained his role thus:

> My duty as a judge is to turn the matter over to the jury in a way which the counsel cannot do, because they each have their own side to fight – they are fighting their case – and it is thought desirable, and has always been found desirable, that the judge, who is supposed to be a person of some experience in the world, and is able to apply that experience to the law, should give his assistance to the jury in considering the case. He is in no sense entitled to dictate to the jury any view as to the facts at all. All the facts of the case are for your consideration. Anything that the judge says is only for your consideration, and anything that has been said by the judge in charging the jury on matters of fact that does not commend itself to their reason or sense, they are quite entitled to reject, and they must act upon their own judgement.[8]

Whether a jury would be willing to reject the strongly-expressed opinion of a judge is another matter, and there were places in his charge where Macdonald expressed his opinions very strongly indeed.

He began, after a grumbling reference to 'this somewhat protracted case', by explaining two general principles of the law. The first was that, whereas a man could not in Scots law completely disinherit his wife or children, there was nothing to say he had to make provision in his will for more distant relations such as nieces and nephews. He was 'master of his own fortune'. Secondly, capacity to make a will did not depend upon the ability to do everything that a man had been accustomed to do in the prime of life:

> . . . a man may be perfectly sound, perfectly of disposing mind, though he may no longer be as fit as he was for the rough business of life, where it calls upon him to exercise mental powers to a great extent.[9]

Macdonald then moved on to consider the particular case before them, and began by restating the two main questions they had to answer: whether Thoms had mental capacity to make his last will and whether, if he had such capacity, he was nonetheless weak and facile and easily imposed upon, and was so imposed upon to make the will and other codicils. He then examined Thoms' history before his health began to break down, and in particular his undoubted eccentricities:

> . . . apparently his great desire was, being a man of a very good-humoured nature, to pass as a funny man. Like most good-humoured people also, he sometimes had irascible fits. People who are keen and good-humoured are often at times irascible. It is very much like the sudden diversion of a stream of water from one direction to another. At one time it may be the water flowing calmly in its bed, and in a moment when you turn round it may be going in somebody else's face. Such a character is a contrast to what is exhibited by people of a more cold temperament, who are neither exuberant on the one hand nor violent upon the other. Some people like the first character best – I must say I do myself. I would rather have a friend who was jolly and good-humoured, though he occasionally lost his temper with me, than a cold uninterested friend who did not give any liveliness to life.[10]

This was one of his Lordship's more subtle observations.

Macdonald stated that Thoms had been a professional success, otherwise he would not have held the offices of Advocate Depute and then Sheriff. He said there was no doubt that he had been extremely proud of his sheriffship and everything connected with it, and that:

> . . . he became very much attached to his Sheriffdom and delighted in the Orcadians, as many other people who have gone to these distant islands have done before him.[11]

He had, moreover, been very attentive both to his Sheriffdom and to his duties. Yet he had these eccentricities which the pursuers founded upon. Macdonald proceeded to list them and comment upon them. On the fining of the cat he said:

> I think I can understand that. Though the cat could not be expected to pay the fines, a great many things that happen in our houses are attributed to the cat, and if there is no other evidence than against the cat, the jokelet of putting a fine against the cat was rather sarcastic. It puts one in mind of what happened to a gentleman who was married to a relation of my own, who lived in a flat in one of the streets of Edinburgh. He was going upstairs in the dark one night, and he met a man coming down and bumped against him and said, 'Who are you?' 'Nobody.' 'You rascal,' he said, 'I have got you at last; you are the man who has been breaking all the china in my house for the last twenty years.'[12]

Having considered all the eccentricities, Macdonald concluded:

> I am afraid we must take it that the late Mr. Thoms, with all respect, was very fond of posing in comedy, very fond of creating a laugh, and indeed many of the witnesses have told us so. I am afraid also we must say that sometimes he slipped out of the role of the low comedian and got rather into the cap and bells of the jester; but still these are not things which, taken by themselves, would be of any consequence, I think, in considering the question of the man's mental capacity.

What the Lord Justice-Clerk called 'the true bone of contention – this Kirkwall cathedral', a pre-restoration view from the 1880s.

He said that no-one during the long years of Thoms' professional life had considered these things more than evidence of jocularity. He had made many friends and retained every one of them, so far as they knew, but not one of them had come forward to say that he attached any importance to these eccentricities. One of the witnesses had said that when he was not making jokes to amuse people he was just like any other man:

> It is clear that any attack on his testamentary powers before he became ill would necessarily fail if it were to be based upon such things as these.

Macdonald thought such things might be used as makeweights in a case where there was solid substantial weight put in the scale in the first instance:

> . . . but I think I may tell you that from the point of view of those who have been accustomed to deal with such cases, they are of no value whatever.[13]

The Lord Justice-Clerk then turned to the question of whether Melrose had used influence to induce Thoms to make the will and codicils. He said there was no direct evidence of that whatever, but there was no need that there should be. It could be inferred from circumstances. There was no doubt that Melrose had had the opportunity, if he could have done it, to influence Thoms. As to whether he had, all Macdonald would say was that this was unlike any case he had ever seen. He said that in such cases one generally found 'pregnant circumstances' inconsistent with the testator being free to act according to his own impulses. Here, the pursuers had something plausible to present, but:

> I must say that wherever there are dissensions among servants such things are always to be found.

Macdonald declined to make further comment, stating that he preferred to leave it to the jury without influencing them at all by any observations of his.[14]

If the jury decided that Melrose had indeed tried to influence Thoms, then they would also have to decide whether Thoms had been amenable to such influence; if, that is, he had been 'weak, facile and easily imposed upon'. If he had not been, then it would not matter if Melrose had tried to influence him. This question, like that of Thoms' capacity to grant his last will, required to be determined by reference to his mental state. It was this mental state which Macdonald discussed next.

He began by saying that the evidence on the question was exceptional, both in the varied character of the witnesses and their trustworthiness:

> Where the obtaining of a will from weak-minded people is alleged, there are generally very few people allowed to have access to them, so that they can see and test the person's capacity. There is generally some not very scrupulous business man mixed up with the proceedings. Gentlemen, in

this particular case, we are absolutely free from any such thing, unless it can be said with justice that Mr. Wood is a not very scrupulous business man. I must say I have heard with some pain – and indeed I was not sure I heard correctly – the observation that was made by the pursuers' counsel about Mr. Wood, that Mr. Wood, from something counsel suggested, must be inferred to have had doubts in regard to the capacity of Mr. Thoms. Gentlemen, Mr. Wood has come here to say that he did not have, and never had, any doubts upon that matter. I am very certain of this, that no man who knows Mr. Wood would fail to accept that as being the expression of his truthful sense of what the case presented to him was. He is a man above suspicion in every way.[15]

Having given this ringing endorsement to one of the defender's principal witnesses, and rapped Cooper's knuckles while he was at it, Macdonald then commended the evidence of Dr Affleck, stating that it was the first time he had ever heard that the doctor who attended a man through a long illness could give evidence of less value than a doctor who had never attended him professionally but was only a casual visitor. He then mentioned the other witnesses who had spoken in favour of Thoms' capacity, the lawyers, secretary of Northern Lights, and his personal secretaries, adding that not a suggestion had been made against either Mr Lessels or Miss Irvine. On the other side stood the two solicitors from Caithness and Shetland, whose evidence he proceeded to dismiss as already mentioned, adding:

> We are all liable to make mistakes, and people sometimes take up wrong-headed views; but if you can only pick out two cases during a man's twenty-five years as Sheriff of a county…I think that is a very thin ground to go upon to make out that the man was not fit to carry out his duties; and, of course, if he was fit to carry out his duties, he was fit to manage his own affairs.

As for the defender's witnesses:

> They all testified distinctly and strongly to the sustained mental capacity of Mr. Thoms in the conduct of business and everything else; and pray observe that all these people, I suppose, without exception, knew all about the facts as to the tawse, and the sweet william, and Acts of Parliament, and all the rest of it.[16]

There was then a digression while Macdonald went over the breakdown in Thoms' physical health and the appointment of Melrose as his attendant. He stressed the trying nature of Melrose's duties and the excellent record he had before being employed by Thoms, while accepting that 'upon more than one occasion' he had broken down and become intoxicated. However, he did not accept Dougall's statement that Melrose was always 'in the blues' with drink, which he took to mean that Melrose was constantly drinking. He did not think it was possible to conceive that Melrose could have fulfilled his duties with the regularity and care that he did unless that had been a 'grossly exaggerated and untrue statement' regarding him. Macdonald pointed out that everyone who came to see Thoms was allowed to see him freely. He said he believed Melrose's statement that the coming of a visitor was a great thing to him because it enabled him to get away a little. He emphasised that Melrose had attended Thoms for eight years without a single holiday, and he was never out of his master's sight except when asleep or for an hour or so when there were visitors:

> I have said already I do not believe – of course you are the judges – I cannot believe on the evidence I have heard that there is any truth in the statements which were made, and made somewhat emphatically by the pursuer, that Mr. Thoms was neglected and ill-treated.

He referred to all the visitors coming day by day and finding everything in order, everything tidy, everything right. He referred to the high character of the witnesses who said this, to the fact that those who could best judge thought Melrose had prolonged the Sheriff's life through the care he took of him. Finally, he referred to the witnesses who said that in Thoms' will Melrose had received nothing more than was reasonable and right for his 'extraordinary services' to Sheriff Thoms.[17]

If the Lord Justice-Clerk had been making his own views fairly clear up to this point, they became clearer still when he concluded his discussion of Thoms' general mental capacity:

> Well, during my long experience, I have never seen a case in which the weight of the evidence was so fatal to the idea of mental incapacity. There is real evidence down to within a short time of his death; and by real evidence I mean evidence which cannot be denied, - the evidence of circumstances, - that down to within a very short time of his death he was much occupied with business, and continued it with correctness, and was firm in maintaining his own views. Have you any doubt about that, gentlemen? I have had the trouble of looking through the whole of this volume from the beginning to end, containing 318 pages of correspondence, with I forget how many letters, and very many of them written with his own hand, and many of them written by his amanuensis or secretary, and from beginning to end of that whole volume I have been unable to find anything indicating that in any way that man was different from having the character of a clever, astute, diligent business man…I say that in the whole of that volume there is not a single thing to suggest extravagance in expenditure, or want of knowledge of his own affairs, or imprudence of any kind with regard to anything he was doing.

There are in these letters which I have read plenty of evidence to the effect that he was not a man who would allow anybody to dictate to him in his business, and that he had a decided will of his own. So I think, gentlemen, if you take that to be so, I think you will agree with me that there is no general evidence tending to shew that he was mentally incapable or mentally weak.[18]

There remained the question of the delusions, and Macdonald gave it short shrift, too, having first taken the trouble to point out to the jury that the allegations of delusions had been a late addition to the pursuers' case. On the clan chiefship, the Lord Justice-Clerk said it was his experience that when people got upon a question of genealogy and wanted to make out their ancestor to be some great person, they always succeeded in doing it:

> . . . people are willing to accept very slipshod evidence in order to persuade themselves that they are connected with some great one.

He thought it might be considered evidence of insanity in some cases if there was no plausible ground for it at all, but he did not think that would be the case merely because the grounds were insufficient. He added that Alfred had not suggested it was an insane delusion when he first agreed to assume the name 'Macthomas' as a condition for inheriting under Thoms' previous will, and that he had no doubt that had Alfred succeeded under the will he would not have attempted to impugn it. Likewise, he did not think Alfred had thought at the time that his uncle seriously believed he wished to kill him, or the doctor would have heard of it at once. As for saying he was poor, this is what people did when they did not want to part with money. This was particularly the case when asked for money for bazaars, and

Thoms and his flags. Caricature accompanying the poem 'A New Northern Streamer' in Ballads of the Bench and Bar.

Macdonald said he would do the same himself. Then there was the alleged delusion about Alfred neglecting his profession. Macdonald said that Thoms might well have been wrong about that, and he might well have acted upon it, but that did not mean he was suffering an insane delusion:

> In point of fact, his nephew was not pushing on; in point of fact, he was away for a long time from his profession, and Mr. Thoms may have taken

up the idea rightly or wrongly that his nephew was making a great deal about that accident from the football [*sic*] and wasting his time.

Then, having passed over the unpainted house, and the two kisses to the niece as being of little significance – the latter, said Macdonald, struck him as an incident of the most natural kind – he strongly directed the jury's attention to Alfred's attempt to have Thoms sign a testamentary writing on the night he died. This was an incident which was:

> . . . a very remarkable one in this case, and which I don't think we have any explanation of, and which I think strongly tends to indicate that the idea of insane delusions is an afterthought.[19]

Returning to Thoms' will, Macdonald expressed one of the questions for the jury in a new and rather loaded way:

> Now, did he understand that will when he dictated it, when he got it written out, when he examined it and made corrections on it with his own hand, and when, towards the end of the reading of it, when it might be expected that his acuteness would be off and he would merely appear to be looking upon it, he made the minute correction which appears on the face of the will? It is a question of fact for you to decide. It is not a question which depends upon doctors…The doctors' evidence is, as it is generally in these cases, conflicting.[20]

He also returned to the question of influence, upon which he had earlier stated his reluctance to make observations, and suggested some other questions for the jury to ask themselves:

> How does the evidence stand? Did Melrose at any time keep or try to keep Mr. Thoms from seeing his friends professionally or socially? If there is evidence that Mr. Thoms was kept from intercourse with others, that would be an important element in this case. That is generally one of the most pregnant circumstances in such cases, where facility is alleged. Has any such effort to keep him under some control been proved in this case? If it has, it would have an important bearing; if it has not, it has a very important bearing the other way.[21]

On what he described as 'the true bone of contention – this Kirkwall cathedral', Macdonald said that there were 'very, very different views' about restoration. 'Architects,' he said, 'are just like doctors – they differ.' But he reminded the jury that Thoms had been told that Dr Rowand Anderson, the foremost authority upon such buildings in Scotland, thought that a very large sum indeed would be required to restore St Magnus as it ought to be restored. What Thoms had left Kirkwall was a large sum, but it was not a sum that could not be spent in full in restoring the cathedral in a way that many architects would like to see done:

It is a great gift, no doubt; but quite possible – very likely – Mr. Thoms' opinion about himself, his exaltation, and desire to appear great in the eyes of people, may have guided him in this particular matter.[22]

There was one last peculiarity of the case that Macdonald wished to mention. This was that the testator had not forgotten his relations. Instead, he had left his nephews what Macdonald said many young men would have been glad to have, even if they had not, unlike these young men, already come into a substantial fortune from their own parents. Then, before a final reiteration of the main questions before them, the Lord Justice-Clerk made one other important direction on the law:

> . . . it is not for the law or for the jury to make a will for anybody, or to direct his property into what they think a more proper channel for it than that which his will expressed, nor to consider whether it is explicable that he should give such a large amount to a particular object. We have to deal solely with the questions of fact, which are to be decided by the evidence and not by guessing what might have been done.[23]

The jury retired at five minutes past three in the afternoon. Half an hour later they returned with their verdict. The foreman stated:

> We unanimously find that the late Sheriff Thoms was of a sound disposing mind when he executed the will of 16th March 1903, and we also find that the late Sheriff Thoms was not weak or facile in mind, or circumvented by Adam Melrose.

The will stood, and St Magnus had its money.[24]

X

Laughter in Paradise

Several of the newspapers across Scotland that had been reporting the trial's progress commented upon the outcome. For the most part, the comments were favourable and dwelt, understandably, on the more humorous aspects of the case. *The Dundee Advertiser* said it had afforded the country 'a first-class amusement for five days'. It continued:

> ... we have no doubt that the vast majority of people will agree that the twelve good men and true have interpreted the evidence aright. Indeed, it is clear that had they decided otherwise a gloomy solemnity would instantly fall upon every elderly gentleman in Scotland at once endowed with a sense of the jocose and property to dispose of at death. They would be merry at risk of raising the dread presumption of the soundness of their 'disposing mind'. They would crack their jokes with the fear of the witness before them, and would pause affrighted in the midst of their playful sallies with the horrified reflection that some day in Court their little extravagance of humour would be brought up against them as cold proof of mental decay.

'Rix' in the *Glasgow Evening News*, on the other hand, expressed in verse a thought that may have occurred to more than a few:

The Privilege of Sheriffship

Though he loved to crack his joke,
Looked for laughter when he spoke;
Though a waistcoat he would wear
Built to fascinate the Fair;
Still, the Sheriff seemed all there.

When he left the Kirkwall bench,
'Now,' said he, 'I must retrench' –
Though some sixty thousand pounds
Might have seemed sufficient grounds
To start motor-cars and hounds.

When he carried in his vest
Gutta-percha of the best,
To repair the female heart
Scarified by Cupid's dart –
That was humour, on his part.

This interpreter of laws
Always kept a pair of tawse
In his pocket, for he felt
Children need a frequent welt
(And he did not wear a belt).

Though his candid soul he prided
On a vest elastic-sided;
Though when mirthfully inclined,
By him Thomas Cats were fined,
He'd a 'sound disposing mind.'

Here's the Moral at the end –
SHERIFFS, as I apprehend,
Though their kin be disinherited,
In manner quite unmerited,
By – what adds to their vexation –
Some cathedral Restoration;
Whatsoe'er they do or say,
Howsoe'er their humour play,
In the most eccentric vein –
They are, *ex officio*, sane.[1]

Appealing as such scepticism may be, especially when viewed in the light of the Lord Justice-Clerk's heavily-weighted charge, there can be little doubt that the verdict was the right one. All that the law requires is that the testator be capable of comprehending the nature and effect of the act of making the will. No-one who reads the evidence of the preparation of Thoms' will could be in any doubt that he understood and approved not just every line but every word of it. There can hardly be one testator in a hundred who has such a detailed knowledge of his own will. Add to that the evidence of the volume of correspondence, Thoms' doctors, clerks, friends and visitors, and it would have been a perverse jury indeed that held the will should fall.

And yet, simply to conclude that Thoms was sane seems somehow inadequate. Some assessment, if not explanation, of his character is called for, given the quite singular way in which he behaved. 'Eccentric' is a rather over-used word, which can include so much as to have hardly any meaning. Moreover, it is sometimes said that the true eccentric does not realise that there is anything unusual or abnormal in his behaviour. If that is true, Thoms was no eccentric, for his was a knowing eccentricity, a self-conscious and wilful desire to be different and to be thought funny. It was, too, a desire to be liked and to be noticed. What factors of nature and nurture combined to produce that desire can only be imagined. Although he was neither the first nor last short person to ensure that the world did not overlook him, there was doubtless more to it than that.

There is something child-like if not childish in a desire always to be the centre of attention, and this quality can be discerned in other aspects of Thoms' behaviour too: the desire to get his own way; the sudden anger when thwarted that would disappear just as quickly; the blithe ignorance of having given offence; the fikes and fads; the playfulness; the kind-heartedness and the generosity. And yet, he had a very grown-up shrewdness, hard-headedness and practicality.

His kindliness and good humour, which the *Glasgow Herald* stated:

> . . . manifested themselves in all directions, and were comprehensive enough to include both his cat and his donkey.[2]

Often combined with that hard-headed practicality. There are numerous examples. Mrs Bruce, for one, spoke of how Thoms, after her husband's death, put himself to considerable trouble more than once on her behalf. He had also taken a great interest in her daughter, characteristically sending her a Christmas card every year, timed to arrive in Christmas morning's post in an envelope inscribed: 'With the Sheriff's Love'.[3] He showed similar concern for another Orkney Sheriff Clerk's daughter. John A. Bruce had been succeeded by Gold the factor's son, Andrew John, but both he and his wife had died within a short time of each other, leaving an orphaned daughter, Winifred. Thoms, who was

179

her godfather, took over payment of the premiums on a life policy for her, and in his will directed his trustee to continue paying them, as well as leaving her a hundred pounds. There were several lawyers to whom he gave advice and assistance at the outset of their careers, including G. F. Mathers who gave evidence, and Duncan J. Robertson who did not.[4] He also advised his Kirkwall landlady and put trade her way, but perhaps the paternalistic interest he took in those he encountered is best illustrated from the account of David Wilson, Chief Officer of the ss *Pole Star*.

Wilson had begun his career on the lighthouse vessels as a seaman on the *Pharos* in 1884. A friend of his mother's knew Thoms, and had asked him to help Wilson if he could, but he was equally willing to help any of the crew. He took pleasure in it, said Wilson, and did it several times. When Wilson applied for a post on one of the Fishery Board steamers, Thoms, who was also a Commissioner there, was most displeased that Wilson had not told him, for if he had he would have been able to help him. On the lighthouse vessels the Sheriff conducted divine service on Sundays and Wilson led the singing. Thoms, he said, was generally liked by the crew. On one occasion he remembered the Sheriff coming back to the vessel from a sale of work on shore where he had bought a small present for every crewman. Wilson kept in touch with Thoms after his retiral, and visited him with his wife and young son at Cluny Drive two months before the Sheriff's death. Feeble as he was, Thoms took time to speak to the little boy and pat him on the head before they left.[5]

It seems Thoms often did 'do good by stealth'. *The Scots Law Times* referred to his: 'many acts of kindness and unostentatious charity to the needy members of the community.'[6] It must, though, be admitted that doing good by fanfare was rather more his style.

Although there were a number of prominent exceptions, many people did like Thoms, despite his pepperiness; and possibly despite his humour too, or at least the more 'elephantine' parts of it. His humour could be sharp and it could be sly, but this was generally not when he was acting the 'funny man'. Then he had a tendency to repeat the same jokes over and over again until, said Duncan J. Robertson, all his friends and acquaintances knew them by heart. According to Robertson:

> . . . he always gave me the impression that all he wrote and said and did was with the view to having his jests and peculiarities included in a life or memoir at some time and I consider that his bequest to the cathedral is quite consistent with his whole character as a means of keeping his memory alive.[7]

Robertson was probably quite right, at least as regards the cathedral. For a man of Thoms' self-regard, the thought that he might be forgotten would have been a painful one. The long years during which he laboured over his numerous wills and codicils show that he was early conscious of his own impending death and anxious to leave something memorable after it. The assiduity with which he erected memorials to his forebears, whether in glass in Dundee Parish Church, in stone in the old kirkyard there, or in print in the clan book, suggests a desire to have the same done to him. And of course he made sure that it was, in the east window of St Magnus.

It took a little while to achieve that memorial, for much had to be done before restoration could commence. First, it had to be decided how the cathedral would be restored, and the arguments and concerns expressed by the architectural witnesses surfaced again almost immediately after the verdict. The following week Dr Thomas S. Clouston, Orkney-born pioneer of psychiatric medicine, wrote to *The Orkney Herald* on the topic. He agreed with the paper's editorial of the previous week that the Town Council should obtain a report on how the building was to be restored, and urged the Council to associate themselves with the County Council, landowners,

Sir Thomas S. Clouston, one of several prominent figures wary of what restoration might entail.

professions and representatives of commerce to form an advisory committee.[8]

Dismantling the old spire of St Magnus Cathedral. (Orkney Library Photographic Archive).

He also wrote to the Marquis of Zetland, as 'historic successor to Earl Rognvald' the builder of the cathedral, to draw his attention to the risk Thoms' legacy implied for the building. While the two architects mentioned in the will, Peace and Blanc, were, he said, good men to carry out a plan fixed on by learned and authoritative architects, neither had ever restored a Norman church or any other old church. Furthermore:

Mr Blanc's style of architecture is, I believe, modern French – a style which is as far from Norman as is possible. Much of what has been done by Mr Peace during the last 10 years is, in the opinions of good judges, bad.

181

Clouston urged Lord Zetland to use his great influence to get Kirkwall Town Council to seek 'really first class and competent advice.'[9]

Whether influenced by such opinions or not, the Magistrates proceeded very carefully. They did form an advisory committee, with representatives of the Church and the parish heritors, and then approached the President of the Royal Institute of British Architects to obtain the names of suitably qualified persons capable of handling the restoration. From the six names received they selected three Edinburgh architects, Blanc, John Kinross and George Mackie Watson, and invited each of them to submit a report with plans and estimates. These were then remitted anonymously for adjudication by an assessor, J. J. Burnet of Glasgow, who had also been appointed on the recommendation of the RIBA President.[10] Kinross's submission featured cast bronze doors, an ornately-carved pulpit and canopy, and paintings to fill the triforium arches,[11] but the plans that the assessor placed first were the rather more conservative ones of Mackie Watson.[12] Even so, there were criticisms of some of his proposals, particularly the tall copper-clad spire and the encaustic-tiled flooring in the choir. His most radical suggestion, to remove the South Transept rose window, was not accepted.[13]

In his original letter to *The Orkney Herald,* Clouston had pointed out that as Earl Rognvald had assessed the whole of the cultivated lands of Orkney for the purpose of building the cathedral, every Orkney man and woman had a 'historic

A postcard of Thoms lampooning the cathedral's benefactor – note the halo - and the proposed restoration, 1909. The 'runes' along the bottom read: 'Saint Magnus Prayer. From the tender mercies of the restorers good Lord deliver us.'. (Orkney Library Photographic Archive).

and moral claim to be heard through their representatives' on how the building was to be restored.[14] Quite a few followed him into the correspondence columns of the local press, where the future of the cathedral proved a perennial topic over the following years. While most comment focused on the architectural aspects of the restoration, there was also resentment at the entire building being given over for the use of the Established Church of Scotland instead of being kept, as Clouston put it, 'above and away from all modern sectarian differences.'[15] Two of the most persistent Kirkwall critics were William Cowan of Tankerness House and the merchant and antiquary, J. W. Cursiter.[16] The former belonged to what might be termed the apoplectic school of letter-writing:

> Clap a copper green nightcap on the head of the Venus de Medici, and ornament the Apollo Belvedere with a cone extinguisher. That's the way to do it; and this is the way the Thoms money is to go – (Bah!!)[17]

In another letter he dismissed Thoms as 'a foolish old woman.'[18] Cursiter by contrast expressed his feelings rather more elegantly:

> Leave it alone as a Father's house to which every prodigal son may, when sick of the husks, have the chance of returning and finding it the same as he left it, and not: 'empty, swept and garnished.'[19]

Some critics went so far as to produce a postcard 'Dedicated to the Provost, Magistrates & Town Council of KIRKWALL in the Orkneys by the Shade of Ruskin and by all true Lovers of our ancient & unadulterated cathedral' poking fun at Thoms and the restoration in both pictures and verse. In the middle of its various lampoons a photograph of the Sheriff sitting cross-legged with his pipe, a bottle and a self-indulgent grin had acquired a halo and the caption 'Saint Magnus restored!', while a supposedly runic inscription at the bottom read: 'Saint Magnus Prayer: From the Tender Mercies of the Restorers Good Lord Deliver Us.'[20]

The restoration eventually began in 1913 and took until 1930 to complete.[21] By 1918 the congregation was able to move into the restored nave and transepts so that work could commence in the choir,[22] and in the spring of 1921 the Thoms memorial window was finished.[23] Although £9,000 from the Thoms' bequest had been, with the sanction of the Court of Session, set aside to fund ongoing maintenance, by the 1950s this had proved to be hopelessly inadequate. In 1958, the Society of the Friends of St Magnus Cathedral was formed to help raise additional funds. [24] Then in the early 1970s it was found that serious structural problems had developed owing to sinking foundations and that there was a danger of the west end of the nave collapsing. £300,000 was raised by an appeal committee and a concealed network of steel girders was installed to save the building.[25]

The restoration funded with Sheriff Thoms' money has generally been viewed as sensitive and beneficial. At any rate, one never hears anyone, in the words of *The Dundee Advertiser* immediately after the case, express: 'vain regrets for the vanished sombre beauty of the weather-toned ruin.'[26]

What would have befallen the cathedral if it had not received Thoms' bequest can only be conjectured. It might well have been restored eventually, but whether on such a scale and to such a standard is another question. The cost in irreparable deterioration in the meantime might also have been great. Thoms' bequest was important not just for enabling a restoration to go ahead, but for ensuring that it did:

> Sheriff Thoms dead has been more potent with the Provost and Magistrates of Kirkwall than Sheriff Thoms alive could have hoped to be. It is doubtful whether in his lifetime the worthy Sheriff could have forced a restoration of St Magnus for twice £60,000; but there is no resisting the Sheriff's 'will' when it takes the shape of a last testament which leaves the necessary amount of money, and stipulates that it shall be expended in this particular manner and no other.[27]

In death he finally managed to force the Kirkwall authorities out of the pessimistic torpor that had frustrated him in life. For this, he had the east window dedicated to him and a new street named after him. It was no more than he deserved.

Time eventually saw Thoms' wishes fulfilled. It also produced some ironies, and the first of these arose a mere four months after the jury's verdict when Frank Towers Cooper KC was promoted to become Sheriff of Caithness, Orkney and Zetland. Memories of the Thoms case were still fresh when he arrived in Kirkwall that August for his first sittings. There was the usual assemblage of county officialdom in the courtroom and there were the usual speeches of welcome, albeit with some slightly unusual references, for if Cooper thought everyone would be too polite to mention his recent doings in the jury court, he was mistaken. His substitute, William Harvey, got the ball rolling. To general laughter he warned his new superior to be careful what he said. When he was taken to see the Earl's Palace and the Bishop's Palace he should not speak about restoring them. He should be chary of expressing the hope that the means and the man might be found. Any words of that kind would be carefully treasured and made a note of, and might give rise to expectations which, said Harvey, at a very distant date, might be doomed to disappointment when his will was opened. W. P. Drever, on behalf of the Orkney Bar, carried on where Sheriff Harvey had left off. Amid his words of welcome, he said that they knew Sheriff Cooper:

> they knew him too well as one of those *illuminati* – one of those evil spirits of Parliament House – (laughter) – who besought the Supreme

Court to say that the blessed bequest of £60,000 was no bequest at all, and worst of all – or best of all – it is wonderful what paradoxes time and place create – to find and declare that the great St George – one of his predecessors in that judgement-seat – was a fool – a born fool – (laughter) – and to rob good Christians of a sacred shrine.

Provost John Sclater, speaking next, steered clear of lawyers' humour, contenting himself with complimenting the new Sheriff on his. He praised him for his honourable conduct of the case and assured him that not one atom of ill-feeling existed over anything he had said in the Supreme Court.

In reply, Cooper entered into the spirit of the occasion. He said he had wondered whether he should arrive in Kirkwall in an armoured train, or if a good strong coat of steel plate would be sufficient:

> At one time while he was crossing the Pentland Firth from the adjoining kingdom of Scotland, he thought he might perhaps exercise his authority as Vice-Admiral of the Pentland Firth – (laughter) – which honour had not yet been definitely conferred upon him – (renewed laughter) – and order the captain of the St Ola to direct his course past these islands, which were not safe – (laughter) – and take him direct to the farthest point of his Sheriffdom at Lerwick, and then send a telegram that he greatly regretted that owing to illness he was unable to come to Kirkwall. (Laughter.)

He added that such feelings had been dispelled by the warmth of his welcome. Later he mentioned the cathedral:

> He would always be an interested spectator, and take a very great interest in the restoration of the cathedral. Old buildings and old things had always had an intense interest for him, and if he could have his way he should like to see every building in the country that had an ancient history and architectural interest restored. Nothing would give more pleasure to him if he could, during his tenure of office, see this magnificent old building, which they had preserved more or less intact – he must not say how much – (laughter) – restored to all its pristine glory. He was very much delighted with the sight of the building, which he had never previously seen, and he hoped that before he was called away to any other place, he would see that building thoroughly restored through the generous gift of a very generous man, and well spent upon an object which was always very near and dear to him. (Applause.)[28]

In the event, Cooper remained Sheriff for only another three months, resigning to contest the Leith Burghs constituency for the Unionists at the ensuing General Election.[29]

His clients had not appealed against the jury's verdict, but they did contest the amount of expenses claimed by Kirkwall Town Council. Thus in January, 1907, almost two years after the trial and over a year after resigning his sheriffship, Cooper found himself back before the Second Division of the Court of Session arguing on behalf of the Thoms siblings that the Provost and Magistrates of Kirkwall were not entitled to the costs of noting precognitions and of citing witnesses who were not in the end examined in court. The Second Division rejected his arguments and awarded Kirkwall the expenses claimed.[30] In total, the pursuers were found liable for £1,784: 18s 11d, of which £412 was due to Kirkwall and £1,372 to Thoms' Trustee.[31] Although the latter amount was largely met by around a thousand pounds of rents and accrued interest owed by the Trustee to Alfred and Harry in respect of the Aberlemno and Crescent properties, the pursuers still had to pay their own lawyers in addition. The whole litigation probably cost them in excess of four or five thousand pounds.[32]

To give some meaning to these figures, £1,400 was the price fetched by Thoms' house at Cluny Drive when it was sold in the autumn of 1905.[33] Adam Melrose had decided immediately after the jury trial that, with the attacks made on him in court and the resulting publicity given to the house, it was impossible for him to continue to live there with any degree of pleasure. The property was therefore sold and Melrose was paid the income from the sale proceeds in lieu of his liferent. He also received a fee for the services he had rendered during the preparation of the defence case, recompense for his expenditure in looking after the house since January 1904, and was allowed to purchase the liferented furniture outright.[34] He moved with his wife and daughter to an address in Montpelier Park, Bruntsfield, where he died aged 78 in December, 1923, almost exactly a year after his wife. Their daughter Susan stayed there till her own death, unmarried, in 1962.[35]

Alfred Thoms remained in practice as a Writer to the Signet in Edinburgh and lived to the advanced age of 86. He died in 1958. Four years earlier he had agreed with Kirkwall Town Council that Aberlemno should be sold to the sitting tenants, the proceeds invested, and the interest paid to him for the remainder of his life. Around the same time he had also done what, in the light of his actions in the will case, may seem a strange thing: he had petitioned the Lord Lyon King of Arms to be recognised as the Chief of Clan MacThomas (albeit with a capital 't'). In fairness, it must be said that in revising his opinion of the 'insane delusion' Alfred Thoms was, like his uncle before him, perfectly entitled to change his mind. He had also had longer than most in which to do so. Moreover, it seems that it was his elder son, not he, who was the driving force behind the application. In 1954, his son had been instrumental in founding the Clan MacThomas Society, and after Alfred's death he dropped the name Thoms, 'resumed' MacThomas and pursued the petition to the Lyon Court with renewed vigour. The petition was eventually granted in May, 1967, thus recognising Alfred's son Patrick Watt MacThomas of Finegand as 18th Hereditary Chief of Clan MacThomas.[36]

Today, Alfred Thoms' grandson is the Clan Chief, or *MacThomaidh Mhor* (but not 'Ye MacComish'). The Clan Society is vigorous, and has branches around the world in the former Dominions and the United States. There are clan gatherings, a clan magazine, clan merchandise (including tartan sashes, t-shirts and tea towels) and even a clan website.[37] On this last, Sheriff Thoms receives a brief mention as 'advocate, bon vivant and philanthropist'. One wonders what he would have made of it all. Perhaps a laughing waistcoat would have been called for.

Thoms' Shetland knitted nightcap and socks on display at the George Waterston Memorial Centre, Fair Isle. (Picture : Anne Sinclair)

187

St Magnus Cathedral, still dominating Kirkwall town centre thanks to Sheriff Thoms. (Drew Kennedy)

188

The dramatic East Window with its scenes of the crucifixion and the ascension and an inscription in memory of Sheriff Thoms. (The Orcadian)

189

Lammas Fair, Kirkwall 1913, watercolour by Stanley Cursiter (Orkney Islands Council)

St Magnus Cathedral, Kirkwall 1914, watercolour by Stanley Cursiter (Orkney Islands Council)

Stained glass window presented to Kirkwall Town Hall by Sheriff Thoms showing King Hakon Hakonson with the Sheriff's Coat of Arms above. His motto, virtutis praemium, means 'the reward of virtue'. (Picture by Martin Findlay).

194

The Nave, St Magnus Cathedral 1914, watercolour by Stanley Cursiter (Orkney Islands Council)

Kirkwall Volunteers 1807, a cartoon originally in the old prison of Kirkwall Tolbooth. It was presented to the County of Orkney by Sheriff Thoms in 1899 and hung in the Jury Room of Kirkwall Sheriff Court. (Picture by Martin Findlay, courtesy of Sheriff Principal Sir Stephen Young, Bart.).

'The Fair of St Olaf, Kirkwall', 1874, by Waller Hugh Paton, RSA, RSW, 1828-95. Presented to the County of Orkney by Sheriff Thoms in 1899 and hung in the Sheriff's chambers at Kirkwall Sheriff Court. Prior to Thoms acquiring it, it had been exhibited with the motto: 'Making good the saying odd/ Near the Church and far from God.' (courtesy of Sheriff Principal Sir Stephen Young, Bart.).

196

Appendix

Thoms in Verse and Song

M. T. Stormonth Darling's *A New Northern Streamer* given in Chapter I
was not the only verse to be inspired by Thoms' doings. The following three
compositions are by Charles Neaves (1800 - 1876), Advocate and man of
letters, Sheriff of Orkney and Shetland 1845 - 1852, and later, as Lord Neaves,
a Senator of the College of Justice. They are reproduced from *Ballads of the
Bench and Bar* (1882).

Th-ms and I.

The High Church is not full,
The service is but dry,
But always as a general rule,
We're present, TH-MS and I.

Others may come and go,
Of Dr. ARNOT shy,
But each week TH-MS his face doth show,
And each three weeks do I.

The Provost sometimes comes,
And Magistrates forbye,
But not so often near as TH-MS,
Nor yet as oft as I.

How glad would ARNOT be,
When casting round his eye,
If many others he could see
As staunch as TH-MS and I!

Then ARNOT speak not soft,
Nor lisp a lullaby,
Lest he below and I aloft
May slumber, TH-MS and I.

Th-ms isn't There

To the High Church I went as the bells had done ringing,
And I sat all alone in the President's chair;
Dr. ARNOT'S soft voice gave a Psalm out for singing,
When I marked in the corner that TH-MS wasn't there.

I scarcely could credit my ocular lenses,
But thought them bewitched with some glamour or glare;
Then I asked: 'Am I fairly bereft of my senses,
Ah no! it's too certain that TH-MS isn't there.'

O! what has come over our constant attendant?
His presence among us we never can spare;
The service on him is so clearly dependent
That we scarce have a *quorum* when TH-MS isn't there.

Is Orkney in need of his interposition?
Is some Danish invasion demanding his care?
Or has Wick broken out into open sedition
Lest the *brand* be abolished – that TH-MS isn't there?

I remember our grief, when consorting with dancers,
If a good vis-à-vis didn't fall to our share.
Now as TH-MS'S bright form as a vis-à-vis answers,
No assembly can charm us if TH-MS isn't there.

I shall send to his house on our very next Sunday,
And make sure of his plans ere to church I repair;
For I fear I might give up the ghost before Monday,
If, with ARNOT inaudible, TH-MS wasn't there.

The Re-opening Services at St. Giles

O Pride is a passion that should be repressed,
Though it isn't so easy to baffle its wiles;
But, if e'er it could lawfully fill a man's breast,
It was *then*, when it throbbed beneath TH-MS' Sunday vest
As the people convened to re-open St. Giles.

The work, thus accomplished, by him was begun;
Of hearty supporters he won us the smiles;
His zeal and good humour shone bright as the sun,
And he well might exult when the business was done,
And the people convened to re-open St. Giles.

For getting subscriptions he knew the best arts;
He brought to the point avaricious old files;
He got into their pockets as well as their hearts;
The stingiest fogie his tribute imparts,
And the people thus meet to re-open St. Giles.

Even now his bland look, with his bag in his hand,
His victims at once to their fate reconciles;
His touching appeal not a soul can withstand,
Though we scarcely expected a double demand
When the people should meet to re-open St. Giles.

But hark! Would that organ so near to JOHN KNOX
Make him think some illusion his fancy beguiles?
Or if not, would he feel it the direst of shocks
That a kist fu' of whistles his memory mocks,
When the people thus meet to re-open St. Giles.

I don't think he would – for no bigot was he
To condemn solemn strains where no blemish defiles;
If from Popery's errors we keep the Kirk free,
I believe he'd be glad our improvements to see,
When the people thus meet to re-open St. Giles.

199

'Tis a splendid success, both within and without!
I would walk to enjoy it a good many miles;
To see Judges and Lawyers and Doctors devout,
And friend TH-MS in his glory thus moving about,
When the people have met to re-open St. Giles.

Rejoice then, dear TH-MS, that your church is renewed,
Or re-edified, say, in the purest of styles;
But let this, I beseech you, be well understood,
Let the *edification within* too be good,
When the people convene to re-visit St. Giles.

The following verses are from a song written by Sheriff-substitute Alexander Nicolson and sung by him when a guest at a Northern Lighthouse Commissioners' dinner on 2nd February, 1872. The full version is given in W. McCombie Smith's book:

Air – 'A Wet Sheet and a Flowing Sea'

O would that I a Sheriff were,
I heard a young man sigh;
O might I but a Sheriff be,
A happy man were I.
My pockets should be lined with gold,
Which now are bare of tin;
My cheeks should wear health's ruddy glow,
Which now are gaunt and thin.

O if I were the Sheriff of
A county by the sea,
I would not envy any man,
However high he be.
I do not mean a Substitute,
Far higher I aspire;
A Sheriff-Depute's place is that
Which stirs my bosom's fire.

The office of a Sheriff is
A good thing in itself;
It bringeth power and dignity,
And a moderate share of pelf.
But ever to my fancy still,
The best of all his rights
Is that he shines with steady ray
Among the Northern Lights.

'Tis pleasant for a single night
Among those lights to shine;
But oh! To be a fixèd star,
I would that lot were mine.
I'd barter all the hopes I have
Lord President to be,
If only I could be made sure
Of a county by the sea.

How joyous on the *Pharos'* deck,
In charge of Captain Graham,
In Public Safety's noble cause
To dare the 'saut sea faem'!
In such a ship, in such a cause,
It's happy I should be
To visit every blessed Light
That guards the Scottish sea.

* * *

In Orkney and in Shetland Isles,
To me it would be joy
To visit every Light that shines
'Twixt farthest Unst and Hoy.
O why did perverse fate to Thoms
That island realm assign?
I like Thoms well, but, truth to tell,
I would his berth were mine.

Punch, 5th March, 1887, published a cartoon and song ridiculing 'The Jolly Commissioners' such as 'Gorging Jack' and 'Guzzling Jimmy' and their cruises of inspection. The song, or shanty, includes the lines:

> Says Guzzling Jim unto Jackee,
> 'Oh, what a lot of Lighthous*es* I see!
>
> 'But they all appear mos' dre'fully shaky
> The Lighthouses appear mos' horr'bly shaky!
> It's very fortch-nate that we came to see.
> Thesh Lighthousesh are not stead*ee*.
>
> 'I think the Lighthouses have been drinking,
> I think the Lighthouses have been drinking,
> They have been taking too much whis*kee*!
> They have been taking too much whis*kee*!'

 This caricature of Thoms is an initial letter from the poem "The Re-opening Services at St Giles' in *Ballads of the Bench and Bar* (1882)

202

Sources, Bibliography & Abbreviations

Andorsen, Harold F. (ed.), (1949), *Memoirs of Lord Salvesen.*

Baikie, Samuel (2001), *Reminiscences of the cathedral Church of St Magnus since 1846 by an Eye Witness.*

Ballads of the Bench and Bar, or Idle Lays of the Parliament House (1882).

Buchan, John (1913), *Andrew Jameson, Lord Ardwall.*

---- (1940), *Memory Hold-the-Door.*

Burke's Landed Gentry of Great Britain, 19th Edition, Volume 1.

Callaghan, Steve and Wilson, Bryce (eds.) (2001), *The Unknown cathedral.*

Census records.

Closed Record: *Closed Record in Reduction Alfred Patrick Macthomas Thoms and Others against William A. Wood (Thoms' Trustee) and Others*, 5th July, 1904, Orkney Library 374.1Y.

The Courier.

Cursiter, Stanley, 'Billy Peace the Provost's Dog', in Howie Firth (ed.) (1995), *In from the Cuithes, An Orkney Anthology.*

Dictionary of National Biography.

Dundee Central Library.

Edinburgh Medical Journal.

Encyclopaedia of the Laws of Scotland (1926).

Evidence: Notes *of Evidence in Jury Trial Thoms and Others v. William A. Wood (Thoms' Trustee) and Others* 4th, 6th, 7th, 8th and 9th February, 1905, Orkney Library 374.1Y.

Ewing, Rev. William (ed.) (1914), *Annals of the Free Church of Scotland 1843-1900.*

Fawcett, Richard (1988), 'Kirkwall cathedral: an Architectural Analysis', in Barbara E. Crawford (ed.) *St Magnus Cathedral and Orkney's Twelfth-Century Renaissance.*

Fereday, R. P. (1986), 'The Lairds and Eighteenth-century Orkney', in R. J. Berry and H. N. Firth (eds.), *The People of Orkney.*

---- (ed.) (2000), *The Autobiography of Samuel Laing of Papdale 1780 – 1868.*

Fraser, John (1935), 'Some Transactions of the Vice-Admiral Depute of Orkney in 1801 – 1803' in *Proceedings of the Orkney Antiquarian Society* volume XIII.

Ginsburg, Madeleine (1982), *Victorian Dress in Photographs.*

Goodfellow, Rev. Alexander (1912), *Sanday Church History.*

---- (1925), *Two Old Pulpit Worthies of Orkney.*

Grant, Sir Francis J. (ed.), (1944), *The Faculty of Advocates in Scotland 1532 – 1943 with Genealogical Notes.*

Hall, Lesley A. (1998), '"The Great Scourge": Syphilis as a medical problem and moral metaphor, 1880 – 1916', posted at www.lesleyahall.net.

Hansard.

Head, Carol (1982), *Old Sewing Machines.*

Hossack, B. H. (1900), *Kirkwall in the Orkneys.*

Hunter, James (1976), *The Making of the Crofting Community.*

John O' Groat Journal.

Kennedy, N. J. D. (1896), 'The Second Division's Progress', viii *Juridical Review,* p 268.

Lindsay, R. S. (1935), *A History of the Mason Lodge of Holyrood House (St Luke's), No.44.*

MacPhail, I. M. M. (1989), *The Crofters' War.*

MacThomas of Finegand, Andrew (2009), *The History of the Clan MacThomas.*

Manson, Thomas (1991), *Lerwick During The Last Half Century (1867 – 1917).*

Manson, T. M. Y. (1996), *Drifting Alone to Norway: the Amazing Adventure of Betty Mouat.*

McGlashan, John (1868), *Practical Notes on the Jurisdiction and Forms of Process in Civil Causes of the Sheriff Courts of Scotland* (4th edition by Hugh Barclay).

Mooney, Harald L. (1975), *The Story of St Magnus Cathedral.*

---- (1989), 'The Twentieth Century', in H. W. M. Cant and H. N. Firth (eds.), *Light in the North.*

Mooney, John (1943), *The cathedral and Royal Burgh of Kirkwall.*

Morton, George A. and Malloch, D. Macleod (1913), *Law and Laughter.*

Mullay, Sandy (1996), *The Edinburgh Encyclopaedia.*

North Highland Archive.

Northern Ensign.

The Northman.

OA: Orkney Archives.

OL: Orkney Library.

Oliver & Boyd's New Edinburgh Almanac and National Repository for the year 1867.

Oliver & Boyd's New Edinburgh Almanac for 1883.

Omond, G. W. T. (1914), *The Lord Advocates of Scotland, Second Series 1834 – 1880.*

The Orcadian.

The Orkney Herald.

Peace's Orkney and Shetland Almanac Advertiser 1895.

Pearsall, Ronald (1969), *The Worm in the Bud: the World of Victorian Sexuality.*

Porter, Roy and Rousseau, G. S. (1998), *Gout the Patrician Malady.*

Public General Statutes.

Queen's Regulations 1879, printed in *The Navy List* July 1885 and reproduced on www.pbenyon.plus.com.

Quétel, Claude (1992), *The History of Syphilis.*

Rendall, Jocelyn (2002), *A Jar of Seed-Corn.*

Schrank, Gilbert (1995), *An Orkney Estate.*

Scots Law Times.

The Scotsman.

Scottish Biographies 1938.

Shaw of Dunfermline, Lord (1921), *Letters to Isabel.*

---- (n.d.), *The Other Bundle.*

Shennan, Hay (1933), *A Judicial Maid-of-all-work.*

The Shetland Times.

Smith, Janet Adam (1965), *John Buchan.*

Smith, John (1907), *The Church in Orkney.*

Smith, William McCombie (1890), *Memoir of the Families of McCombie and Thoms* (Second edition).

Smout, T. C. (1986), *A Century of the Scottish People 1830-1950.*

Society of Writers to Her Majesty's Signet, *Regulations respecting Apprentices and Intrants to the Society*, 1st February, 1897, printed in *The Court of Session and Sheriff Court Annual 1898-99.*

Statutory Registers of Births, Marriages & Deaths.

Thomson, William P. L. (2000), *The Little General and the Rousay Crofters* (2nd edition).

Tidy, Henry Letheby (1930), *A Synopsis of Medicine* (5th edition).

The Times.

Tudor, John R. (1883), *The Orkneys and Shetland; their Past and Present State.*

Tweedsmuir, Lady (1947), *John Buchan by his Wife and Friends.*

Wilson, A. (1911), *The cathedral Church of St Magnus, Kirkwall, Orkney; Notes on its History, Present State, and Proposed Restoration.*

www.bankof England.co.uk/education/Pages/inflation/calculator

www.caithness.org

www.clanmacthomas.org

Notes

Chapter 1

1   Fawcett (1988) p 102.

2   The Bank of England inflation calculator gives the value of £60,000 in 1903 as £6,178,064.51 in 2012 (http://www.bankof England.co.uk/education/Pages/inflation/calculator/index1.aspx). However, if one proceeds on the basis that each 1903 pound sterling was represented by a gold sovereign containing 8 grams of 22 carat gold, current gold values give an equivalent figure of almost twelve million pounds.

3   Will of George Hunter Macthomas Thoms dated 16th March, 1903, and registered in the Books of Council and Session 14th January, 1904. Ownership of the cathedral was vested in the Provost and Magistrates by virtue of the burgh's royal charters.

4   *Evidence* p 65 (A. P. M. Thoms); Grant, p 207.

5   1881 Census.

6   McCombie Smith, Chapters VI & VII; Grant, p 207; *Scots Law Times* 31st October, 1903; *The Orkney Herald* 4th November, 1903; *The Shetland Times* 31st October, 1903; OA K10/12/2/1 Precognition of Thomas William Ranken. He was appointed an Advocate-Depute by Lord Advocate James Moncreiff in 1862, and also served under his successor George Young from 1869. His appointment would have fallen when Moncreiff was out of office during the Conservative administration of 1866-8; *Encyclopaedia of the Laws of Scotland* vol v, p 183; Omond*; Oliver & Boyd's Almanac 1867*.

7   In full 'Sheriff of the Sheriffdom of the Shires of Caithness, Orkney and Shetland' (Commission in favour of George Hunter Thoms, Esquire, Advocate, entered in OA SC11/1/12 Diet Book of the Sheriff Court of Orkney 1863-1876, 22nd August, 1870).

8   At Burravoe in Shetland; Stromness and St Margaret's Hope in Orkney; and Thurso and Lybster in Caithness.

9   For a fuller account of the confusing nomenclature of Sheriffs, see note 13 in Chapter 4 below.

10 McGlashan, Chapter I; Sheriff Courts (Scotland) Acts 1838 and 1853; Sheriffs (Scotland) Act 1870; OA D99/1/1 Diary of James Robertson 22nd and 23rd August, 1870.

11 Shennan, p 11.

12 OA K10/12/2/3 Precognition of D. P. Henderson Esquire of Stemster; OA K10/12/2/1 Precognition of Gifford Gray; he was also a curler, a bowler and a fisherman (McCombie Smith, p 188).

13 *Habits of Good Society* (c 1860) quoted Ginsburg. Just over a century later the fashion was revived in shirts.

14 *Evidence* p 2 (Rev. John Mackenzie Gibson).

15 OA K10/12/2/3 Precognitions of Col. James Honyman Henderson and D. P. Henderson Esq, of Stemster.

16 *Evidence* p 2 (Rev. John Mackenzie Gibson).

17 OA D99/1/1 Diary of James Robertson, Friday 19th August, 1870.

18 OA K10/12/2/1 Precognition of Mrs Jane Heddle Bruce.

19 OA K10/12/2/1 Precognition of Mrs Jane Heddle Bruce.

20 *Evidence* p 241 (Lord Ardwall); Shennan, pp 9ff.

21 The Court of Session Act 1830 abolished the High Court of Admiralty in Scotland and transferred its jurisdiction to the Court of Session and the Sheriff Courts. Inferior Admiralty jurisdictions, however, though no longer strictly necessary, were permitted to continue. All Thoms' predecessors after 1830 continued to hold the office of Vice Admiral, although his immediate predecessor, Adam Gifford, does not appear to have had it officially confirmed by the Admiralty. Thoms petitioned the Admiralty in 1872 but did not receive their commission until 25th August, 1883 - OA K10/12/2/1 Precognition of Thomas William Ranken and extracts from the Admiralty Court Diet Book.

22 Shennan, p 9.

23 *Queen's Regulations* 1879.

24 Shennan, p 9. Gregory's Mixture is a compound of ground rhubarb root, ginger and magnesia, the legacy to a grateful posterity of James Gregory (1753 – 1821), controversialist and Professor of Medicine at Edinburgh University. Thoms wore the uniform on 'state occasions' (OA K10/12/2/1 Precognition of T. W. Ranken), and most years was seen wearing it in the Lord High Commissioner's procession to the opening of the General Assembly (*The Shetland Times* 30th May, 1891).

25 OA K10/12/2/3 Precognition of D. P. Henderson Esquire of Stemster; OA K10/12/2/3 Precognition of Adam Melrose.

26 *Evidence* p 323 (Lord Justice-Clerk's charge). Thoms was not unique. Tudor urged those visiting Fair Isle to take a pocket enema with them: 'One or two lives might have been saved here, and in Foula, had this simple means of relief been within reach.' (Tudor (1883), p 430).

27 T. Manson, p 258.

28 T. Manson, p 234; *Evidence* pp 266-7 (William Cowper). He also had a memorial window installed in St Mary's Parish Church, Dundee, in honour of his ancestors (McCombie Smith, pp 175 & 215).

29 *Evidence* p 2 (the Rev. John Mackenzie Gibson). The pair of Thoms' socks on display in Fair Isle have been darned (information from Anne Sinclair).

30 OA K10/12/2/1 Precognition of William Roger Mackintosh, quoting from his *The Orcadian* report of the occasion. The lecture on darning was probably that delivered by Thoms on an occasion in the early 1870s when he took the chair at a penny reading organised by the Kirkwall Young Men's Literary Association (K 10/12/2/1 Precognition of Mrs Isabella Baikie Bremner or Fyffe or Bailey).

31 Shennan, p 9.

32 *The Scotsman*, 25th January, 1882; *The Shetland Times*, 28th January, 1882.

33 Fraser. Another version of this story, described as one preserved by the burghers of Kirkwall, is found in the *Northman* (Kirkwall) 31st December, 1892, copied from the *Scottish Leader*. According to it, Thoms had sent word out to a visiting British man-of-war that he was to pay a 'state visit' and the crew were all lined up on deck to receive him: 'After some little difficulty had been overcome in climbing up the man-of-war's side, the Vice-Admiral, panting, reached the deck. Here he found all the men on the broad grin. It was plain they were smiling at him, and even the officers looked uncommonly pleasant. Having satisfied himself by a hurried glance that his uniform was all right, the Vice-Admiral shook hands with the officers, and after being shown over the ship took his departure. The sailors were still smiling, and the cause of their mirth was disclosed to the Sheriff when he overheard an old salt growl – "Call himself an admiral, when he boarded us on the wrong side!"'

34 *Ballads of the Bench and Bar,* pp 30-31. The author was M. T. (later Lord) Stormonth Darling (Shennan, p 10). The poem is also reproduced by McCombie Smith, pp 186-7, adding an explanatory note that a set of flags always consists of two, the smaller being for windier weather.

35 *The Shetland Times* 21st August, 1880.

36 OA K10/12/3/1 Print of documents for the defenders, May, 1904; OA K10/12/2/1 Precognition of Alexander Sutherland, SSC. If the sketch is indeed by Sambourne it does not bear much resemblance to his published work.

37 *The Shetland Times,* 18th August, 1888.

38 *The Shetland Times,* 1st September, 1888.

39 *The Shetland Times,* 4th August, 1883.

40 T. Manson, p 253. The stone was laid 31st July, 1883.

41 Subsequently Schoor & Co, then Schoor, Muir & Co.

42 OA K10/12/2/1 Precognition of Mrs Muir; *Peace's Orkney and Shetland Almanac Advertiser 1895* advertisement for Messrs Schoor & Co.

43 *The Scotsman,* 7th June, 1886.

44 *The Scotsman,* 30th October, 1886.

45 *Northman,* 31st December ,1892.

46 *The Shetland Times,* 13th November ,1886.

47 *The Shetland Times,* 29th May, 1886, quoting the *North British Advertiser.*

48 'It is said that not one could be induced to come, on account of some silly notion that something unbecoming was required in the matter of dress! This is not creditable to Unst.' Basil R. Anderson, *The Shetland Times*, 13th November, 1886.

49 *The Shetland Times*, 29th May, 1886, quoting the *North British Advertiser*.

50 *The Shetland Times*, 13th November, 1886.

51 *The Shetland Times*, 29th May, 1886.

52 T. M. Y. Manson; *The Shetland Times*, 13th November,1886.

53 *The Shetland Times*, 8th May, 1886.

54 *The Scotsman*, 15th October, 1886.

55 *The Shetland Times*, 28th August, 1886.

56 *The Shetland Times*, 29th May, 1886, quoting the *North British Advertiser*.

57 OA K10/12/2/1 Precognition of Mrs Muir; *Peace's Orkney and Shetland Almanac Advertiser 1895* advertisement for Messrs. Schoor & Co.

58 OA K10/12/1/6 Precognition of David Munro Kirkness.

59 The Free Library got £50, the Balfour Hospital £100, and Kirkwall Burgh School a medal for the best girl, as well as the books mentioned below – OA K10/12/1/6 Precognition of Nicol Spence; K10/12/2/1 Precognition of John McEwan M.A.

60 OA K10/12/2/1 Precognition of Duncan J. Robertson.

61 The cathedral was almost certainly a topic of conversation at dinner on the day Thoms was sworn in as Sheriff. One of his fellow guests at Robertson's table was the expert on the building, Sir Henry Dryden (OA D99/1/1 Diary of James Robertson, Monday 22nd August, 1870).

62 OA K10/12/2/1 Precognition of Isaac Costie.

63 *The Orkney Herald*, 29th July, 1891; *The Scotsman*, 24th July, 1891.

64 OA K10/12/1/6 Precognition of Nicol Spence.

65 *Evidence* pp 265- 267 (William Cowper).

66 OA K10/12/2/1 Precognition of William Roger Mackintosh, quoting from his *The Orcadian* report. It should not, however, be thought that the magistrates did not want the building restored or did not wish for some means of doing so to materialise. In 1898, when Thoms refused Provost Nicol Spence's request for a subscription for some other purpose on the grounds that he could not afford it, the Provost replied that he was disappointed to hear it, as he had always lived in hope that Thoms was to do for Kirkwall cathedral what Dr Chambers had done for St Giles: an intriguing piece of evidence, the possible significance of which was not explored (OA K10/12/1/6 Precognition of Nicol Spence).

67 *Evidence* pp 310-11 (James S. S. Logie, MD).

68 McCombie Smith, p 185.

69 First edition 1859, second edition, edited by H. J. E. Fraser, 1874; McCombie Smith, p 179; *Scots Law Times*, 31st October, 1903.

70 OA K10/12/3/1 Print of documents for the defenders, May, 1904.

71 McCombie Smith, pp 185 & 188; *Oliver & Boyd's Almanac for 1883*.

72 McCombie Smith, p 180. The past tense is curious. It may simply reflect the past tense of his involvement in the restoration. Certainly his funeral was taken by the minister of St Giles, and there is no mention in the case records of his having transferred his religious allegiance elsewhere. However, he told the rector of Kirkwall's Episcopal Church that he almost always attended divine worship there when in the town (OA K10/12/2/1 Precognition of Rev. J. B. Craven). There were also attempts by his relatives' counsel to make the point that he was not a religious man.

73 McCombie Smith's account, possibly written by Thoms himself (see below), does not make his father's Free Church loyalties explicit (p 175), and they did not prevent his father being one of the ancestors honoured in the stained glass window Thoms funded in the parish church.

74 *Ballads of the Bench and Bar*, p 26 ('Th-ms and I'), p 68 ('Th-ms isn't there'), and p 82 ('The re-opening services at St Giles'). See Appendix.

75 McCombie Smith, p 185. Thoms was initiated in Lodge St David No.36, Edinburgh, on 27th December, 1851, and subsequently also joined the Lodge of Holyrood House (St Luke's) No.44 (information from John Stevens; Lindsay, volume II, p 748). As well as holding a number of other Masonic offices, on at

least one occasion Thoms deputised for the Grand Master Mason at a meeting of the Grand Lodge of Scotland (*The Orkney Herald*, 9th July, 1884).

76 McCombie Smith, pp 180-1.

77 *Evidence* p 19 (Isabella Dougall).

78 *The Orkney Herald*, 6th March, 1878.

79 *Evidence* p 18 (Isabella Dougall).

80 In his tribute in Kirkwall Sheriff Court, Sheriff Cosens said that at the time he first knew him (presumably when Cosens went to the Bar in 1884), Thoms did not enjoy much practice or seem to care for any (*The Orkney Herald*, 4th November, 1903).

81 www.caithness.org

82 *Evidence* pp 43-4, 47 (Nurse M. Morrison); p 147 (Dr J. O. Affleck); OA K10/12/1/6 Precognition of Benjamin D. C. Bell; OA K10/12/2/3 Precognition of D. P. Henderson Esquire of Stemster.

83 *Evidence* pp 4 & 9 (Rev. J. M. Gibson); p 31 (M. Bullions); p 57 (Alfred P. M. Thoms).

84 *Evidence* p 13 (Rev. J. M. Gibson).

85 *Evidence* p 4 (Rev. J. M. Gibson).

86 OA K10/12/2/1 Precognition of Andrew Stewart (legs to be made by the carpenter of the *Pole Star*); OA K10/12/1/6 Precognition of Mrs. Agnes Frisken or Grant (going to see Angus Buchanan, Solicitor, to see if he could get him a new pair); *Evidence* p 263 (G. F. Mathers W.S.).

87 *Evidence* p 215 (John Lessels); p 241 (Lord Ardwall).

88 *Evidence* p 91 (D. K. Murray); Copy Record, &c. in Appeal William Peace Drever v. The Orkney Steam Navigation Company Limited, Second Division, 22nd October, 1897, in possession of the author.

89 *Evidence* pp 253-4 (T. W. Ranken).

90 OA K10/12/2/1 Precognition of Miss Margaret Yorston.

91 OA K10/12/2/3 Precognition of Adam Melrose.

92 K10/12/1/6 Precognition of Mrs Agnes Frisken or Grant.

93 *Evidence* p 91 (D. K. Murray); *Evidence* p 23 (Isabella Dougall).

94 *Evidence* p 311 (James S. S. Logie); *Evidence* p 315 (Mrs Elizabeth Lees or Peace); OA K10/12/2/1 Precognitions of Alexander Sutherland and William Roger Mackintosh.

95 *Evidence* p 193 (Adam Melrose).

96 *Evidence* p 56 (Alfred P. M. Thoms).

97 *Evidence* p 196 (Adam Melrose).

98 *Evidence* p 4 (Rev. J. M. Gibson).

99 OA K10/12/2/3 Precognition of Adam Melrose; *Evidence* pp 63-4 (Alfred P. M. Thoms); Register of Deaths for the District of Morningside.

Chapter 2

1 –

2 The account of Alfred Thoms' relations with his uncle is, unless otherwise stated, drawn from *Evidence* pp 53-78 (Alfred P. M. Thoms).

3 OA K10/12/2/3 Precognition of Miss Emily Irvine.

4 The fees in 1897 totalled £345:1s:1d for the three- or five-year indentured apprenticeship (three years for Alfred as he was a graduate), with £137:17s:0d thereafter on becoming an intrant (*Regulations respecting Apprentices and Intrants to the Society*, 1st February, 1897). These fees had changed little in the preceding ten years (information from the WS Society).

5 *Evidence* p 56 (Alfred P. M. Thoms).

6 *Evidence* p 58 (Alfred P. M. Thoms).

7 now known as 'Ancient MacThomas' (MacThomas, p 89).

8 *Evidence* p 18 (Isabella Dougall); p 47 (Nurse Margaret Morrison).

9 *Evidence* p 88 (William McCombie Smith).

10 *Evidence* p 314-5 (Mrs Elizabeth Lees or Peace).

11 *The Shetland Times*, 21st February, 1891.

12 OA K10/12/2/1 Precognition of Mrs Jane Heddle Bruce.

13 *Evidence* p 6 (Rev. J. Mackenzie Gibson).

14 Thoms' solicitor, J. P. Wood, WS, expressed the opinion privately that Alfred had 'behaved in a manly way' about the matter (OA K10/11/2/11 Memorandum to enable Counsel to consider as to the Defence in the action for the reduction of Sheriff Thoms' will, etc, 18th May, 1904).

15 *Evidence* p 176 (John Philp Wood WS).

16 *Evidence* p 298 (Professor John Glaister); Copies of the wills and codicils from 1893 onwards are to be found in OA K10/12/3/1 Print of Documents for the Defenders, May, 1904.

17 OA K10/12/2/1 Precognition of Thomas William Ranken. The Ladies' Vestry is now the souvenir shop. On the inside wall Thoms' coat of arms can still be seen, painted and gilded, above the inscription: 'To the Glory of God and In Honour of S. Margaret. 1891.'

18 OA K10/12/2/3 Precognition of Adam Melrose; *Evidence* p 65 (Alfred P. M. Thoms). Alfred specifically mentions the undertaker also being a joiner. Presumably a man of Thoms' class would have been expected to patronise one of the more upmarket firms that devoted themselves exclusively to funeral direction.

19 OA K10/1/1 Thoms Bequest Minute Book No 1 3rd February, 1904 – 20th August, 1912, p 8 (3rd February 1904). Kirkwall Town Council may have told Alfred later that they would have been prepared to settle the matter amicably had they not been dissuaded by the Trustee's solicitors (OA K10/11/2/3/1 Draft letter to A. P. M. Thoms, 1906). Parties unwilling to compromise often blame their lawyers.

20 *Closed Record.*

21 OA K10/12/2/3 Precognition of Adam Melrose.

22 Unlike Scots criminal trials, with their juries of fifteen, civil jury trials are an import from England so have the smaller juries favoured there. They also have opening speeches by counsel, which likewise do not feature in criminal procedure.

23 *Scots Law Times*, 17th June, 1899.

24 *The Orkney Herald*, 8th February, 1905. Being a government law officer did not then preclude private practice. Although Salvesen was appointed Solicitor-General the week before the trial, Scott Dickson had been Lord Advocate since 1903 and Solicitor-General before that. It may be that they gave Alfred advice that he was unwilling to take.

25 He was given a judicial life peerage as Lord Shaw of Dunfermline, but on his retiral in 1929 was raised to the hereditary peerage as the 1st Baron Craigmyle.

26 Shaw's notice in the *Dictionary of National Biography*, written by his successor Lord Macmillan, is singularly sniffy, not only disparaging his talents in the field of pure law as opposed to advocacy, but suggesting that he had unacceptably cut corners in pursuing his ambitions.

27 He was the grandfather of the Lord Clyde who presided in the South Ronaldsay inquiry.

28 OA K10/1/1 Thoms Bequest Minute Book No 1 3rd February, 1904 – 20th August, 1912, pp 32 and 34.

29 Cooper was appointed Sheriff of Chancery and McClure Sheriff of Argyll (*Scots Law Times*, 11th February, 1905). McClure became Sheriff of Aberdeen, Banff and Kincardine in 1920, Garson Sheriff-substitute at Portree in 1929, and Jameson Sheriff-substitute at Edinburgh in 1923 (Grant).

30 1891 Census.

31 Sutherland 1874-6, Ross 1876-80, Perth 1880-5 (Grant, p 130).

32 *Evidence* p 323 (Lord Justice-Clerk's charge).

33 *Evidence* pp 321-3 (Lord Justice-Clerk's charge).

34 *The Scotsman*, 6th February, 1905.

35 *Evidence* p 30 (Margaret Bullions); p 103 (Mrs Isabella Gellatly Thoms or Smith).

36 *Evidence* p 46 (Nurse Margaret Morrrison).

37 *Evidence* p 242 (Lord Ardwall).

38 *Evidence* p 46 (Nurse Margaret Morrison); p 3 (Rev. J. Mackenzie Gibson).

39 OA K10/12/1/6 Precognition of Mrs Agnes Frisken or Grant. Afterwards she remarked to her husband that the Sheriff might have given the boy a sixpence instead of frightening him like that.

40 He added that as far as he understood 'the whole family were somewhat queer.' OA K10/12/2/1 Precognition of the Rev. J. B. Craven. Craven, too, had rejected a Free Church upbringing. He was a son of the Rev. John E. Craven, Minister of the Free Kirk at Bucksburn, Aberdeen (*The Orkney Herald* 23ʳᵈ April, 1924).

41 OA K10/12/2/1 Precognition of Miss Margaret Yorston.

42 OA K10/12/1/6 Precognition of David Wilson.

43 OA K10/11/2/11 Memorandum to enable Counsel to consider as to the Defence in the action for the reduction of Sheriff Thoms' will, etc., 18ᵗʰ May, 1904; *Evidence* p 12 (Rev. J. Mackenzie Gibson).

44 OA K10/12/1/6 Precognition of David Wilson.

45 OA K10/12/2/1 Precognition of Mrs Jane Heddle Bruce.

46 *Evidence* p 316 (Mrs Bruce).

47 OA K10/12/1/6 Precognition of Miss Hester Bruce.

48 OA K10/12/2/1 Precognition of Andrew Stewart.

49 *Evidence* p 246 (Sheriff Hay Shennan).

50 OA K10/12/2/1 Precognition of James Cullen Grierson; *Evidence* p 94 (Grierson).

51 OA K10/12/1/6 Precognition of Mrs Agnes Frisken or Grant.

52 *Evidence* p 122 (Miss Helen Jane Fleming – taken on commission at Rome).

53 OA K10/12/2/1 Precognition of James Cullen Grierson.

54 OA K10/12/2/1 Precognition of James Cullen Grierson; *Evidence* p 94 (Grierson).

55 A precognition is a statement noted by a solicitor or clerk from a prospective witness in the course of or prior to court proceedings. Typically, each side's witnesses will be precognosced on behalf of the side calling them and also on behalf of the other. This gives the respective solicitors or counsel an idea of what each witness can speak to, but witnesses can sometimes embarrassingly fail to 'come up to precognition'. Much depends upon the skill of the person who takes the precognition as to whether it truly reflects the probable evidence of the witness. Precognitions are neither read over nor signed by the witness, and need therefore to be treated at times with some caution. They have no force in the proceedings where only evidence on oath is accepted. Sworn precognitions made before the Sheriff are quite different items.

56 Despite the 'sneers of his own circle and the dislike of "the trade".' *The Shetland Times,* 6ᵗʰ August, 1892, quoting from a profile in *The Sunbeam Magazine.*

Chapter 3

1 –

2 Shaw (1921), p 253.

3 Ivory and his family visited Thoms at Cluny Drive - OA K10/12/2/3 Precognition of Adam Melrose.

4 Gladstone's Irish Land Act of 1881 had granted fair rents, security of tenure and free sale of tenancies.

5 For the 'Highland Land War' see Hunter, chapters 8 and 9.

6 One of his obituaries noted that 'the speedy restoration of order was largely due to the firmness and ability with which he handled a very difficult situation'(*Scots Law Times,* 13ᵗʰ November, 1915).

7 MacPhail, p 114.

8 Regulations by the Sheriff of Caithness, Orkney and Shetland for Apprentices, dated 27ᵗʰ February and registered 2ⁿᵈ March, 1871; Curriculum for Apprentices dated 29ᵗʰ November and registered 7ᵗʰ December, 1871, Kirkwall Sheriff Court Diet Book OA SC 11/1/12.

9 Procurators (Scotland) Act 1865, repealed 1873. McGlashan Chapter X.

10 OA K10/12/2/3 Precognitions of Robert S W Leith and William Cowper. The latter states that after the Society of Procurators of Orkney was established in 1889, Thoms gave them £60 for their library in 1890, £22:15:2 in 1892, and a guinea in each subsequent year until he resigned his sheriffship in 1899.

11 *The Shetland Times,* 24ᵗʰ August, 1889. A Shetland Faculty was not formed until February, 1983.

12 OA K10/12/2/3 Precognition of Robert S. W. Leith.

13 Thomson, pp 138 & 140. The use of such naval vessels to transport officials and others around was common. *The Shetland Times* of 22nd February, 1890, criticised the use of the gunboat *Firm* to move some Customs officers' families. A Caithness acquaintance of Thoms encountered him at Wick one very stormy day in oilskins, sou'wester and a foul temper because the gunboat *Jackal*, for which he had wired to take him over to Orkney, had not come because of the weather (OA K10/12/2/3 Precognition of D. P. Henderson, Esq. of Stemster).

14 *John O' Groat Journal*, 30th September, 1890.

15 *The Shetland Times*, 13th June, 1891.

16 *The Shetland Times*, 3rd October, 1891.

17 *The Orkney Herald*, 29th April, 1885.

18 *The Orkney Herald*, 3rd February, 1886; *The Shetland Times*, 20th March, 1886.

19 OA K10/12/2/1 Precognition of William Roger Mackintosh.

20 Shaw (1921), p 253.

21 *The Orcadian*, 26th December, 1885.

22 OL *Answers for John Macrae, SSC, Procurator-Fiscal of Orkney to the Bill of Suspension for the Rev. Matthew Armour v the said John Macrae*, March 6th, 1886.

23 Mackenzie was present on only the first day of the trial.

24 *The Orcadian*, 26th December, 1885; *The Orkney Herald*, 23rd December, 1885; OL *Answers for John Macrae SSC, Procurator-Fiscal of Orkney to Bill of Suspension for the Rev Matthew Armour*, March 6th, 1886. *The Orcadian* reported:- 'As showing the state of feeling in town, we may mention that on Monday morning, when Mr Cursiter, one of the witnesses, went to open his shop, he found the premises had been all smeared in a most disgusting fashion. The dastardly act is condemned on all hands, and we understand the police have been put on night duty ever since.'

25 *The Orkney Herald*, 3rd February, 1886.

26 Goodfellow (1925), p 185.

27 Goodfellow (1925), p 188.

28 Perhaps even in the same congregation as Armour. The latter for a time in the 1840s spent his New Year holidays in Dundee and attended St Peter's Free Church, the one in which Thoms' father was an elder (Goodfellow (1912), p 180).

29 Goodfellow (1925), pp 187-8; *The Orkney Herald*, 24th August, 1887. Goodfellow says Thoms was forced to apologise by the Lord Advocate. Although responsibility for matters relating to the administration of justice in Scotland still then lay with the Home Secretary (until September that year when the Scottish Secretary's powers were extended by the Secretary for Scotland Act 1887 [50 & 51 Vict. c. 52]), he performed his duties with the advice and assistance of the Lord Advocate. The Conservative Lord Advocate of 1887 was the Lord Justice-Clerk of 1905, John H. A. Macdonald.

30 Mellis's father was Free Church minister at Tealing in Forfarshire (*The Orkney Herald*, 9th November, 1887; Ewing, Vol. I, p 265). Thoms was not, of course, born into a Free Church family, being aged eleven when the Disruption led to the formation of that church. Goodfellow (1925), p 177, while referring to the three 'renegade Free Church men' who were the 'principal personages engaged in this prosecution business', does not name them, but the third must have been Macrae. Such changes of denomination were not uncommon. Macrae's funeral in 1888 was conducted in three rooms of his house at Crantit, St Ola, by his own minister, the Episcopalian Rev. J. B. Craven, a son of the Free Kirk manse, and the two ministers of the cathedral, one of whom, the Rev. John Rutherford, had been a minister of the United Presbyterian Church (*The Orkney Herald*, 19th September, 1888; J. Smith (1907), p 68).

31 Goodfellow (1925), p 185.

32 *The Orkney Herald*, 9th November, 1887.

33 *The Shetland Times*, 13th August, 1887. The fines were paid.

34 *The Orcadian*, 3rd September, 1887.

35 *Evidence* p 91 (David Keith Murray).

36 *The Shetland Times*, 12th March, 1892.

37 Solicitors in each Sheriff Court district took it in turns to act free of charge as agents for the poor. Before a potential litigant could be admitted to the Poor's Roll, however, he had to have a probable cause of

action and produce a certificate confirming his poverty granted by the Parish Minister, or two elders, or the heritor on whose lands he resided. A refusal to grant a certificate could result in the minister or others being summoned to appear before the court to give evidence on the matter and possibly found liable in expenses (McGlashan, pp 340-347). McGlashan gives a lengthy list of examples where parties had or had not been deemed impoverished enough to be admitted to the roll.

38   *The Shetland Times*, 4th August, 1883.

39   *The Times*, 25th August, 1887.

40   *The Shetland Times*, 15th September, 1888.

41   *The Scotsman*, 5th April, 1871.

42   *The Shetland Times*, 26th September, 1891.

43   off Shore Street, now demolished.

44   *The Orkney Herald*, 2nd September, 1885.

45   OA K10/12/2/1 Precognition of Alexander Sutherland, SSC.

46   OA K10/12/2/1 Precognition of Isaac Costie.

47   *The Shetland Times*, 13th August, 1887.

48   *The Orcadian*, 3rd September, 1887.

49   OA K10/12/2/1 Precognition of Thomas Hutchison.

50   OA K10/12/2/1 Precognition of Alexander Sutherland, SSC.

51   *The Shetland Times*, 20th August ,1887.

52   *The Orkney Herald*, 29th July, 1891.

53   *The Orcadian*, 3rd September, 1887.

54   *The Shetland Times*, 24th August, 1889.

55   OA K10/12/2/1 Precognition of J. Kirkland Galloway. His last, hearsay, example is possibly a garbled account of the Wick incident, mentioned below, involving a transcript of evidence.

56   OA K10/12/2/1 Precognition of James Cullen Grierson.

57   OA K10/12/2/1 Precognition of James Cullen Grierson.

58   OA K10/12/2/1 Precognition of Alexander Sutherland, SSC.

59   OA K10/12/2/1 Precognition of Alexander Sutherland, SSC.

60   OA K10/12/2/1 Precognition of Alexander Sutherland, SSC.

61   *John O' Groat Journal*, 29th February, 1888.

62   *John O' Groat Journal*, 6th December, 1892.

63   *The Shetland Times*, 1st February, 1890. In fact the Secretary of State only had power to remove Sheriffs-substitute.

64   OA K10/12/2/1 Precognition of William Roger Mackintosh.

65   *Evidence* p 214 (John Lessels); *The Shetland Times*, 19th April, 1884.

66   *The Orcadian*, 20th August, 1887.

67   see, eg, *The Shetland Times*, 24th August, 1889.

68   *The Shetland Times*, 8th November, 1890.

69   *Scots Law Times*, 15th May, 1897, quoting Dove Wilson's *Sheriff Court Practice* (1890).

70   OA K10/12/1/6 Precognitions of John Small and John S. Tulloch.

71   OA K10/12/1/6 Precognition of Nicol Spence.

72   Although it was alleged that Thoms removed eighteen pages, he insisted that he had only removed one sheet of four pages (*John O' Groat Journal*, 5th February, 1889; *The Scotsman*, 19th March, 1889).

73   OA K10/12/2/3 Precognition of D. P. Henderson Esq., of Stemster.

74   *The Shetland Times*, 12th May, 1888.

75   OA K10/12/2/3 Precognition of D. P. Henderson Esq., of Stemster.

76   OA K10/12/2/3 Precognition of Robert S. W. Leith.

77   *Evidence* p 92 (Shaw's cross-examination of D. K. Murray).

78 OA K10/12/2/3 Precognition of Robert S. W. Leith. Leith says it was Symon but adds that he was now a solicitor in Lerwick. Symon practised in Edinburgh.

79 *John O' Groat Journal,* 28th November, 1930.

80 *The Shetland Times,* 4th August, 1883.

81 Sheriffs (Scotland) Act 1747; *John O' Groat Journal,* 8th February, 1888

Chapter 4

1 –

2 eg, the case of the initials carved on the cathedral tower (*The Orkney Herald,* 29th July, 1891). In the case of a Latheronwheel fish curer who had falsified a fishing agreement, after the defence had called the local doctor and Provost Rae of Wick to testify to the accused's previous good character, the Sheriff declared that his good character only aggravated the crime, and sentenced him to the maximum permissible two years' imprisonment (*The Orkney Herald,* 8th May, 1878). The accused was called Alexander Sutherland. The lawyer of that name was the son of Alexander Sutherland, fish curer, Wick, who does not appear to have been the same man. Sutherland is one of the most common names in Caithness.

3 OA K10/12/2/3 Precognition of Robert S. W. Leith.

4 Harper's father had been Principal of the United Presbyterian College. The Rev. Ebenezer Erskine (1680 - 1754) and his brother Ralph led the First Secession from the Established Church of Scotland in 1733.

5 OA K10/12/2/1 Precognition of Alexander Sutherland, SSC.

6 OA K10/12/2/1 Precognition of James Cullen Grierson.

7 *The Shetland Times,* 17th December, 1887.

8 *The Shetland Times,* 26th September, 1891.

9 i.e. Town Clerk of Pulteneytown, then administered separately from the Royal Burgh of Wick.

10 Information from David Sutherland.

11 *Scots Law Times,* 30th January, 1904 (profile of Georgeson), 21st December, 1907 (obituary of Hector Sutherland); *John O' Groat Journal,* 28th May, 1897 (obituary of G. M. Sutherland), 28th November, 1930 (obituary of Alexander Sutherland); Register of Deaths in the Parish of Kirkintilloch, 1919 (David Cormack).

12 *John O' Groat Journal,* 12th October, 1887.

13 Although their motion in fact used the archaic term 'Sheriff-Depute' to refer to Thoms' office, in their speeches the Caithness lawyers used 'Sheriff Principal'. To avoid confusion, the latter term is used here throughout. The original office of Sheriff or Sheriff Principal was hereditary, passing with the ownership of land. Its holders, often having no legal training, appointed Sheriffs-Depute to carry out their legal duties, and these Deputes in turn appointed Substitutes. When the heritable jurisdictions were abolished after the '45, the Sheriff-Depute survived although no longer a depute of anyone. The Circuit Courts (Scotland) Act 1828 provided that the Sheriff-Depute could be referred to simply as Sheriff, and all Sheriff Court statutes from 1853 onwards used that term exclusively. Despite this, 'Sheriff', 'Sheriff-Depute' and 'Sheriff Principal' all continued to be used. Thoms liked to correct anyone who called him Sheriff Principal that the office did not exist.

14 Caldwell rejoined the Liberal Party in 1892 and was MP for Mid-Lanarkshire from 1894 to 1910 (*The Scotsman,* 27th April, 1925).

15 *John O' Groat Journal,* 18th July, 1888.

16 *John O' Groat Journal,* 25th July, 1888.

17 *John O' Groat Journal,* 25th July, 1888.

18 *John O' Groat Journal,* 1st August, 1888; *Northern Ensign,* 1st August, 1888.

19 North Highland Archive, Minutes of Wick Town Council 30th August, 1888.

20 *John O' Groat Journal,* 21st November, 1888; *Northern Ensign,* 21st November, 1888.

21 *John O' Groat Journal,* 8th August, 1888, 8th July, 1890.

22 Referred to again as 'Sheriff-Depute' (see note 13 above).

23 *John O' Groat Journal,* 5th February, 1889.

24 *The Scotsman,* 19th March, 1889; *Hansard,* 28th March, 1889.

25 *The Shetland Times,* 23rd February, 1889.

26 e.g. from the *Elgin Courant & Courier* reported in the *John O' Groat Journal,* 1st August, 1888.

27 *John O' Groat Journal,* 28th November, 1930.

28 One of the principal Crown witnesses was D. W. Georgeson, and prosecuting counsel was A. L. McClure, Kirkwall's counsel in the will case. *John O' Groat Journal,* 22nd June, 1900.

29 *John O' Groat Journal,* 30th December, 1890.

30 *John O' Groat Journal,* 16th June, 1891; *The Shetland Times,* 20th June, 1891, 30th January, 1892; OA K10/12/2/3 Precognition of John Philp Wood, WS.

31 Shennan, p 9.

32 Shennan, p 36.

33 *The Orkney Herald,* 4th November, 1903; *Scots Law Times,* 9th January, 1904.

34 Gilbert Schrank (1995), *An Orkney Estate,* p 90. James Cullen Grierson would also commit suicide, on 3rd July, 1915, aged 51. His death certificate, perhaps reflecting the conventional thinking of the period, states that he was of unsound mind at the time (Register of Deaths for the District of Lerwick). It is said that he had got drunk in Whalsay while on duty with the RNR and was facing a court martial (information from Brian Smith).

35 *The Orcadian,* 20th August, 1887, see above.

36 OA K10/12/2/1 Precognition of J. Kirkland Galloway.

37 OA K10/12/1/6 Precognition of John S. Tulloch.

38 OA K10/12/1/6 Precognition of John Small.

39 OA K10/12/2/3 Precognition of Robert S. W. Leith.

40 OA K10/12/2/1 Precognition of Alexander Sutherland SSC.

41 *John O' Groat Journal,* 30th August, 1892. The Wick substitute then was David J. Mackenzie. He had moved there from Lerwick in 1891.

42 Shaw, *The Other Bundle,* p 78.

43 Andorsen, pp 149-152.

44 Kennedy. He begins by quoting an earlier critical article of 1888.

45 OA K10/12/2/1 Precognition of Duncan J. Robertson.

46 OA K10/12/2/1 Precognition of J. B. Anderson.

47 George Hunter Macthomas Thoms Gray, born Albany Street, Lerwick, 11th July, 1895 (Register of Births for the District of Lerwick and Gulberwick). Admittedly, the Sheriff had dropped hints that he would like the child named after him. When the father asked Thoms his full name, Thoms suggested that to give the child all his names might be rather a burden (OA K10/12/2/1 Precognition of Gifford Gray).

48 *The Shetland Times,* 19th April, 1884. Thoms had just donated £45 to cover the cost of ventilating the Lerwick sewers, and the paper also referred to his offer to guarantee the remaining costs of Lerwick Harbour works the previous year.

49 OA K10/12/2/1 Precognition of Alexander Sutherland, SSC; *The Shetland Times,* 23rd January, 1904. Despite losing its frame at some point, the picture survived and was eventually restored, reframed and put on display in the new Shetland Museum in 2007.

50 *Evidence* pp 90–93 (David Keith Murray).

51 *Evidence* p 328 (Lord Justice-Clerk's charge); a rather unexpected remark to come from a senior judge.

Chapter 5

1 Shennan, p 10.

2 OA K10/12/2/1 Precognition of Obadiah Sutherland.

3 *Evidence* p 323 (Lord Justice-Clerk's charge).

4 *Evidence* pp 17-18 (Isabella Dougall); Shennan, p 10.

5 OA K10/12/2/1 Precognition of Miss Margaret Yorston.

6   OA K10/12/2/1 Precognition of Mrs Muir.

7   *Evidence* pp 17-20 (Isabella Dougall); pp 29-31 (Margaret Bullions).

8   OA K10/12/2/1 Precognition of Mrs Isabella Baikie Bremner or Fyffe or Bailey.

9   OA K10/12/2/1 Precognition of Miss Margaret Yorston.

10 *Evidence* p 2 (Rev. J. Mackenzie Gibson).

11 OA K10/12/2/1 Precognition of Mrs Isabella Baikie Bremner or Fyffe or Bailey.

12 *Evidence* p 18 (Isabella Dougall).

13 *Evidence* p 125 (Miss Helen Jane Fleming).

14 *Evidence* p 2 (Rev. J. Mackenzie Gibson).

15 *Evidence* p 18 (Isabella Dougall).

16 *Evidence* p 125 (Miss Helen Jane Fleming).

17 OA K10/12/2/3 Precognition of D. P. Henderson, Esq. of Stemster.

18 OA K10/12/2/1 Precognition of Mrs Isabella Baikie Bremner or Fyffe or Bailey.

19 OA K10/12/2/1 Precognition of Obadiah Sutherland.

20 OA D99/1/1 Diary of Sheriff James Robertson, Saturday, 16th August, 1873. Geddes was probably an army officer, William Loraine Geddes, Captain in the 53rd Regiment of Foot and brother-in-law of F. W. Traill-Burroughs the laird of Rousay.

21 *Evidence* pp 30 – 31 (Margaret Bullions).

22 *Evidence* p 18 (Isabella Dougall); p 30 (Margaret Bullions); only the latter mentions the glass.

23 *Evidence* p 102 (Mrs Isabella Gellatly Thoms or Smith).

24 *Evidence* pp 30 (Margaret Bullions); p 102 (Mrs Isabella Gellatly Thoms or Smith).

25 *Evidence* p 102 (Mrs Isabella Gellatly Thoms or Smith).

26 *Evidence* p 322 (Lord Justice-Clerk's charge).

27 *Evidence* p 3 (Rev. J. Mackenzie Gibson).

28 *Evidence* p 111 (Mrs Isabella Gellatly Thoms or Smith).

29 *Evidence* pp 30 (Margaret Bullions); p 20 (Isabella Dougall).

30 *The Orkney Herald* 15th February, 1905. This may be the animal Thoms was referring to in 1873 when he mentioned in a letter to Sheriff James Robertson that 'Lady' had glanders or a bad cold (OA D99/1/1 Diary of Sheriff James Robertson, 16th July, 1873).

31 OA K10/12/2/1 Precognition of James Cullen Grierson.

32 Shennan, p 10.

33 Register of Deaths for the District of Morningside.

34 *Closed Record,* p 19.

35 *Evidence* p 329 (Lord Justice-Clerk's charge).

36 *Evidence* p 136 (Dr Alexander Bruce).

37 *Evidence* p 286 (Shaw's examination-in-chief of Professor John Glaister).

38 *Evidence* p 147 (Dr J. O. Affleck).

39 *Henry IV, Part 2*, Act I, Scene ii.

40 Respectively Sydney Smith and Thomas Sydenham, both quoted in Porter and Rousseau p 3.

41 *Evidence* p 137 (Dr Alexander Bruce).

42 Porter and Rousseau p 4.

43 *Evidence* p 240 (Lord Ardwall).

44 Tidy, p222.

45 OA K10/12/2/3 Precognition of Dr Affleck.

46 *Evidence* p 3 (Rev. J. Mackenzie Gibson).

47 *The Scotsman* 6th February, 1905.

48 *John O' Groat Journal*, 4th May, 1887.

49 On 9th October, 1889, to a 51-year-old spinster Elizabeth Watson Wemyss (Register of Marriages in the United District of St Andrews and St Leonards in the County of Fife).

50 *Evidence* p 9 (Rev. J. Mackenzie Gibson).

51 Fereday (1986), p 242.

52 Examples from a slightly earlier period are the mistresses and children of George Traill of Holland, Papa Westray (1773–1840), nicknamed 'the Parish Bull' on account of his proclivities (Rendall, p 13). His lawful son, Thomas, was Thoms' 'smoking and imbibing' companion of 1873, later bankrupted through his taste for high living. The illegitimate son of Thoms' other friend Captain John Baikie was acknowledged, and rose to be a prominent Kirkwall wood merchant and contractor (Register of Deaths for the District of Kirkwall 1899; Baikie, pp 18-19).

53 Smout (1986), pp 163-5.

54 Pearsall, p 267.

55 *The Scotsman,* 6th February, 1905.

56 *Evidence* p 16 (Rev. J. Mackenzie Gibson).

57 Tidy, pp 222–228, 855.

58 Hall (1998).

59 Quétel (1992), pp 103-4.

60 *Evidence* p 7 (Rev. J. Mackenzie Gibson).

61 *Evidence* p 20 (Isabella Dougall).

62 *Evidence* p 49 (Nurse Margaret Morrison).

63 *Evidence* p 43 (Nurse Margaret Morrison).

64 *Evidence* p 44 (Nurse Margaret Morrison).

65 *Evidence* p 27 (Isabella Dougall). Dougall says this was McPherson, but Nurse Morrison says McPherson was the one who dropped the book and then resigned. Dougall lists the various menservants as Stewart, Reid, Murray, McPherson, Mackenzie and Hay. She misses out Gibson (*Evidence* p 27).

66 *Evidence* p 47 (Nurse Margaret Morrison).

67 *Evidence* pp 43ff (Nurse Margaret Morrison).

68 *Evidence* pp 44-5 (Nurse Margaret Morrison).

69 *Evidence* p 191 (Adam Melrose).

70 *Evidence* p 269 (John A. Forrest, WS).

71 Mr Hamilton Bruce (OA K10/12/2/3 Precognition of Adam Melrose). This presumably was R.T. Hamilton Bruce, the dedicatee of W. E. Henley's poem 'Invictus'.

72 *Evidence* p 45 (Nurse Margaret Morrison).

73 *Evidence* p 148 (Dr J. O. Affleck).

74 OA K10/12/2/3 Precognition of Adam Melrose.

75 *Evidence* p 194 (Adam Melrose).

76 OA K10/12/2/3 Precognition of Adam Melrose.

77 His starting salary, on entering Thoms' service on 14th November, 1895, had been five pounds a month, but was increased four months later (*Evidence* p 197 (Adam Melrose)).

78 *Evidence* p 199 (Adam Melrose).

79 OA K10/12/1/6 Precognition of David Munro Kirkness.

80 *Evidence* p 21 (Isabella Dougall).

81 *Evidence* p 23 (Isabella Dougall).

82 *Evidence* p 33 (Margaret Bullions) ; *The Scotsman,* 6th February, 1905.

83 *Evidence* p 48 (Nurse Margaret Morrison); *The Scotsman,* 6th February, 1905.

84 *Evidence* p 33 (Margaret Bullions); p 39 (Elizabeth Coghill).

85 *Evidence* p 23 (Isabella Dougall).

86 *Evidence* p 21 (Isabella Dougall).

87 *Evidence* pp 21 & 27 (Isabella Dougall).

88 *Evidence* pp 210–213 (James Hay).

89 *Evidence* p 45 (Nurse Margaret Morrison).

90 *Evidence* p 33 (Margaret Bullions).

91 *Evidence* p 33 (Margaret Bullions), p 38 (Elizabeth Coghill).

92 *Evidence* pp 21-2 (Isabella Dougall).

93 *Evidence* p 8 (Rev. J. Mackenzie Gibson), p 148 (Dr. J. O. Affleck).

94 *Evidence* p 33 (Margaret Bullions).

95 *Evidence* p 20 (Isabella Dougall).

96 *Evidence* p 25 (Isabella Dougall).

97 *Evidence* pp 60-1 (Alfred P. M. Thoms).

98 *Evidence* p 27 (Isabella Dougall).

99 *Evidence* p 192 (Adam Melrose).

100 OA K10/12/1/6 Precognition of Mrs Agnes Frisken or Grant.

101 *Evidence* p 36 (Margaret Bullions).

102 *Henry IV, Part 2,* Act I, Scene ii.

103 *Evidence* p 11 (Rev. J. Mackenzie Gibson).

104 *Evidence* p 229 (Miss Emily Irvine).

105 *Evidence* p 48 (Nurse Margaret Morrison).

106 OA K10/12/2/1 Precognition of Andrew Walls.

107 The same amount as the postage on the card. OA K10/12/2/1 Precognition of T. W. Ranken.

108 *Evidence* p 6 (Rev. J. Mackenzie Gibson).

109 *Evidence* p 105 (Mrs Isabella Gellatly Thoms or Smith). He spoke rather more favourably on the subject in 1888 when formally opening the third day of the St Bernard's Church Bazaar: 'If the Church of Scotland was to prosper in the future, she must be content to leave old-fashioned ways, and enter upon a war against the world in the shape of bazaars, and conquer it. His justification of bazaars had always been that if the Established Church was to keep its ground it must resort to the voluntary efforts of its members, and give them a lesson in what he ventured to say was the privilege of giving.' (*The Scotsman,* 5th March, 1888).

110 *The Scotsman,* 8th February, 1905.

111 *Evidence* pp 213-5 (John Lessels).

112 *Evidence* p 230 (Miss Emily Irvine); in 1898 Thoms, refusing a subscription to Duncan J. Robertson in Kirkwall, closed his letter: 'Thanking you for the opportunity you have afforded me.' (OA D20/4/19/5 George H M Thoms, 13 Charlotte Square, Edinburgh to Duncan J Robertson, 14th March 1898).

113 *Evidence* pp 312-3 (James S. S. Logie, MD).

114 *Evidence* p 6 (Rev. J. Mackenzie Gibson).

115 *Evidence* p 236 (Miss Emily Irvine).

116 *Evidence* p 134 (George Currie, C.A.).

117 *Evidence* p 105 (Mrs. Isabella Gellatly Thoms or Smith).

118 *Evidence* p 6 (Rev. J. Mackenzie Gibson); p 62 (A. P. M. Thoms).

119 *Evidence* p 7 (Rev. J. Mackenzie Gibson); p 48 (Nurse Margaret Morrison).

120 *Evidence* p 48 (Nurse Margaret Morrison).

121 *Evidence* p 20 (Isabella Dougall).

122 *Evidence* p 32 (Margaret Bullions).

123 *Evidence* p 24 (Isabella Dougall).

124 *Evidence* p 192 (Adam Melrose).

125 *Evidence* p 26 (Isabella Dougall).

126 *Evidence* pp 216-7 (John Lessels).

127 *Evidence* pp 36-7 (Margaret Bullions).

128 *Evidence* pp216-7, 222 (John Lessels).

129 *Evidence* p 19 (Isabella Dougall); p 43 (Elizabeth Coghill).

130 *Evidence* p 106 (Mrs Isabella Gellatly Thoms or Smith).

131 *Evidence* p 19 (Isabella Dougall).

132 *Evidence* p 106 (Mrs Isabella Gellatly Thoms or Smith).

133 *Evidence* p 29 (Isabella Dougall).

134 *Evidence* pp 214, 223 (John Lessels).

135 *Evidence* p 220 (John Lessels).

136 *Evidence* p 24 (Isabella Dougall). Nurse Morrison said she saw Melrose mixing up the salts and giving it to Thoms as mineral water. When she challenged Melrose, he allegedly replied, 'It is good enough for an old thing like that; he ought to have been dead long ago.' (*Evidence* p 49).

137 *Evidence* p 49 (Nurse Margaret Morrison).

138 *Evidence* p 48 (Nurse Margaret Morrison).

139 *Evidence* pp 23-4 (Isabella Dougall).

140 *Evidence* p 46 (Nurse Margaret Morrison).

141 *Evidence* p 23 (Isabella Dougall).

142 *Evidence* p 57 (A. P. M. Thoms).

143 *Evidence* p 22 (Isabella Dougall).

144 *Evidence* p 34 (Margaret Bullions).

145 *Evidence* p 49 (Nurse Margaret Morrison).

146 *Evidence* p 22 (Isabella Dougall).

147 *Evidence* p 107 (Mrs Isabella Gellatly Thoms or Smith).

148 *Evidence* p 34 (Margaret Bullions); p 39 (Elizabeth Coghill).

149 *Evidence* p 39 (Elizabeth Coghill).

150 *Evidence* pp 193, 195, 205, 209 (Adam Melrose).

151 *Evidence* p 222 (John Lessels).

152 *Evidence* p 15 (Rev J. Mackenzie Gibson).

153 *Evidence* pp 148-9, 158 (Dr J. O. Affleck).

154 *Evidence* p 15 (Rev. J. Mackenzie Gibson), p 150 (Dr J. O. Affleck).

155 probably St Cuthbert's – see Mullay, pp323-4.

156 *Evidence* pp 197, 210 (Adam Melrose).

157 *Evidence* p 6 (Rev. J. Mackenzie Gibson).

158 *Evidence* pp 192-4 (Adam Melrose); OA K10/12/2/3 Precognition of Adam Melrose; *The Orkney Herald,* 8th February, 1905.

159 Melrose records one of the visitors being Ramsay the carpenter and undertaker of Torphichen Street, calling about the Sheriff's coffin (OA K10/12/2/3 Precognition of Adam Melrose).

160 *The Shetland Times,* 30th January, 1904. The completed epitaph reads: 'Erected over the cremated remains of George Hunter Macthomas Thoms of Aberlemno, F.R.S.E., &c., &c., Advocate, Emeritus Sheriff of Caithness, Orkney and Shetland, and who was associated as Vice-Chairman with Dr. William Chambers of Glenormiston, in the restoration of St. Giles' cathedral, Edinburgh, 1879. Born at Dundee 3rd June 1831. Died at Edinburgh 25th October 1903. Aged 72 years. Mr. Thoms' coat of arms is registered 1881.' (*Evidence* p 65 (A. P. M. Thoms)).

161 OA K10/12/2/3 Precognition of Adam Melrose.

Chapter 6

1 –

2 *Evidence* p 46 (Margaret Morrison).

3   *Evidence* p 4 (Rev. J. Mackenzie Gibson).

4   *Evidence* pp 4-5 (Rev. J. Mackenzie Gibson).

5   *Evidence* p 13 (Rev. J. Mackenzie Gibson).

6   *The Scotsman,* 6th February, 1905.

7   *Evidence* p 19 (Isabella Dougall).

8   *Evidence* p 41 (Elizabeth Coghill).

9   *Evidence* p 31 (Margaret Bullions).

10 *Evidence* p 42 (Elizabeth Coghill).

11 *Evidence* p 25 (Isabella Dougall); p 35 (Margaret Bullions). He told Bullions that he would come back to say good-bye, which suggests a reluctance to face up to what parting with these servants entailed rather than any confusion over what was happening.

12 Mrs Dougall received a drawing-room walnut table, a walnut couch and four chairs (*Evidence* p 28); Bullions a lady's easy-chair covered with the Thoms' tartan (p 36); and Coghill a fancy drawing-room ebonised chair (p 42).

13 *Evidence* pp 40-1 (Elizabeth Coghill).

14 *Evidence* p 41 (Elizabeth Coghill).

15 *Evidence* p 42 (Elizabeth Coghill).

16 *Evidence* p 47 (Nurse Margaret Morrison).

17 *Evidence* p 46 (Nurse Margaret Morrison).

18 *Evidence* p 48 (Nurse Margaret Morrison).

19 *The Scotsman,* 7th February, 1905.

20 Register of Deaths in the District of St George and City of Edinburgh.

21 *Evidence* p 53 (A. P. M. Thoms).

22 *Evidence* p 55 (A. P. M. Thoms).

23 *Evidence* p 57 (A. P. M. Thoms).

24 *Evidence* pp 60-1 (A. P. M. Thoms).

25 *Evidence* pp 66-7 (A. P. M. Thoms).

26 *Evidence* pp 67-8 (A. P. M. Thoms).

27 *Evidence* p69 (A. P. M. Thoms).

28 The official transcript of the evidence sometimes records a witness's affirmative answer to a question as if it were a statement by the witness of the matter affirmed. This, therefore, was probably: 'Have you looked at these Acts?' – 'Yes.' The statement about the Grand Hotel may well fall into the same category. Elsewhere, eg in Cooper's re-examination of Harry Thoms quoted below, the shorthand writer gave a more sober record of an exchange than did the newspaper reporters. Whilst remaining an accurate record of the facts spoken to, it removes some of the colour and rhythm of the questioning.

29 *Evidence* pp 69-70 (A. P. M. Thoms).

30 *Evidence* p 70 (A. P. M. Thoms).

31 *Evidence* p 71 (A. P. M. Thoms).

32 *Evidence* pp 72-3 (A. P. M. Thoms).

33 *Evidence* pp 73-4 (A. P. M. Thoms).

34 *Evidence* pp 74-5 (A. P. M. Thoms).

35 *Evidence* pp 75-6 (A. P. M. Thoms).

36 *Evidence* pp 76-8 (A. P. M. Thoms).

37 *Evidence* p 68 (A. P. M. Thoms).

38 *Evidence* pp 78-80 (H. J. M. Thoms).

39 *The Scotsman,* 7th February, 1905. The official court shorthand writer rendered this exchange: '(Q.) "What do you hope your brother Mr. Alfred Thoms will do as regards the members of the family?" (A.) "I think reasonably he might give us a share, especially as I am joining him in the action."'(*Evidence* pp 80-81).

40 *Evidence* pp 81-2 (Mrs Grace Catherine Thoms or Hallowes).

41 *Evidence* pp 83-8 (Emily Thoms and Edith Thoms).

42 *Evidence* p 88 (William McCombie Smith).

43 According to the records of Dundee Town Council, the area in question was about $2^4/_5$ acres and consisted of sloping ground not intended to be built on at the south end of the Crescent development next to the made-up ground adjoining the Caledonian Railway line. When conveyed to the town, it was to be thrown open to public use as a westward extension of the Magdalen Green ('Minute of Meeting of Sub-committee of the Sub-committee [*sic*] of the Works Committee of the Town Council of Dundee, 21st February, 1896' in *Minutes of Meetings of the Town Council of Dundee and its Committees 1895-6*, Dundee Central Library, D42.6).

44 *Evidence* pp 89-90 (Robert Blackadder).

45 Baikie, p 10.

46 Hossack, p 286.

47 J. Mooney, pp 75-7; Baikie.

48 Hossack, pp 36-7; Fereday (2000), p 178 n 4 & p 184 n 94; *Evidence* p 267 (William Cowper), pp 282-5 (H. J. Blanc).

49 *Evidence* pp 94-8 (Alexander Ross, LLD).

50 *Evidence* pp 99-100 (Thomas Ross).

51 *Evidence* p 101 (Mrs Isabella Gellatly Thoms or Smith).

52 *Evidence* p 103 (Mrs Isabella Gellatly Thoms or Smith).

53 The 'Agenoria' lock-stitch machine was patented by the Franklin Sewing Machine Company, Birmingham in 1870, and manufactured there by it and a number of other companies until 1883 (Head, p 19). 'Perpigena' is probably a mishearing of 'Papagena', the heroine of Mozart's *The Magic Flute*.

54 *Evidence* pp 101-2 (Mrs Isabella Gellatly Thoms or Smith).

55 *Evidence* p 105 (Mrs Isabella Gellatly Thoms or Smith).

56 *Evidence* p 110 (Mrs Isabella Gellatly Thoms or Smith).

57 *Evidence* p 112 (Mrs Isabella Gellatly Thoms or Smith).

58 *Evidence* p 110 (Mrs Isabella Gellatly Thoms or Smith).

59 *Evidence* pp 129-33 (Dr Robert Fleming).

60 *Evidence* p 139 (Dr Alexander Bruce).

61 *Evidence* p 141 (Dr Alexander Bruce).

62 *Evidence* p 141 (David Yellowlees).

63 *Evidence* p 142 (David Yellowlees).

64 *Evidence* p 142 (David Yellowlees).

65 *Evidence* pp 142-3 (David Yellowlees).

66 *Evidence* p 143 (David Yellowlees).

67 *Evidence* pp 143-4 (David Yellowlees).

68 *The Scotsman,* 7th February, 1905.

69 *Evidence* pp 144-5 (David Yellowlees).

70 *Evidence* p 146 (David Yellowlees).

71 *The Courier,* 7th February, 1905.

72 *Scots Law Times,* 15th October, 1898.

Chapter 7

1 OA K10/11/2/3/1 Draft letter to A. P. M. Thoms, 1906.

2 *The Courier,* 8th February, 1905.

3 *The Scotsman,* 8th February, 1905.

4 He would receive a knighthood in 1911 (*Edinburgh Medical Journal*, 1922, volume xxix, p 254).

5   *Edinburgh Medical Journal*, 1922, volume xxix, p 256.

6   *Edinburgh Medical Journal*, 1922, volume xxix, pp 256-257.

7   *Evidence* p 150 (Dr J. O. Affleck).

8   *Evidence* pp 147-152 (Dr J. O. Affleck).

9   *Evidence* p 158 (Dr J. O. Affleck).

10 *Evidence* pp 156-7 (Dr J. O. Affleck).

11 *Evidence* p 158 (Dr J. O. Affleck).

12 Dr Affleck's austere bachelor existence was enlivened by a love of literature and foreign travel (*Edinburgh Medical Journal*, 1922, volume xxix, p 257).

13 *Evidence* p 164 (Dr A. Black).

14 *Evidence* p 227 (Miss Emily Irvine).

15 *Evidence* p 170 (John Philp Wood WS).

16 *Evidence* pp 227-229 (Miss Emily Irvine).

17 *Evidence* pp 170-3 (John Philp Wood WS).

18 *Evidence* p 187 (John Philp Wood WS).

19 Blanc was one of the architects recommended by Thoms to advise on the details of the restoration and was, as Thoms pointed out, a member of the Royal Scottish Academy in Edinburgh, not an Associate of the Royal Academy in London (*Evidence* pp 188-9 (Joseph Inglis WS)).

20 *Evidence* pp 187-190 (Joseph Inglis WS and William Yeaman).

21 *Evidence* p 174 (John Philp Wood, WS).

22 *Evidence* p 173 (John Philp Wood WS).

23 *Evidence* p 165 (John Philp Wood WS).

24 *Evidence* p 167 (John Philp Wood WS).

25 *Evidence* pp 168-0 (John Philp Wood WS).

26 Afterwards Lord Kinross, Lord Justice-General and Lord President of the Court of Session. He died in office a fortnight before the Thoms case came to trial, so tributes to his abilities and judgement were still fresh in everyone's minds.

27 *Evidence* p 175 (John Philp Wood WS); *The Orkney Herald,* 8th February, 1905.

28 *Evidence* pp 175-6 (John Philp Wood WS).

29 *Evidence* p 176 (John Philp Wood WS).

30 *Evidence* p 177 (John Philp Wood WS).

31 *Evidence* p 191 (Adam Melrose).

32 *Evidence* pp 191-7 (Adam Melrose); *The Scotsman,* 8th February, 1905.

33 *Evidence* p 192 (Adam Melrose).

34 *Evidence* pp 198-9 (Adam Melrose).

35 *Evidence* p 203 (Adam Melrose).

36 *Evidence* p 205 (Adam Melrose).

37 *Evidence* pp 201-2 (Adam Melrose).

38 *Evidence* pp 201-2 (Adam Melrose).

39 *The Scotsman,* 8th February, 1905.

40 *Evidence* pp 205-7 (Adam Melrose).

41 *Evidence* p 208 (Adam Melrose).

42 *Evidence* p 209 (Adam Melrose).

43 *Evidence* p 209 (Adam Melrose).

44 OA K10/12/2/3 Precognition of Adam Melrose.

45 *Evidence* p 216 (John Lessels). The wage increase was four months after Melrose was engaged, so presumably he twice threatened to resign, unless Nurse Morrison was mistaken in dating the incident recalled by her to one week into his employment.

46 *Evidence* p 217 (John Lessels).

47 *Evidence* p 218 (John Lessels).

48 *Evidence* p 220 (John Lessels).

49 *Evidence* pp 222-3 (John Lessels).

50 *Evidence* p 225 (Miss Emily Irvine).

51 *Evidence* pp 225-7 (Miss Emily Irvine).

52 *Evidence* p 239 (Miss Emily Irvine).

53 *Evidence* p 238 (Miss Emily Irvine).

Chapter 8

1 Buchan (1940), p 83; (1913).

2 Janet Adam Smith, p 66.

3 Lady Tweedsmuir, p 48.

4 *Evidence* pp 238-9 (Lord Ardwall); *The Orkney Herald,* 15th February, 1905.

5 The other story is slightly better. When counsel appearing before him said he would now address the question of commission received by the witness, which he had been forgetting, Ardwall rejoined, 'Ah, don't commit the omission of omitting the commission.' - Morton & Malloch, pp 193-4.

6 *The Orkney Herald,* 15th February, 1905.

7 Of Tangwick in Shetland, Sheriff of Renfrew and Bute, Vice-Dean of the Faculty of Advocates, etc.

8 *Evidence* pp 239-41.

9 *The Orkney Herald,* 15th February, 1905.

10 *The Orkney Herald,* 15th February, 1905.

11 This question is not given in the reports, but has been reconstructed from the way the answer is given.

12 *Evidence* pp 242-5 (Lord Ardwall); *The Orkney Herald,* 15th February, 1905.

13 Married 22nd April, 1903, at the Parish Church of St Saviour, Pimlico (Register of Marriages in the District of St George, Hanover Square, London).

14 *Evidence* p 79 (H. J. M. Thoms).

15 The Inventory of Thoms' estate lists two paintings of Scapa by Sam Bough, as well as three coast scenes and one loch scene, some of which may also have been in Orkney (OA K10/11/2/4/1).

16 This may have been the 'watercolour painting of Saint Giles cathedral by Doyle, with relative Key' which Thoms bequeathed to Wood his solicitor. The inventory lists a colour lithograph of St Giles in the drawing-room, which may be a reference to the same picture. Whether the original or a reproduction, it seems to have been *The Bells of St Giles* by Conan Doyle's father Charles Altamont Doyle.

17 *Evidence* p 257 (T. W. Ranken).

18 *Evidence* pp 254-5 (T. W. Ranken).

19 *Evidence* pp 258-9 (T. W. Ranken).

20 *Evidence* p 258 (T. W. Ranken).

21 *Evidence* p 260 (T. W. Ranken).

22 *Evidence* pp 260-2 (Mrs Fanny Ranken).

23 Not, as a legal typist of 1904 had it, 'a Greek Mexican'(OA K10/12/2/3 Precognition of William Cowper).

24 *Evidence* p 265 (William Cowper).

25 OA K10/12/2/1 (Precognition of John McEwan MA).

26 *Evidence* p 266 (William Cowper).

27 *The Orkney Herald,* 15th February, 1905.

28 *The Orkney Herald,* 15th February, 1905.

29 *Evidence* p 269 (John A. Forrest WS).

30 *Evidence* pp 270-1 (William A. Wood CA); *The Orkney Herald,* 15th February, 1905.

31 *Evidence* pp 271-77 (Walter Wood Robertson).

32 *Evidence* pp 277-9 (Walter Wood Robertson).

33 *Evidence* pp 279-80 (Walter Wood Robertson); *The Orkney Herald,* 15th February, 1905.

34 *The Orkney Herald,* 15th February, 1905 (the newspaper gives the quotation partly in indirect speech).

35 *The Orkney Herald,* 15th February, 1905.

36 *Evidence* p 280 (Walter Wood Robertson).

37 *Evidence* p 280 (Walter Wood Robertson).

38 Robertson's son, Walter James Robertson, had been called to the Scots Bar in 1896 (*Scottish Biographies 1938*).

39 *Evidence* pp 280-1 (Walter Wood Robertson); *The Orkney Herald,* 15th February, 1905.

40 *Evidence* pp 281-2 (Walter Wood Robertson).

41 *Evidence* pp 282-5 (Hippolyte J. Blanc).

42 *Evidence* pp 285-7 (Professor John Glaister).

43 *Evidence* p 288 (Professor John Glaister).

44 *Evidence* p 289 (Professor John Glaister).

45 *Evidence* p 291 (Professor John Glaister).

46 *Evidence* pp 292-3 (Professor John Glaister).

47 *Evidence* pp 294-5 (Professor John Glaister).

48 *Evidence* pp 295-6 (Professor John Glaister); *The Orkney Herald,* 15th February, 1905.

49 *Evidence* p 297 (Professor John Glaister).

50 *Evidence* pp 297-9 (Professor John Glaister); *The Orkney Herald,* 15th February, 1905.

51 *Evidence* p 300 (Professor John Glaister); *The Orkney Herald,* 15th February, 1905.

52 *Evidence* pp 300-1 (Professor John Glaister); *The Orkney Herald,* 15th February, 1905.

53 5th April, 1905, (Register of Marriages for the District of St Giles and City of Edinburgh). Clouston had been an acquaintance of Thoms, too (OA K10/12/1/6 Precognition of Dr Benjamin D. C. Bell).

54 *Evidence* pp 301-4 (Dr David Wallace).

55 *Evidence* pp 305-9 (Andrew Gold).

56 *Evidence* p 147 (Dr J. O. Affleck).

57 *Evidence* pp 310-13 (James S. S. Logie, MD).

58 Probably observed by 'Billy', the Provost's old dog, whose favourite station from which to watch the world go by was just inside the pillar at the entrance to the courtyard (Cursiter, p 124).

59 Hossack, *op. cit.* p 34; the plate is illustrated on p 37.

60 Now in the possession of the author. It bears the inscription 'To Brother Provost Peace D.P.G.M.C.O&Z [ie Depute Provincial Grand Master Caithness, Orkney and Zetland] From Geo H M Thoms PGM.C.O&Z March 1890.'

61 *Evidence* pp 313-5 (Mrs Elizabeth Lees or Peace).

62 number 24.

63 OA K10/12/1/6 Precognition of Miss Hester Bruce.

64 *Evidence* pp 315-7 (Mrs Jean Heddle Bruce).

Chapter 9

1 *The Scotsman,* 3rd August, 1915.

2 *The Scots Law Times,* 16th October, 1915.

3 Shennan said this is what Thoms did, but he was writing many years later, and there is no mention of such a practice in the evidence (Shennan, p 10).

4 *The Orkney Herald,* 15th February, 1905.

5 Shaw (1921) pp 254-5.

6 *The Orkney Herald,* 15th February, 1905.

7   *The Scots Law Times*, 26th June, 1915.

8   *Evidence* p 336 (Lord Justice-Clerk's charge).

9   *Evidence* pp 319-21 (Lord Justice-Clerk's charge).

10   *Evidence* pp 321-2 (Lord Justice-Clerk's charge).

11   *Evidence* p 322 (Lord Justice-Clerk's charge).

12   *Evidence* p 323 (Lord Justice-Clerk's charge).

13   *Evidence* pp 233-4 (Lord Justice-Clerk's charge).

14   *Evidence* pp 324-5 (Lord Justice-Clerk's charge).

15   *Evidence* pp 326-7 (Lord Justice-Clerk's charge).

16   *Evidence* pp 327-8 (Lord Justice-Clerk's charge).

17   *Evidence* pp 329-30 (Lord Justice-Clerk's charge).

18   *Evidence* p 331 (Lord Justice-Clerk's charge).

19   *Evidence* pp 332-4 (Lord Justice-Clerk's charge).

20   *Evidence* p 336 (Lord Justice-Clerk's charge).

21   *Evidence* p 337 (Lord Justice-Clerk's charge).

22   *Evidence* p 338 (Lord Justice-Clerk's charge).

23   *Evidence* p 339 (Lord Justice-Clerk's charge).

24   *The Orkney Herald*, 15th February, 1905.

Chapter 10

1   *The Orkney Herald*, 15th February, 1905.

2   Quoted *The Orkney Herald*, 15th February, 1905.

3   OA K10/12/2/1 Precognition of Mrs Jane Heddle Bruce.

4   OA K10/12/2/1 Precognition of Duncan John Robertson.

5   OA K10/12/1/6 Precognition of David Wilson.

6   *The Scots Law Times*, 31st October, 1903.

7   OA K10/12/2/1 Precognition of Duncan John Robertson.

8   *The Orkney Herald*, 22nd February, 1905.

9   Copy letter, T. S. Clouston, Edinburgh, to the Marquis of Zetland, 13th March, 1905, in the possession of the author.

10   Wilson, (1911) pp 10-11; OA K10/2/1 Advisory Committee Minute Book, 1907-1910.

11   Callaghan and Wilson, pp 41 & 45-7; OA K10/2/1 Advisory Committee Minute Book, 1907-1910.

12   The plans of Kinross were placed second and those of Blanc third (OA K10/2/1 Advisory Committee Minute Book, 1907-1910).

13   Wilson, pp 12-14 & 19-20.

14   *The Orkney Herald*, 22nd February, 1905.

15   *The Orkney Herald*, 22nd February, 1905; see for example the letter from 'A Dissenter' in *The Orkney Herald*, 18th December, 1908.

16   Cowan, then well into his eighties, was the father of William Dover Baikie and Alfred Baikie, respectively tenth and eleventh lairds of Tankerness, each of whom had changed his name to Baikie upon inheriting the estate. Cursiter was the uncle of the artist Stanley Cursiter, latterly H.M. Painter and Limner in Scotland, whose paintings of the cathedral restoration are reproduced in this book.

17   *The Orkney Herald*, 30th December, 1908.

18   *The Orkney Herald*, 7th April, 1909.

19   *The Orkney Herald*, 13th January, 1909.

20   Orkney Library Photographic Archive.

21   H. L. Mooney (1975), p 8.

22 H. L. Mooney (1989), p 103.

23 *The Orkney Herald,* 27th April, 1921.

24 H. L. Mooney (1975), p 8.

25 Callaghan and Wilson, p 43.

26 *The Orkney Herald,* 15th February, 1905.

27 Wilson, p 9.

28 *The Orkney Herald,* 9th August, 1905.

29 Cooper saw his Liberal opponent's majority increase from 817 to 2,812. Although selected again to fight the seat, poor health forced him to withdraw. He died suddenly in August, 1915, when undergoing treatment for a heart complaint. Hunter and Clyde were pall-bearers at his funeral (*Scots Law Times* 5th November and 23rd December, 1905, 27th January, 1906, and 16th October, 1915; *The Scotsman* 3rd and 7th August, 1915).

30 (1907) 14 *Scots Law Times Reports,* p 635.

31 *The Orkney Herald,* 16th January, 1907.

32 Judicial expenses awarded against a party in an action are more restricted than those charged by lawyers to their clients. Here, the Auditor of Court had whittled down the accounts of the Trustee and Kirkwall from £2,534 and £839 respectively (*The Orkney Herald,* 16th January, 1907).

33 This was less than expected for such a house, but the building of Corrennie Drive had destroyed the views to the south and the purchaser argued that he would have to spend £100 to install electric light and fit proper grates in the three public rooms in place of the gas fires favoured by Thoms (OA K10/1/1 Thoms Bequest Minute Book No 1, 3rd February, 1904 – 20th August, 1912, p 71 (16th October, 1905)).

34 OA K10/11/2/4/5 Copy Deed of Consent by the Provost and Magistrates of the Royal Burgh of Kirkwall and Adam Melrose and Mrs Janet Melrose in favour of W. A. Wood CA as Trustee therein mentioned dated 3rd April, 1906, and subsequent dates; OA K10/1/1 Thoms Bequest Minute Book No 1, 3rd February, 1904 – 20th August, 1912, pp 56-80 (10th March to 30th December, 1905).

35 Register of Deaths in the District of Morningside and City of Edinburgh.

36 *Burke's Landed Gentry of Great Britain,* 19th Edition, Volume 1; www.clanmacthomas.org; MacThomas, pp 97-8. A few months after his father's death, Patrick MacThomas wrote Kirkwall Town Council to see if he could purchase two or three acres of land from his great-uncle's Forfarshire estate and thus entitle himself to the territorial designation 'of Aberlemno', but the Council, having sold the property, was unable to help (OA K10/9/2 – 22nd November, 1958, P. W. MacThomas (formerly Thoms), Little Wilbraham, nr. Cambridge to The Clerk of the Town Council of Kirkwall, and draft reply pencilled thereon).

37 www.clanmacthomas.org

Index of persons mentioned in the text
[excluding references to Sheriff Thoms himself]

Gold, Andrew, 157
Gold, Andrew John, 179
Gold, Mrs Andrew J., 179
Gold, Miss Winifred, 179
Goodfellow, Rev. Alexander, 39, 40
Goodlad & Coutts, Messrs, 43
Graeme, A. M. Sutherland-, of Graemeshall, 88
Grant, Mrs Agnes Frisken or, 29, 30, 80
Grant, Superintendent Alexander, 13, 29, 35
Gray, Superintendent Gifford, 62
Grierson, A. J., of Quendale, 31
Grierson, James Cullen, 31-2, 33, **45**, 45, 49, 61, 64, 103, 172

H.

Hallowes, Mrs Grace Thoms or, (Sheriff's niece), 25, 94, 102
Harper, Sheriff Ebenezer Erskine, 46, 48, 51, **52**, 52-3, 55
Harvey, Sheriff William, 184
Hay, James, 77, 130
Heddle, William J., **128**
Howman, Matthew L., **128**
Hunter, William (later Lord Hunter), 26, 27, 166

I.

Inglis, Joseph, WS, 121
Irvine, Miss Emily, 24, 82, 88, 119-20, 132-3, 135, 164, 172
Irvine, Mrs Mary, 24
Irvine, Rev. Walter, 132
Ivory, Sheriff William, 33-4, **34**

J.

Jameson, Andrew, *see* Ardwall, Lord
Jameson, John G., 26, 27, 139
Jamieson, Rev. John, 40

K.

Kinross, John, 182
Kinross, Lord, *see* Balfour, John Blair,
Kirkness, David M., 11-13

L.

Leith, Robert S. W., 48-9, 51, 61
Lessels, John, 81-2, 83, 100, 127, 130-1, 172
Liberty, Messrs, 12
Liddle, Thomas H., **128**
Lloyd-George, David (1st Earl Lloyd-George), 26
Logie, James S. S., MD, 14, 82, 157, 168
Logie, Mrs J. S. S., 14
Low, Thomas Peace, **128**

M.

Macdonald, Alexander, 43
Macdonald, Sir John H. A., Lord Justice-Clerk, 26, **27**, 27, 28, 64, 65, 91, 92, 96, 107, 110, 139-40, 144, 145, 161, 164, 167, 168-76, 179
MacGibbon, David, 107

Y.

Z.

Paul J. Sutherland

Paul J. Sutherland grew up within sight of St Magnus Cathedral. He attended Kirkwall Grammar School and the University of Edinburgh, graduating with Honours in Law in 1989. After qualifying as a solicitor, he worked in private practice in Orkney before moving to Shetland in 1999 to work in local government.

He has contributed to *The Making of Modern Orkney* (1995) and *New Orkney Antiquarian Journal volume 4* (2009), and is the author of *Morton Lodge No 89, 250 Years of a Lerwick Institution* (2012).

Although, like Sheriff Thoms, he is both a lawyer and a bachelor, he claims no eccentricities beyond an interest in old books, old cars and old-time dancing. He lives in Lerwick.